REFERENCE

NEW CENTURY BIBLE

General Editors

RONALD E. CLEMENTS

M.A., B.D., PH.D. (Old Testament)

MATTHEW BLACK

D.D., D.LITT., F.B.A. (New Testament)

1 and 2 Corinthians

NEW CENTURY BIBLE

1 and 2 Corinthians

NEW CENTURY BIBLE

Based on the Revised Standard Version

---

1 and 2 Corinthians

Edited by

F. F. BRUCE, D.D.

Rylands Professor of Biblical Criticism and Exegesis
University of Manchester

OLIPHANTS

OLIPHANTS
MARSHALL, MORGAN AND SCOTT, LTD.
BLUNDELL HOUSE
GOODWOOD ROAD
LONDON S.E.14

ISBN 0 551 00600 5

Printed in Great Britain by
Butler & Tanner Ltd, Frome and London

To
David and Jean Payne

CONTENTS

CONTENTS

PREFACE

In completing this commentary I eagerly seize the opportunity to express my thanks to Principal Matthew Black for inviting me to undertake it, and thus providing the necessary stimulus to deepen my acquaintance with the fascinating mind of Paul. I suspected before, and now I know, that no one can begin to plumb the depths of his personality without making a close study of his relations with the church in Corinth, as these are reflected in his Corinthian correspondence. True, I count not myself to have apprehended the full measure of his character in all its warmth and versatility, but one cannot spend the time required for a work of this kind without profiting greatly by the apostle's constant company.

To many previous expositors of these letters I am, naturally, much indebted. One of them calls for special mention. About half the commentary on 1 Corinthians had been written when Professor C. K. Barrett's superb volume on this epistle appeared in the Black (Harper) series. Source critics may try to discern traces of its influence on my treatment of 1 C. 9–16; I shall not be greatly surprised if they are successful.

My gratitude must also be expressed to Miss Margaret Hogg, who typed my manuscript and compiled the indexes.

F.F.B.

ABBREVIATIONS

BIBLICAL

OLD TESTAMENT (*OT*)

Gen.	Jg.	1 Chr.	Ps.	Lam.	Ob.	Hag.
Exod.	Ru.	2 Chr.	Prov.	Ezek.	Jon.	Zech.
Lev.	1 Sam.	Ezr.	Ec.	Dan.	Mic.	Mal.
Num.	2 Sam.	Neh.	Ca.	Hos.	Nah.	
Dt.	1 Kg.	Est.	Isa.	Jl	Hab.	
Jos.	2 Kg.	Job	Jer.	Am.	Zeph.	

APOCRYPHA (*Apoc.*)

1 Esd.	Tob.	Ad. Est.	Sir.	S. 3 Ch.	Bel.	1 Mac
2 Esd.	Jdt.	Wis.	Bar.	Sus.	Man.	2 Mac.
			Ep. Jer.			

NEW TESTAMENT (*NT*)

Mt.	Ac.	Gal.	1 Th.	Tit.	1 Pet.	3 Jn
Mk	Rom.	Eph.	2 Th.	Phm.	2 Pet.	Jude
Lk.	1 C.	Phil.	1 Tim.	Heb.	1 Jn	Rev.
Jn	2 C.	Col.	2 Tim.	Jas	2 Jn	

DEAD SEA SCROLLS

1QIs	First Isaiah Scroll
1QIs^b	Second Isaiah Scroll
1QLevi	Second Testament of Levi
1QpHab	Habakkuk Commentary
1QS	Rule of the Community (Manual of Discipline)
1QSa (= 1Q28a)	Rule of the Community (Appendix)
1QSb (= 1Q28b)	Collection of Benedictions
1QM	War of the Sons of Light against the Sons of Darkness
1QH	Hymns of Thanksgiving

4QFlor	Florilegium, Cave 4
4QPatr	Patriarchal Blessing, Cave 4
CD	Fragments of a Zadokite work (Damascus Document)

GENERAL

AJA	*American Journal of Archaeology*
Ant.	*Antiquities* (Josephus)
Apoc. Mos.	*Apocalypse of Moses*
Asc. Isa.	*Ascension of Isaiah*
AV	*Authorized Version*
Bauer–Arndt–Gingrich	W. Bauer, *A Greek–English Lexicon of the New Testament and Other Early Christian Literature*, translated by W. F. Arndt and F. W. Gingrich (Cambridge, 1957)
BJ	*De Bello Judaico* (Josephus's *Jewish War*)
BJRL	*Bulletin of the John Rylands Library* (Manchester)
BNTC	*Black's New Testament Commentaries*
BZNW	*Beihefte zur Zeitschrift für die neutestamentliche Wissenschaft*
CBC	*Cambridge Bible Commentary*
CBQ	*Catholic Biblical Quarterly*
CD	See under **Dead Sea Scrolls** (above)
CIG	*Corpus Inscriptionum Graecarum*
CIL	*Corpus Inscriptionum Latinarum*
CNT	*Commentaire du Nouveau Testament*
Conf. Ling.	*De Confusione Linguarum* (Philo, *On the Confusion of Tongues*)
Diss.	*Dissertationes* (Epictetus)
EB	*Études Bibliques*
EGT	*Expositor's Greek Testament*
Ep.	*Epistle*
Eph.	*Letter to the Ephesians* (Ignatius)
E.T.	English Translation
ExB	*Expositor's Bible*
ExT	*Expository Times*
Geog.	*Geographica* (Strabo)

Haer.	*Adversus Haereses* (Irenaeus, *Against Heresies*)
HDB	Hasting's *Dictionary of the Bible*
HE	*Historia Ecclesiastica* (Eusebius)
Hist.	*History*
HNT	*Handbuch zum Neuen Testament*
HTR	*Harvard Theological Review*
IB	*Interpreter's Bible*
ICC	*International Critical Commentary*
ILS	*Inscriptiones Latinae Selectae* (ed. H. Dessau)
INT	*Introduction to the New Testament*
JBL	*Journal of Biblical Literature*
JJS	*Journal of Jewish Studies*
Jos.	Josephus
JTS	*Journal of Theological Studies*
Jub.	Jubilees
KEK	*Kritisch–Exegetischer Kommentar* (*Meyer-Kommentar*)
Leg. alleg.	*Legum Allegoriae* (Philo, *Allegorical Interpretation*)
LXX	Septuagint
MNTC	*Moffatt New Testament Commentary*
MT	Massoretic Text
NEB	*New English Bible*
NICNT	*New International Commentary on the New Testament*
NovT	*Novum Testamentum*
n.s.	new series
NTD	*Das Neue Testament Deutsch*
NTS	*New Testament Studies*
Opif. mundi	*De Opificio Mundi* (Philo, *On the Creation of the World*
Or. Sib.	*Sibylline Oracles*
P	*Papyrus*
P.Ox.	*Oxyrhynchus Papyri*
RB	*Revue Biblique*
RNT	*Das Regensburger Neue Testament*
RSV	*Revised Standard Version*
RV	*Revised Version*

SJT	*Scottish Journal of Theology*
Spec. leg.	*De Specialibus Legibus* (Philo, *On Special Laws*)
TB	Babylonian Talmud
Test. Gad (etc.)	*Testament of Gad* (etc., in *Testaments of the Twelve Patriarchs*)
TR	Textus Receptus
TWNT	*Theologisches Wörterbuch zum Neuen Testament*, ed. G. Kittel and G. Friedrich (Stuttgart, 1933 ff.), E.T. (Grand Rapids, 1964 ff.)
WC	*Westminster Commentaries*
ZK	*Zahn-Kommentar*
ZNW	*Zeitschrift für die neutestamentliche Wissenschaft*

SELECT BIBLIOGRAPHY

1 and 2 Corinthians

COMMENTARIES

Kuss, O. (*RNT*, 1941)
Lietzmann, H., revised by Kümmel, W. G. (*HNT*, 1949[4])
Thrall, M. E. (*CBC*, 1965)
Wendland, H. D. (*NTD*, 1964[10])

OTHER LITERATURE

Barrett, C. K., 'Cephas and Corinth', in *Abraham unser Vater. Festschrift für O. Michel*, ed. O. Betz etc. (1963), pp. 1ff.
Barrett, C. K., 'Christianity at Corinth', *BJRL* 46 (1963–4), pp. 269ff.
Buck, C. H., 'The Collection for the Saints', *HTR* 43 (1950), pp. 1ff.
Lake, K., *The Earlier Epistles of St. Paul* (1914[2]), pp. 102ff.
Lütgert, W., *Freiheitspredigt und Schwarmgeister in Korinth* (1908)
Manson, T. W., *Studies in the Gospels and Epistles* (1962), pp. 190ff.
Schlatter, A., *Paulus, der Bote Jesu* (1934)
Schmithals, W., *Die Gnosis in Korinth* (1965[2])

1 Corinthians

COMMENTARIES

Allo, E. B. (*EB*, 1935)
Bachmann, P. (*ZK*, 1936[4])
Barrett, C. K. (*BNTC*, 1968)
Calvin, J. (1546); E.T. by J. W. Fraser (1960)
Conzelman, H. (*KEK*, 1969)
Craig, C. T. (*IB*, 1953)
Edwards, T. C. (1903)
Findlay, G. G. (*EGT*, 1900)
Godet, F. (1886); E.T. by A. Cusin (1886)
Goudge, H. L. (*WC*, 1926[2])
Grosheide, F. W. (*NICNT*, 1954[2])
Héring, J. (*CNT*, 1949); E.T. by A. W. Heathcote and P. J. Allcock (1962)
Hodge, C. (1857; reprinted 1953)
Kelly, W. (1878)
Lightfoot, J. B., *Notes on the Epistles of St. Paul* (1895), pp. 137ff.
Moffatt, J. (*MNTC*, 1938)
Robertson, A., and Plummer, A. (*ICC*, 1929[2])

OTHER LITERATURE

Barrett, C. K., 'Things Sacrificed to Idols', *NTS* 11 (1964–5), pp. 138ff.

15

Dean, J. T., *St. Paul and Corinth* (1947)

Deluz, G., *A Companion to 1 Corinthians* (1959); E.T. by G. E. Watt (1963)

Hurd, J. C., *The Origin of 1 Corinthians* (1965)

Isaksson, A., *Marriage and Ministry in the New Temple* (1965)

Wilckens, U., *Weisheit und Torheit* (1959)

2 Corinthians

COMMENTARIES

Allo, E. B. (*EB*, 1937)

Bachmann, P. (*ZK*, 1922⁴)

Bernard, J. H. (*EGT*, 1903)

Calvin, J. (1547); E.T. by T. A. Smail (1964)

Denney, J. (*ExB*, 1894)

Filson, F. V. (*IB*, 1953)

Goudge, H. L. (*WC*, 1927)

Héring, J. (*CNT*, 1950); E.T. by A. W. Heathcote and P. J. Allcock (1967)

Hodge, C. (1860; reprinted 1950)

Hughes, P. E. (*NICNT*, 1962²)

Isaacs, W. H. (1920)

Kelly, W. (1882)

Menzies, A. (1912)

Plummer, A. (*ICC*, 1915)

Strachan, R. H. (*MNTC*, 1935)

Windisch, H. (*KEK*, 1924⁹)

OTHER LITERATURE

Bornkamm, G., *Die Vorgeschichte des sogenannten Zweiten Korintherbriefes* (1961)

Bultmann, R., *Exegetische Probleme des zweiten Korintherbriefes* (1947)

Friedrich, G., 'Die Gegner des Paulus im 2. Korintherbrief' in *Abraham unser Vater, Festschrift für O. Michel*, ed. O. Betz etc. (1963), pp. 181ff.

Georgi, D., *Die Gegner des Paulus im 2. Korintherbrief* (1964)

Käsemann, E., 'Die Legitimität des Apostels', *ZNW* 41 (1942), pp. 33ff.

Kennedy, J. H. *The Second and Third Epistles of St. Paul to the Corinthians* (1900)

Prümm, K., *Diakonia Pneumatos*, 3 vols. (1960–7)

Stephenson, A. M. G., 'A Defence of the Integrity of 2 Corinthians', in *The Authorship and Integrity of the New Testament* (K. Aland, etc.), 1965, pp. 82ff.

INTRODUCTION

to

1 Corinthians

INTRODUCTION TO 1 CORINTHIANS

1. FOUNDATION OF THE CORINTHIAN CHURCH

Corinth, an ancient city of Greece, was situated on the Isthmus of Corinth, where it commanded the land-routes between Northern Greece and the Peloponnese and, through the harbours of Lechaeum on the west and Cenchreae on the east, early became an emporium of Mediterranean trade. The city was built on the north side of the Acrocorinthus, which rises 1,900 feet above the plain, and served the Corinthians as their citadel. It contained an inexhaustible water supply in the fountain of Peirene.

The city, thanks to its maritime commerce, enjoyed great prosperity. It acquired a reputation for luxury, and its name became proverbial for sexual licence. It was a centre of the worship of Aphrodite, whose temple stood on the summit of the Acrocorinthus. At the foot of the citadel stood the temple of Melicertes, patron of seafarers; his name is a hellenized form of Melkart, once the chief deity of Tyre. The Isthmian Games, over which Corinth presided, and in which all the Greek city-states participated, were held every two years; at them the sea-god Poseidon was specially honoured.

Corinth survived many crises in Greek history, but suffered disaster at the hands of the Romans in 146 B.C. In retribution for the leading part it had played in the revolt of the Achaian League against the overlordship of Rome, the Roman general L. Mummius razed it to the ground, sold its population into slavery and confiscated its territory to the Roman state. It lay derelict for a century, and was then refounded by Julius Caesar as a Roman colony, under the name *Laus Iulia Corinthiensis*. While it retained its own colonial administration, it was from 27 B.C. the seat of government of the Roman province of Achaia.

Roman Corinth quickly regained the prosperity of its predecessor. At the narrowest point of the Isthmus a sort of shipway (Gk *diolkos*) was constructed, on which smaller vessels were dragged across the $3\frac{1}{2}$ miles between the Corinthian and Saronic Gulfs. With the old prosperity the old reputation for sexual laxity also returned: the temple of Aphrodite was staffed by 1,000 female

18

slaves dedicated to her worship, who are said to have made the
city a tourist attraction and enhanced its prosperity (Strabo,
Geog. VIII. vi. 20). The cult-statue of Aphrodite was attired in the
armour of the war-god Ares, with his helmet for a foot-rest and
his shield for a mirror. This background helps to explain the
necessity for the repeated warnings against fornication in Paul's
Corinthian correspondence.

As Corinth was a Roman colony, its citizens were Romans,
probably freedmen from Italy, but the population was augmented
by Greeks and Levantines, including Jews. According to Ac. 18.4
ff., there was a synagogue and a considerable Jewish community
in Corinth when Paul visited it about A.D. 50. While the 'synagogue of the Hebrews' referred to in the note on 2 C. 11.22
appears, from the style of the lettering on its lintel, to be later than
the apostolic age, it may have stood on the same site as the
synagogue where Paul debated during the first weeks of his stay
in the city.

Christianity came to Corinth when Paul arrived there from
Athens, soon after his evangelization of Macedonia. It was on his
arrival in Corinth that he first made the acquaintance of Priscilla
and Aquila (cf. 1 C. 16.19), who were among the Jews recently
expelled from Rome by edict of Claudius (*c.* A.D. 49). According to
the recurrent pattern of Paul's procedure as recorded in Acts, he
made the synagogue of Corinth his first base of operations, arguing
that the Messiah was Jesus in accordance with the *OT* scriptures
and, as the Western text says, 'inserting the name of the Lord
Jesus' at appropriate points in the lessons (Ac. 18.4). When, as
usually happened, the synagogue authorities could tolerate him
no longer, he moved to other headquarters, next door to the
synagogue, where one of his converts, a Gentile God-fearer named
Titius Justus, probably a citizen of Corinth, had a commodious
house (see note on Gaius, 1 C. 1.14). Here Paul continued to
proclaim salvation through Christ crucified, and the number of
his converts increased rapidly.

On July 1, A.D. 51 (less probably A.D. 52), Lucius Junius Gallio
arrived in Corinth as proconsul of Achaia. (From a rescript of
Claudius to the Delphians (W. Dittenberger, *Sylloge Inscriptionum
Graecarum* II³, 801) Gallio is known to have been proconsul of
Achaia in the period of Claudius's 26th acclamation as *imperator*—
a period known from other inscriptions (*CIL* III. 476, VI. 1256) to

cover the first seven months of A.D. 52.) Soon after his arrival, some leaders of the Jewish colony in Corinth tried to prosecute Paul before his tribunal on a charge of propagating an illegal religion. Gallio's refusal to take up the case, because he judged the dispute to be one internal to the Jewish community, regarding points of legal and religious interpretation, was tantamount in practice to a ruling that Christianity was a variety of Judaism and as such entitled to a share in the protection which Roman law extended to the Jewish religion, provided that public order was maintained. Thanks to this ruling (which may well have been followed as a precedent by other magistrates) Paul continued his apostolic activity with impunity not only in Corinth, where he spent eighteen months in all, but in other parts of the Roman world for the next ten years. He left Corinth in the spring of (probably) A.D. 52, and after a brief visit to Palestine, returned to the Aegean area, where he spent the greater part of the following three years in Ephesus. His Ephesian ministry and the period immediately succeeding it provide the setting for his Corinthian correspondence.

2. CHRISTIANITY IN CORINTH

The church at Corinth, as reflected in the Corinthian correspondence, supplies an example of the sea-change the gospel was apt to suffer when it was assimilated to a Hellenistic environment. Paul, for example, viewed the indwelling Spirit in the followers of Christ as the firstfruits of the heritage of glory which would be theirs in fullness at the parousia; by life in the Spirit they enjoyed in anticipation the life of the coming resurrection age. For one strand of Hellenistic thought the possession of the Spirit, the heavenly essence, was the all-important matter: the crowning achievement of Christ was the impartation of the Spirit. His crucifixion was significant mainly as the means by which he had outwitted and conquered the 'principalities and powers' that were hostile to men and would have prevented them from enjoying the heavenly gift. But now that they enjoyed the heavenly gift, they had 'arrived'; the kingdom was theirs already (cf. 1 C. 4.8ff.). What could the hope of resurrection add by way of bliss to those who knew themselves here and now to be 'men of the Spirit'? Let others know the exalted Christ as he was proclaimed to them by Paul or Apollos or Peter; they were in direct touch with him by the Spirit, and had no need of such intermediaries. We shall not be far wrong if we identify the people who argued thus with the 'Christ party' whose existence is probably implied in 1 C. 1.12.

The same attitude appears in the exaggerated estimate placed by some Corinthian Christians on the more spectacular and ecstatic 'spiritual gifts'—especially glossolalia. It is evident that, while Paul does not rule out glossolalia as a manifestation of the Spirit (he possessed the gift himself), he is eager to persuade the Corinthians that there were other spiritual gifts which, while not so impressive, were much more helpful in building up the community. Such a manifestation as glossolalia was not peculiar to Christianity: Greece had long experience of Pythian prophecy and Dionysiac enthusiasm. Hence Paul insists that it is not the pheno- menon of 'tongues' or prophesying in itself that evidences the presence and activity of the Holy Spirit, but the actual content of the utterance (1 C. 12.1–3). Self-evidently such an utterance as 'Jesus be cursed!' could not come by inspiration of the Spirit of God; it has been suggested that this utterance expresses the atti- tude of those *pneumatici* who insisted on their relation to the heavenly Christ and repudiated all reference to the earthly ministry of Jesus, but Paul is more probably envisaging an extreme instance for the sake of his argument.

It would be anachronistic to call them 'Gnostics'—a term which is best reserved for adherents of the various schools of Gnosticism which appear in the second century A.D.—but their doctrine might legitimately be called 'incipient Gnosticism'; at least one can appreciate from the Corinthian correspondence 'into how con- genial a soil the seeds of Gnosticism were about to fall' (R. Law, *The Tests of Life* (1909), p. 28). These 'men of the Spirit' certainly set much store by wisdom (*sophia*) and knowledge (*gnōsis*), assessing them (as Paul maintains) by secular standards, whereas in the gospel of Christ crucified God had turned these standards upside down and made them look foolish. The 'knowledge' which they cultivated, if it was not accompanied by Christian love, was not calculated to build up the Christian community or strengthen its fellowship; there was a temptation to despise fellow-Christians who were not so far advanced in knowledge and to show no patience in face of their unenlightened scruples in matters of food and sex.

The 'men of knowledge' held that, since the body was but a temporary expedient, bodily actions were morally and religiously indifferent.

Paul, the most liberal and emancipated of first-century Christians, could go a long way with these 'men of knowledge': he agreed with them, for instance, that the flesh of animals which had been sacrificed to pagan deities was none the worse for that and that Christians might eat it with a good conscience, but he was always prepared voluntarily to restrict his liberty in such matters if its exercise might harm the conscience of a less emancipated Christian. On the other hand, while food was ethically and spiritually indifferent, sexual relations were not: they had profound and lasting effects on the personality. So, if he echoed these people's slogan 'All things are lawful', he immediately qualified it with a 'but . . .' (cf. 1 C. 6.12; 10.23).

But it was not only against this perversion of Christian liberty into libertinism that he had to put the Corinthian church on its guard. There were some members of the church who, perhaps by reaction against the pervasive immorality of Corinthian life, or in anticipation of the ascetic Gnosticism of the second century, embraced a cult of severity to the body and thought it best to renounce married life. There were others who were influenced by the Jewish Christianity which had its headquarters in Jerusalem, treating, for example, the prohibition of 'what has been sacrificed to idols' in the apostolic decree of Ac. 15.29 as permanently binding on Gentile Christendom. There are indications here and there in the correspondence that some visitors to Corinth, disapproving of Paul's 'laxity' in this regard (as it seemed to them), tried to impose a stricter regimen on his converts. While Paul was foremost in restricting his liberty in the interests of others, and recommended this example of his to his converts, he insisted that such restrictions must be self-imposed, and condemned any attempt at imposing them from without as a threat to the gospel of free grace. Moreover, in so far as such visitors (whether authorized to do so or not) invoked the names of the original apostles—Peter and his colleagues—their action, in Paul's eyes, amounted to a breach of the agreement which he and Barnabas had reached with the Jerusalem leaders a few years before, providing that the latter would concentrate on the evangelization of Jews and leave the Gentile mission-field to Paul and Barnabas (Gal. 2.1–10). It is difficult

not to connect these visitors and those influenced by them with the
'Cephas party' of 1 C. 1.12.

In countering these tendencies at Corinth which threatened the
liberty of the gospel and the unity of the church, Paul thus had to
campaign simultaneously on more than one front. This is one
reason for the difficulty which modern readers find in understanding these letters. Another reason is that they are full of allusions to
persons and incidents well known to Paul and his readers, but
(apart from these allusions) quite unknown to us. In reading them,
we often find ourselves in the position of people listening to one end
of a telephone conversation and trying, not very successfully, to
reconstruct what is being said at the other end. There are many
interpretative problems in the Corinthian correspondence the
solutions to which can hardly be more than intelligent guesses.

3. OCCASION, STRUCTURE AND DATE OF
1 CORINTHIANS

In the course of his Ephesian ministry, Paul received disquieting
news about the ethical principles and practices of his converts at
Corinth. In particular, some of them had not broken completely
with the besetting vice of Corinth, and indeed saw no reason why
they should. He therefore sent them a letter directing them not to
associate with fornicators, meaning that the presence of such people
must not be tolerated within their fellowship. We know of this
letter only from a reference to it in 1 C. 5.9.–11; it may be distinguished as the 'previous letter' or 'Corinthians A'. Some commentators have suggested that part of it may survive in Paul's
extant Corinthian correspondence, on the hypothesis that one or
both of our two Letters to the Corinthians are composite recon-
structions—in 1 C. 6, for example (as suggested by G. Bornkamm,
Die Vorgeschichte des sogenannten Zweiten Korintherbriefes (1961),
pp. 34ff., n. 131), or in 2 C. 6.14–7.1 (where, however, the one subject we know to have been treated in the 'previous letter' is not
mentioned; see pp. 213ff.)—but more probably it has disappeared
altogether.

Some time later, Paul had a communication, either by letter
or through a personal visit, from 'Chloe's people', as he calls
them (perhaps members of a household church in Corinth), which

indicated a growth of party-spirit in the Corinthian church. There was a tendency to form 'schools', each claiming the name of a leading figure in the Christian world (Paul, Apollos or Cephas) or using the name of Christ himself in a partisan sense. Paul reacted to this news by dictating a letter in which he reproached his friends at Corinth for this and other undesirable tendencies, showing how they were impoverishing themselves by this behaviour, and promised (or threatened, if that was how they viewed the prospect) to visit them soon. Meanwhile, he was sending Timothy to visit them—he may indeed have already set out.

This letter, which we may call 'Corinthians B', was practically ready for despatch (1 C. 1–4) when a further communication came to Paul from Corinth which moved him to dictate much more of it. This communication took the form of a letter from the Corinthian church in which the writers assured Paul that they remembered his teaching and observed the 'traditions' which they had received from him, and sought his ruling or advice on a variety of questions, including marriage and divorce, food that had been sacrificed to idols, the exercise of spiritual gifts in the church, and the collection which they had heard he was organizing for the believers in Jerusalem. In addition, the bearers of this letter—probably Stephanas, Fortunatus and Achaicus (1 C. 16.17)—gave him an oral account of further disturbing tendencies in the church: illicit sexual relations were still condoned in some quarters (they mentioned one specially flagrant instance), there were cases of members of the church suing one another in the pagan law-courts, and the conduct at church meetings left much to be desired. Paul therefore continued to dictate more of 'Corinthians B', first dealing with his visitors' oral reports about sexual laxity and litigiousness (1 C. 5–6) and then taking up one by one the points raised in the Corinthians' letter (1 C. 7–16). Some of their questions may have involved the elucidation of points made in his previous letter ('Corinthians A'); there is insufficient evidence for the suggestion that they were puzzled by changes in Paul's attitude to some of these issues since he first came to Corinth (cf. the stimulating reconstruction of 'Paul's Dialogue with the Corinthian Church' in J. C. Hurd, *The Origin of 1 Corinthians*, 1965).

When 'Corinthians B' (1 C. 1–16) was complete, it was taken to Corinth possibly by Stephanas and his companions.

We can readily recognize these stages in the composition of 1 C., which may have extended over a period of some weeks. This is sufficient to account for such discrepancies as have been detected, for example, in references to the visit of Timothy (apparently certain in 4.17, less certain in 16.10f.) and of Paul himself ('soon' in 4.19, after staying at Ephesus until Pentecost and then passing through Macedonia in 16.5–9). Among recent commentators, J. Héring discerns two separate letters—an earlier one (consisting of 1.1–8.13; 10.23–11.1; 16.1–4, 10–14), perhaps taken back to Corinth by Chloe's people, and a later one (consisting of 9.1–10.22; 11.2–15.58, with chapter 13 inserted in the wrong place; 16.5–9, 15–24), taken back by Stephanas—which were later put together by an editor. Even such a relatively simple editorial process as this involves greater improbabilities than does the acceptance of the integrity of the letter; still greater improbabilities beset the more elaborate partition theories that have been propounded from time to time.

As for the date of 1 Corinthians, it was completed some time before Pentecost (16.8) and some parts of chapter 15 would have special point if they were composed around Eastertide (see note on 15.20). The year was apparently Paul's last year in Ephesus (probably A.D. 55), for a year or so later (2 C. 8.10; 9.2) he had left Ephesus and was in Macedonia (2 C. 2.12f.; 7.5; 8.1ff.; 9.2).

ANALYSIS OF 1 CORINTHIANS

FIRST SECTION **1.1–9** PROLOGUE.
    (a) **1.1–3** Salutation.
    (b) **1.4–9** Thanksgiving.

SECOND SECTION **1.10–4.21** PAUL DEALS WITH THE REPORT RECEIVED
        FROM CHLOE'S PEOPLE.
    (a) **1.10–17** Party strife.
    (b) **1.18–2.5** The proclamation of Christ crucified.
       i. **1.18–31** *Divine and secular wisdom.*
      ii. **2.1–5** *Paul's reliance on spiritual power.*
    (c) **2.6–13** The hidden wisdom of God.
    (d) **2.14–3.4** Spiritual, unspiritual and fleshly men.
       i. **2.14–16** *The source of spiritual insight.*
      ii. **3.1–4** *Milk for spiritual infants.*

THE FIRST LETTER OF PAUL TO THE
CORINTHIANS

PROLOGUE 1.1-9

**1.1. called by the will of God to be an apostle of Christ
Jesus:** this fuller wording combines 'called to be an apostle' (cf.
Rom. 1.1) and 'an apostle . . . by the will of God' (cf. 2 C. 1.1;
Eph. 1.1; Col. 1.1; 2 Tim. 1.1). The word-order **Christ Jesus** is
preferred by Paul to 'Jesus Christ'. **our brother Sosthenes:** if
this is 'Sosthenes, the ruler of the synagogue' in Corinth, whose
rough usage by the bystanders at Gallio's tribunal is described in
Acts 18.17, then, like his colleague or predecessor Crispus (see
verse 14 below), he became a Christian. The identity cannot be
proved. But since no other mention of Sosthenes occurs in Paul's
epistles, his inclusion in the salutation here is best explained if he
was someone well known to the Corinthian church who was with
Paul in Ephesus at the time of writing.

2. To the church of God which is at Corinth: the designation **the church of God** is commonly used by Paul of the church
in a particular locality; cf. the plural 'the churches of God' in
11.16. The **church of God** comprises all believers in Christ in
Corinth; they are further described as **those sanctified in Christ
Jesus**, i.e. set apart by God to be his holy people by virtue of their
faith-union with Christ, through which they share his risen life—
this is what is meant by the characteristically Pauline locution **in
Christ (Jesus).** In other words, they are **called to be saints** (cf.
Rom. 1.7), 'saints by divine calling'. **in every place:** a reference
either to churches in Achaia outside Corinth (cf. 2 C. 1.1), like
the church at Cenchreae (Rom. 16.1), or to churches founded by
apostles other than Paul. The latter interpretation is rendered the
more probable by **both their Lord and ours** (cf. 15.11, 'I or
they'). There is Jewish attestation for the use of **place** in the sense
'place of worship'. To **call on the name of our Lord Jesus
Christ** is to confess faith in him (cf. the quotation and application
of Jl 2.32 in Rom. 10.13f.).

3. Grace to you and peace . . .: A characteristically Christian
greeting (cf. Rom. 1.7; 2 C. 1.2; Gal. 1.3, etc.).

THANKSGIVING **1.4–9**

4. I give thanks to God always: after the initial salutation, Paul generally begins his letters with thanksgiving on his readers' account (cf. Rom. 1.8; Phil. 1.3; Col. 1.3; 1 Th. 1.2; 2 Th. 1.3; Phm. 4).

because of the grace of God: manifested especially in spiritual gifts.

5. with all speech and all knowledge: by **speech** (*logos*) he may mean 'eloquence'—the ability to express their **knowledge** (*gnōsis*). The Corinthian Christians evidently set much store by this **knowledge.** Far from depreciating it, Paul speaks highly of it as a gift of the Spirit (12.8), but warns them that unless it is accompanied by love, the greatest gift of all, it is liable to inflate them instead of building them up (8.1b). They prized **knowledge** because they believed it gave them access to the divine mysteries (cf. 2.6ff.), but it probably did not have for them the more technical sense of *gnōsis* associated with the developed Gnosticism of the following century. They may be described as 'gnosticizing' rather than 'Gnostic'.

6. the testimony to Christ was confirmed among you: the truth of the gospel was corroborated by their receiving these spiritual gifts, a regular experience in apostolic times (cf. Gal. 3.2–5; Heb. 2.3b–4).

7. as you wait for the revealing of our Lord Jesus Christ: his **revealing** (*apokalypsis*) is his parousia or coming in glory (cf. v. 5; 15.23), the object of lively expectation on the part of the earliest Christians.

8. the day of our Lord Jesus Christ: another expression for his parousia. The Old Testament 'day of the LORD' is thus christianized (cf. 3.13; 5.5; 2 C. 1.14). By Christ's sustaining power they will stand **guiltless** before him on that day.

9. God is faithful: Paul's confidence is that God, who has begun a good work by calling them **into the fellowship of his Son** will complete it by preserving them to the end (cf. Phil. 1.6).

PAUL DEALS WITH THE REPORT RECEIVED FROM
CHLOE'S PEOPLE 1.10–4.21

PARTY STRIFE 1.10–17

10. that there be no dissensions among you: lit. 'n
schisms' (Gk *schismata*). These had not developed yet, but if th
quarrelling and party-spirit described in the following sentenc
were allowed to develop unchecked, outright division might b
the result. As yet they formed one united church, in spite of thes
internal tensions. **that you be united in the same mind an**
the same judgment: cf. Phil. 2.2.

11. Chloe's people: Chloe is not otherwise known, but she wa
probably a woman of substance with a 'household' of servant
some of whom, members of the Corinthian church, had recentl
visited Paul or sent him a letter and given him news of the churc

12. I belong to Paul: if there was a tendency to form parti
and claim the leadership of various outstanding men, it wa
natural that some of the Corinthian Christians should consid
that their primary loyalty was to the apostle who first brought th
gospel to their city. But Paul deprecated this misuse of his name
much as the similar use of other leaders' names. Such partisanshi
was in line with the tendency in contemporary paganism to exa
religious teachers to the status of *theioi anthrōpoi*, men possessir
divine qualities.

I belong to Apollos: the learned Jew of Alexandria, who w
taught 'the way of God more accurately' by Priscilla and Aqui
when he visited Ephesus in A.D. 52 (shortly after Paul's departu
from Corinth), and then, crossing to Achaia, gave great help to th
Christian cause in Corinth when 'he powerfully confuted the Je
in public, showing by the scriptures that the Christ was Jesus' (A
18.24–28). His eloquence and skill in biblical interpretatio
perhaps along the allegorical lines characteristic of his native cit
made a deep impression on some members of the church, wh
regarded themselves as belonging to his school. There seems to ha
been no sense of personal rivalry between Paul and Apoll
however.

I belong to Cephas: Paul prefers to use this hellenized form
Aramaic *kēpā*, 'rock' (cf. Jn 1.42); other New Testament writ
use the Greek translation *Petros*. Peter may have paid a person

visit to Corinth; in any case there was a group of people in the church who invoked his authority and claimed to be his followers, and who may have represented a judaizing tendency which (unlike that attacked in Galatians) did not insist on circumcision but did insist (*inter alia*) on the food-restrictions imposed on Gentile Christians by the Jerusalem decree (Ac. 15.28f.; cf. 1 C. 8.1ff.; 10.25ff.). If Peter had any responsibility for this group, Paul could well have regarded this as a breach of the agreement of Gal. 2.6–10.

I belong to Christ: This could be Paul's retort to the other party slogans, or it could designate a fourth party in the church. Paul's affirmation in 2 C. 10.7, 'If any one is confident that he is Christ's, let him remind himself that as he is Christ's, so are we', might be quoted in support of either interpretation, but is probably irrelevant to the present passage (see p. 231). The indignant question **Is Christ divided?** (verse 13) implies that **Christ** was being used as a party name. When the probable tendencies of the other parties mentioned here are compared with tendencies referred to in the general argument of the letter, a process of elimination suggests that the 'Christ party' consisted of the self-styled 'spiritual men', the *illuminati* 'for whom "Christ" meant something like "God, freedom, and immortality", where "God" means a refined philosophical monotheism; "freedom" means emancipation from the puritanical rigours of Palestinian barbarian authorities into the wider air of self-realisation; and "immortality" means the sound Greek doctrine as opposed to the crude Jewish notion of the Resurrection' (T. W. Manson, *Studies in the Gospels and Epistles* (1962), p. 207).

13. Was Paul crucified for you? Or were you baptized in the name of Paul?: As the answer to the former question is 'No, it was Christ who was crucified for us', so the answer to the second question is 'No, it was in (better, 'into') Christ's name that we were baptized' (cf. Ac. 8.16; 19.5). To be baptized into the name of Christ is hardly distinguishable from being 'baptized into Christ' (Gal. 3.27; cf. Rom. 6.3), i.e. being incorporated into him (cf. 1 C. 12.13).

14. I baptized none of you except Crispus and Gaius: Crispus was the ruler of the synagogue in which Paul preached when first he came to Corinth; his conversion is related in Acts 18.8. He and Gaius were two of Paul's earliest converts in Corinth;

B

hence Paul baptized them himself. Gaius is probably 'Gaius, who is host to me and to the whole church' (Rom. 16.23); he has been plausibly identified with Titius Justus, the Corinthian 'God-fearer' (a Gentile who joined in Jewish worship without becoming a full convert or proselyte) who lived next door to the synagogue and placed his house at Paul's disposal when he was no longer allowed to preach in the synagogue (Acts 18.7). Gaius Titius Justus would be a complete Roman name (*praenomen, nomen gentile, cognomen*).

15. lest any should say that you were baptized in my name: so far was Paul from encouraging the cult of personality. It is not that baptism was unimportant to him, but baptism was equally valid whether administered by an apostle or by any other Christian, and Paul preferred that it should be administered by one of his colleagues, e.g. Silas or Timothy (Acts 18.5) or by one of his early converts such as Crispus or Gaius.

16. I did baptize also the household of Stephanas: 'the first converts in Achaia', according to 16.15 (cf. also 16.17). This parenthesis may be a later insertion; perhaps Stephanas on his arrival reminded Paul that he had baptized him and his family too.

17. not with eloquent wisdom: Paul took care that his hearers should not be so impressed with a rhetorical style or powers of logical reasoning that their attention might be distracted from the message itself. A passage from the *Corpus Hermeticum* is quoted as a parallel: 'The words of the Greeks cannot carry conviction: this is Greek philosophy, a mere noise of words. But our speech consists not of mere words but of utterances most replete with efficacy' (xvi. 2). It is, however, a purely verbal parallel; there is probably no literary dependence.

THE PROCLAMATION OF CHRIST CRUCIFIED **1.18–2.5**

Divine and secular wisdom **1.18–31**

18. the word of the cross: the message whose central theme is the cross of Christ. It produces opposite effects in those **who are perishing** (on the way to perdition; cf. 2.6) and those **who are being saved** (on the way to eternal life and glory; cf. 2.7). Since **folly** is here set over against **the power of God**, 'weakness' is implied along with the former and 'wisdom' along with the latter.

19. 'I will destroy . . .': a quotation from Isa. 29.14, belonging to a context which has provided recurring *NT testimonia*.

20. Where is the wise man? Where is the scribe? Where is the debater . . .?: an echo rather than a quotation of Isa. 33.18, where the collapse of the Assyrian plans against Jerusalem is celebrated (cf. also Job. 12.17; Isa. 19.12). By adding **of this age . . . of the world** Paul shows that it is secular wisdom that he is depreciating by contrast with the wisdom of God revealed in 'the word of the cross'.

21. it pleased God through the folly of what we preach to save those who believe: Greek wisdom and philosophy, says Paul, had neither led men to the knowledge of God nor brought them deliverance from sin; but these ends had now been achieved by **the folly** of the *kērygma*, the message proclaimed by the apostles. It was by the standards of secular wisdom that this message was one of **folly**, not in God's estimation or in the apostles' reckoning. But by accomplishing through this message what secular wisdom had been unable to accomplish, God had turned that wisdom into folly.

22. Jews demand signs: confirmatory tokens of divine power (cf. Mk 8.11f.; Mt. 16.1–4; Jn 2.18); but 'the word of the cross' appeared to be a proclamation of human weakness.
and Greeks seek wisdom: whereas 'the word of the cross' was by their standards a message of folly: over and above the disgrace of crucifixion, how could any one accept as lord and deliverer a man who had not sufficient wit to save himself from so ghastly a death, or look to such a man as an exponent of wisdom?

23. Christ crucified, a stumbling block to Jews: to Jews the idea of a crucified Messiah was a contradiction in terms: upon the Messiah the divine blessing rested in the highest degree (Isa. 11.2), whereas on 'a hanged man' the divine curse was expressly invoked (Dt. 21.23; cf. Gal. 3.13).
folly to Gentiles: Paul uses the terms 'Greeks' and 'Gentiles' interchangeably as counterpart to 'Jews'.

24. to those who are called: called as in 1.2; cf. Rom. 8.28, 30 ('called according to his purpose').
the power of God and the wisdom of God: the power of God in conquering the forces of evil and redeeming men from their control; **the wisdom of God** in solving by means of **Christ crucified** the problem which had defeated secular wisdom. The identification of Christ with **the wisdom of God** in primitive Christianity carries with it the ascription to him of the functions

predicated of personified Wisdom in the Wisdom literature of the *OT* and inter-testamental period, especially as God's agent in revelation and creation (cf. 8.6.). What is emphasized above all, however, is his agency in redemption (cf. verse 30).

25. wiser than men . . . stronger than men: a compendious construction, meaning 'wiser than men's wisdom, . . . stronger than men's power'.

26. not many . . . wise . . . powerful . . . noble: an indication of the social and cultural level of the church of Corinth and probably the majority of Gentile churches. Selina, Countess of Huntingdon, thanked God for the letter 'm' in 'many'; a few members, like Erastus, the city treasurer (Rom. 16.23), occupied fairly influential positions.

27–8. God chose what is foolish . . .: the Old Testament does not lack instances of God's deliberate choice of people or instruments that were foolish, weak, despised and mere nonentities by ordinary standards in order to accomplish his purpose; in this regard the gospel marked no change of procedure on his part. By this means, and pre-eminently so by the gospel, he annuls all conventional canons of wisdom, power, reputation and value. Nothing could be more subversive of these canons in the first-century Graeco-Roman world than the proclamation of a crucified man exalted as Lord over the universe.

29. so that no human being might boast: for this emphatic note in Paul's presentation of the gospel cf. Rom. 3.27; 4.2; Eph. 2.9.

30. He is the source of your life in Christ Jesus: that is, of your new, spiritual life (lit. 'from him you are in Christ Jesus'). He is the source of physical life too, but Paul's present concern is with **life in Christ Jesus** (cf. verse 2).
whom God made our wisdom, our righteousness and sanctification and redemption: the last three substantives are not correlative with **wisdom**; they denote aspects of the wisdom which believers find in Christ, in whom they are justified (see note on 2 C. 5.21), sanctified and redeemed (cf. 6.11).

31. 'Let him who boasts, boast of the Lord': a near-quotation from Jer. 9.24. It has been suggested that Paul recollects a sermon preached on the 9th day of the month Ab, one of the great fast-days of the Jewish year, for which the *haphṭarah*, or prophetic lesson, was Jer. 8.13–9.24 (H. St. J. Thackeray, *The*

Septuagint and Jewish Worship (1920), pp. 80ff., especially pp. 96f.);
but this is quite doubtful.

Paul's reliance on spiritual power 2.1–5

2.1. proclaiming the testimony of God: For **testimony**
(*martyrion*) some important early texts (including probably the
earliest of all, *P⁴⁶*) read 'mystery' (*mystērion*). The former reading is
in line with 1.6, the latter with 2.7. The gospel was both the message
to which the apostles bore witness and the divine revelation,
previously concealed, which they made known.

**2. I decided to know nothing among you except Jesus
Christ and him crucified:** cf. 1.23. This was no new policy on
Paul's part, adopted (as some have thought) because of the ill
success of another approach at Athens (Ac. 17.22–31): it was his
regular practice (cf. Gal. 3.1).

3. in weakness and in much fear and trembling: this
probably does not refer to his general state of health; it might
refer to reaction after his recent experiences in Macedonia and
Athens and concern for his friends in Thessalonica, whom he had
been compelled to leave so precipitately (1 Th. 3.1–5), but more to
a sense of complete personal inadequacy in view of the task of
evangelizing such a city as Corinth. This is the background of the
encouragement given to him in Ac. 18.9f.

4. in plausible words of wisdom: Gk *en peithois sophias
logos*, for which we should perhaps read 'in plausibility of wisdom'
(*en peithoi sophias*), a reading supported by *P⁴⁶*.
in demonstration of the Spirit and power: if Paul's words
carried conviction, that conviction was produced, not by any
eloquence or reasoning skill of his, but by the power of the Spirit
applying the message to the hearers' conscience.

5. that your faith might not rest in the wisdom of men:
Paul may have in mind some visitors to Corinth after his departure
who tried to improve on his work; in any case, the precaution was
necessary in view of the Corinthians' high regard for secular
wisdom. **but in the power of God:** the preaching of Christ
crucified, made effective in them by the Spirit.

THE HIDDEN WISDOM OF GOD 2.6–13

6. among the mature we do impart wisdom: some of the
Corinthian Christians, especially perhaps after hearing Apollos

and other visitors, were inclined to dismiss Paul's teaching as elementary, ABC stuff. He assures them that he has more advanced teaching to impart to those who are spiritually **mature** (*teleioi*, a word used in mystery religions of the 'initiated'), but evidently he does not regard the Corinthians as sufficiently mature to assimilate this wisdom (cf. 3.1–3). Spiritual maturity, his whole letter suggests, depends not so much on knowledge (*gnōsis*), in which they were not deficient, as on love (*agapē*).

not a wisdom of this age or of the rulers of this age: the wisdom of which Paul speaks is not secular wisdom, which is dominated by the rulers (*archontes*) or powers that control the current climate of opinion. These powers are **doomed to pass away:** they are on the way out, because Christ is now reigning (cf. 15.24f.) and their dominion is at an end (cf. Col. 2.15).

7. a secret and hidden wisdom of God: lit. 'God's wisdom in a mystery, the (wisdom which has been) hidden'. In *NT*, as in the Qumran literature, a mystery is commonly some aspect of God's eschatological purpose, formerly obscure, which is now made known by a further revelation; in *NT* this eschatological purpose is fulfilled in Christ (cf. 2 C. 1.19f.). It is evident that the mystery of which Paul speaks here is not something additional to the saving message of Christ crucified; it is in Christ crucified that the wisdom of God is embodied. It consists rather in the more detailed unfolding of the divine purpose summed up in Christ crucified (see note on 13.2a).

which God decreed before the ages: this is expanded in Eph. 3.2–12, where the 'mystery of Christ, . . . hidden for ages in God' is now divulged as 'the manifold wisdom of God . . . to the principalities and powers in the heavenly places . . . according to the eternal purpose which he has realized in Christ Jesus our Lord'. There is substance in H. Schlier's remark that it is in the Epistle to the Ephesians that **the secret and hidden wisdom of God,** on which Paul does not enlarge here to the Corinthians, is imparted 'among the mature' (*Der Brief an die Epheser* (1965[5]), pp. 21f.).

for our glorification: for the glorifying of the people of God as the climax of his saving purpose, cf. Rom. 8.30; this glorifying consists in their attaining perfect conformity to the exalted Christ.

8. None of the rulers of this age understood this: this is true of the human authorities responsible for the condemnation of Christ (cf. Ac. 4.25–28; 3.17f.), but Paul is thinking rather of the powers in the spiritual realm by which the human authorities were impelled on their chosen course.

they would not have crucified the Lord of glory: thus ensuring their own doom. Cf. Col. 2.15, where the passion of Christ is portrayed as his victorious struggle against aggressive 'principalities and powers'; a hint of this probably appears here and there in the Gospels (cf. Lk. 22.53, 'the power of darkness'; Jn 12.31; 14.30; 16.11, 'the ruler of this world'). The **Lord of glory** himself embodies the divine fulness and it is by union with him that his people are to be glorified: the *archontes* had no inkling of his true being when they imagined they had him at their mercy.

9. **'What no eye has seen . . .':** the introductory words **as it is written** imply that this is a quotation from an authoritative document, but the document cannot be identified. The words resemble Isa. 64.4, but are not a direct quotation of it. Origen on Mt. 27.9 (cf. Jerome on Isa. 64.4; Ambrosiaster on 1 C. 2.9) says they appear in the *Secrets (Apocalypse) of Elijah*, but they are not in the fragment of that (probably post-Pauline) work which has survived. They are frequently quoted in the early Christian centuries, especially by Gnostic writers, because they lent themselves readily to a Gnostic interpretation. Before the end of the second century they were ascribed to Jesus (cf. *Acts of Peter* 39; *Gospel of Thomas* 17). The language of 1 Jn 1.1 could be a deliberate rebuttal of their Gnostic interpretation.

10. **God has revealed to us through the Spirit:** whatever the original force of the quotation was, Paul declares that the wonderful mysteries **which God has prepared for those who love him** are accessible **through the Spirit** to all believers. This is no esoteric knowledge, confined to an inner ring of select initiates.

the Spirit searches . . . the depths of God: in later Gnosticism **depths** connoted recondite knowledge; here it refers to the revelation of the divine essence and purpose. Paul may have in mind Job 11.7, 'Can you find out the deep things of God?' (although the LXX rendering is quite different).

11–12. **we have received: we** is emphatic (Gk *hēmeis*); he means 'we believers in Christ' as distinct from followers of secular wisdom. He takes it for granted that his readers as well as himself have received the Spirit (cf. 3.16; 6.19; 12.13); but the wisdom which the Spirit imparts can be acquired only by diligent study, with humble and receptive minds; and the Corinthian Christians gave little evidence of progress in this study.

not the spirit of the world (by which secular wisdom is informed) **but the Spirit which is from God:** for the antithesis cf. Rom. 8.15 ('not . . . the spirit of slavery . . . but . . . the spirit of sonship'); 2 Tim. 1.7 ('not . . . a spirit of timidity but a spirit of power and love and self-control').

that we might understand the gifts bestowed on us by God: as a man's own spirit best understands his inner thoughts, so the Spirit of God alone can grasp divine truths (verse 11), and alone can interpret to those within whom he dwells 'the things that are freely given to us by God' (*RV*).

13. in words not taught by human wisdom but taught by the Spirit: the implication is that divine truths should not be communicated in rhetorical forms suitable for secular wisdom; the Spirit supplies the language as well as the substance of revelation.

interpreting spiritual truths to those who possess the Spirit: lit. 'to spiritual (men)', the adjective *pneumatikois* being construed as dative of the indirect object; but it could equally well be taken as an instrumental dative, as in the first of the two alternative marginal renderings, 'interpreting spiritual truths in spiritual language', which suits the preceding words better.

SPIRITUAL, UNSPIRITUAL AND FLESHLY MEN 2.14–3.4

The source of spiritual insight 2.14–16

14. The unspiritual man: lit. the 'soulish' man (Gk *psychikos*), the man who is controlled by his 'soul' (*psychē*) or natural self. The distinction between the adjectives *psychikos* and *pneumatikos* ('spiritual') recurs in 15.44–46, where the present mortal body of 'earth' is called the *sōma psychikon* (*RSV* 'physical body'), while the resurrection body, which is immortal and heavenly, is called the *sōma pneumatikon* ('spiritual body'). There the distinction between the two kinds of body is based on the fact that the first Adam was created 'a living *psychē*' (Gen. 2.7) whereas Christ, the last Adam, the firstfruits of the resurrection order, has become 'a life-giving spirit (*pneuma*)'. Everything that belongs to our heritage from the first Adam, the father of our mortal humanity, is therefore *psychikon*; everything which we derive from union with the exalted

Christ, the head of the new creation, is *pneumatikon*, the more so as
it is conveyed to us by the Spirit. Hence the **unspiritual** (unregenerate) **man** is the man who is exclusively 'in Adam'. Since he
has not received the Spirit, **the gifts of the Spirit . . . are folly
to him;** he lacks the organ by which alone they can be appreciated.

15. The spiritual man, the man who has received the Spirit
of God and is a member of the risen Christ, **judges all things:** or
'discerns' them; the same verb *anakrinō* is used as at the end of
verse 14. By **all things** we should understand 'the gifts bestowed
on us by God' (verse 12).

but is himself to be judged (discerned) **by no one:** elsewhere
in the letter this epigram is spelt out in practical terms, as when
Paul says (4.3f.), 'with me it is a very small thing that I should be
judged by you or by any human court. I do not even judge myself.
. . . It is the Lord who judges me' (where the three occurrences of
'judge' represent Gk. *anakrinō*, as here). It is plain throughout that
he recognizes the value of self-judgment (11.31), constructive
criticism (11.17ff.) and community discipline (5.3ff.); but ultimately the man of God is answerable to God alone, and in any
case he cannot be assessed at all by those who have not the same
Spirit as he has received.

**16. 'For who has known the mind of the Lord so as to
instruct him?':** a quotation from Isa. 40.13 (also quoted in Rom.
11.34), where Gk. *nous* ('mind') renders Hebrew *rûaḥ* ('spirit').
But we (emphatic, as in verse 12) **have the mind of Christ:**
the man who by the Spirit is united to Christ shares **the mind of
Christ;** what is impossible for the 'unspiritual' man, to know **the
mind of the Lord**, is now open to him.

Milk for spiritual infants 3.1–4

**3.1. But . . . I could not address you as spiritual men,
but as men of the flesh:** Here a third category, that of **men of
the flesh** (*sarkinoi*), is added to the 'unspiritual' and 'spiritual'
men of 2.14f. This threefold division is not the later Gnostic
(Valentinian) division of mankind into 'spiritual' (*pneumatikon*),
'earthy' (*choïkon*) and 'soulish' (*psychikon*), of which the 'spiritual'
kind (*genos*) partakes of heavenly wisdom and is destined for
perfection, the 'earthy' is doomed to corruption, and the 'soulish'
will rest in an intermediate state of refreshment, if it strives after
the better part, but otherwise it also goes to corruption (Irenaeus,

Haer. I. vii. 5). For Paul, while all 'unspiritual' men are **men of the flesh**, it is possible even for those who are in some sense **spiritual men** to be so described. The Corinthian Christians had received the Spirit, but they did not live as those who had received him; indulgence in party-strife was not a 'spiritual' activity, but a 'fleshly' one. They had not yet begun to produce the 'fruit of the Spirit' (Gal. 5.22), but continued to indulge in some at least of the 'works of the flesh', among which dissension and party spirit are listed (Gal. 5.20). By **flesh** in this sense Paul does not mean the body, but fallen humanity with the sum-total of sinful propensities inherited by natural birth. That these should persist in men who have received the Spirit is part of the paradox which finds expression in Paul's repeated injunctions to his readers to be what they are—to be in practical conduct what they are by divine calling as members of Christ (see note on 5.7). Far from being 'mature' (2.6), these Corinthians were still **babes in Christ.**

2. As such they had to be fed on **milk, not solid food.** This analogy was commonplace in contemporary pedagogics; for *NT* parallels cf. Heb. 5.12–14, where those who ought by this time to have attained maturity are admonished for not having passed beyond the milk stage, and 1 Pet. 2.2, where new converts are encouraged to acquire an appetite for 'the pure spiritual milk' that they may grow up to full health. Paul was perhaps blamed for not giving his converts such advanced 'knowledge' as some subsequent teachers had given them; his reply is that they are not yet able to digest it. But the **solid food** of which he speaks is the 'secret and hidden wisdom' of 2.7; it is the fuller exposition of Christ crucified. If they treated this as 'milk for babes' in comparison with the kind of knowledge for which they craved, that showed that they were still applying the standards of secular wisdom and maintaining the attitude of 'men of the flesh'.

3. jealousy (*zēlos*) **and strife** (*eris*)**:** these are included in the 'works of the flesh' in Gal. 5.20 (cf. 2 C. 12.20); men of the Spirit ought to have got rid of such things. Of these two, *eris* is always bad; *zēlos* may be good (cf. 2 C. 7.7, 11; 9.2; 11.2), in which case it is usually translated 'zeal'.

4. 'I belong to Paul' . . . **'I belong to Apollos':** This was reprehensible enough, but while only the partisans of Paul and Apollos are referred to here, it was from other parties that Paul's chief trouble came. He avoids giving any appearance of an attack on Peter, but Apollos and his followers presented no challenge to Paul's apostleship (cf. 4.6). Partisanship was consonant with the wisdom of men (the leading philosophical schools of Greece invoked the names of their founders and chief teachers), but not with 'the mind of Christ'.

GOD'S FIELD AND GOD'S BUILDING 3.5–17

5. Apollos and **Paul** were but **servants** (*diakonoi*) of Christ, each performing the task assigned to him by his Master.

6–8. I planted, Apollos watered, but God gave the growth: The service of God is first compared to a field, in which each servant has his allotted work to do. While Paul **planted** the gospel seed in Corinth, he regards Apollos's activity there after his own departure as perfectly normal and proper: **Apollos watered** the seed; but it was God, not the planter or the waterer, who made it grow. The planter and the waterer will be paid their appropriate **wages** on the 'day of Christ' (cf. 3.13; 4.5).

9. we are fellow workers for God: lit. 'God's fellow-workers' (*RV*, *NEB*), which may mean that Paul and Apollos work together **for God** or work together 'with God' (*AV*); in the present context they are God's servants, not his partners; the former rendering is therefore far preferable (cf. note on 2 C. 6.1).

you are . . . God's building: Paul now changes the figure of a field for that of a building, more particularly a temple. These two figures appear side by side in Qumran literature, e.g. in 1 QS viii.5f. ('the council of the community shall be established in truth as an eternal plantation, a holy house for Israel'); see on verses 16f.

10. I laid a foundation, and another man is building upon it: in the field, Paul plants the seed and Apollos waters it; when the figure is changed, Paul lays the **foundation** (as he had done in founding the Corinthian church) and someone else lays the upper courses. But this other person is evidently not Apollos: no exception was taken to Apollos's watering what Paul had sown, but there is a more critical note in the references to building on the foundation Paul had laid. In the light of Paul's own policy not to 'build on another man's foundation' (Rom. 15.20)—and especially so in Rome—we may not be far astray in discerning here an allusion to the Peter party and even, perhaps, in identifying **another man** with Peter himself. In any case, care must be exercised over the quality of the material and workmanship that go into building on the foundation.

11. For no other foundation can any one lay than that which is laid, which is Jesus Christ: it is conceivable that some of the Peter party, depreciating Paul's apostolic claims, had told the Corinthians that it was to Peter that Jesus said 'you are Peter, and on this rock (*petra*) I will build my church' (Mt. 16.18). Paul assures them that the only **foundation** that can be laid for the church is Christ himself, and that was the foundation which Paul had laid at Corinth with his preaching of 'Jesus Christ and him crucified'. The concept of Christ as the foundation—natural in itself—was strengthened in the early church by the use of Isa. 28.16 ('Behold, I am laying in Zion for a foundation a stone, a tested stone . . .') frequently conflated with other 'stone' passages in *OT*, as a *testimonium* of Christ (cf. Rom. 9.33; 1 Pet. 2.6). No one else, whatever the meaning of his name, could fill this rôle.

12–15. The quality of the foundation could not be disputed, but the state of the building depended on what was erected on this foundation. Was the material durable, like **gold, silver, precious stones**, or combustible, like **wood, hay, stubble?** In a fire which broke out suddenly and spread rapidly through one of those ancient cities, structures of durable material would survive with little damage, while wooden shacks would go up in smoke. Paul had taught his converts the basic truths of the gospel. What kind of teaching had others given them? Was it teaching that would stand the fiery test of persecution? Above all, was it teaching that would stand the searching test of final judgment on **the Day**? The quality of the material and the workmanship alike would then be shown for what it really was: the faithful servant would **receive a reward**, while faulty workmanship would be consumed, and the worker would **suffer loss.** He himself would **be saved**, like a man pulled to safety through the smoke and flames of his burning house, for his salvation depends on God's grace, not on his own works; but he would have nothing to show for all his labour.

16. Do you not know . . .?: the question may suggest previous catechetical instruction (cf. 6.2, 3, 9, 15, 16, 19, etc.).
that you are God's temple: the 'building' of v. 9 is more closely defined as a sanctuary (Gk *naos*) for God to inhabit. The idea of the believing community, especially the community of the end-time, as a living temple of God, in contrast to a 'house made with

hands', is found both in the Qumran texts (cf. 1 QS v.5f., viii.4ff., 9.5f., where the Qumran community is a 'holy house' [*bêt qôdeš*] and its priestly members or its inner council a 'holy of holies' [*qôdeš qôdāšîm*]) and in *NT* (cf. 2 C. 6.14; Eph. 2.20ff.; 1 Pet. 2.4ff.; also Heb. 3.6; 9.11f., 23f.; Jn 2.19ff.; Ac. 7.48). But in the *NT* community the distinction between 'holy house' and 'holy of holies' disappears. **and that God's Spirit dwells in you:** cf. Eph. 2.22. In the Qumran teaching the institution of the 'holy house' is associated with the laying of the 'foundation of holy spirit for eternal truth' (1 QS ix.3f.); there the 'holy spirit' is bestowed as a sign of the end-time, but does not acquire the personal quality which is commonly found in the *NT* doctrine. The *OT* background may be recognized in Ezek. 11.19f.; 36.25–27; 37.26–28, with spiritualization of the 'sanctuary' which is to be 'in the midst of them for evermore'. For the body of the individual member of a community as a temple of the Holy Spirit cf. 1 C. 6.19. See B. Gärtner, *The Temple and the Community in Qumran and the NT* (1965), especially pp. 56ff.

17. If any one destroys God's temple, God will destroy him: the temple of God can be destroyed, or defiled (Gk *phtheirō*), by party-spirit and quarrelling, so let them beware; the punishment for such sacrilege will fit the crime (cf. 11.30).

For God's temple is holy: because his Spirit dwells in it, just as the tabernacle in the wilderness and the temple in Jerusalem were holy because his 'name' or his 'glory' dwelt there.

and that temple you are: a reaffirmation of verse 16a.

STEWARDS OF THE MYSTERIES OF GOD 3.18–4.5

Warning and encouragement 3.18–23

18–20. Let no one deceive himself: Paul reverts to the theme of wisdom and folly; if God's wisdom is folly by the standards of this world, **the wisdom of this world is folly with God,** and it is God's assessment that counts in the end. Let them learn to evaluate everything in the light of divine wisdom. Two further *OT* texts underline this lesson (in addition to those quoted in 1.19f.), from Job 5.13a and Ps. 94.11a.

craftiness: Gk *panourgia*, 'cunning' in 2 C. 4.2; 11.3; see notes on 2 C. 11.3; 12.16.

21. So let no one boast of men: by claiming one only of the servants of God as leader they are not only showing their enslavement to secular fashions; they are impoverishing themselves, for all the servants of God are equally theirs. In fact **all things** are theirs because of their union with Christ, who is Lord of all things; they are 'heirs of God and fellow heirs with Christ' (Rom. 8.17). In Stoic literature the theme that the wise man possesses everything is a commonplace; for Paul, the truly wise man is he who has embraced the wisdom of God in Christ crucified.

22. whether Paul or Apollos or Cephas: as in 1.12, and unlike 3.4ff., he includes **Cephas** along with **Apollos** and himself—not necessarily 'because here Paul is writing somewhat rhetorically and is off his guard' (C. K. Barrett, in *Abraham unser Vater* (1963), p. 5) but because he deliberately makes his readers' heritage in Christ as comprehensive as possible.

or the world or life or death or the present or the future: this rhetorical piling up of terms is similar to the catalogue in Rom. 8.38f. of the things which cannot separate the believer from the love of God; **the world** is not reproduced there, but it is relevant here because they are to inherit it (cf. Rom. 4.13, where Abraham's 'descendants' are his spiritual children) and to exercise authority over it (cf. 6.2).

23. and you are Christ's: not one group of them only (cf. 1.12) but all of them together.

and Christ is God's: as they themselves, together with the universe are under the authority of Christ, so Christ himself is subordinate to God, the author of all (cf. 8.6; 11.3; 15.28).

The one valid judgment 4.1-5

4.1. servants of Christ and stewards of the mysteries of God: this is how the apostles and other eminent teachers should be looked upon, not as party-leaders. The word **servants** (Gk *hypēretai*) is different from that so rendered in 3.5 (Gk *diakonoi*), but in practice there is little distinction between them. The 'steward' (Gk *oikonomos*) was the servant entrusted with the administration of his master's business or property; his responsibility was to devote his time, ability and energy to his master's interests, not to his own. The apostles were **stewards** entrusted with the administration of **the mysteries of God**, i.e. the truths of the gospel.

2. it is required of stewards that they be found trust-

worthy: unlike the dishonest steward of the parable, who squandered his master's goods (Lk. 16.1ff.). Their trustworthiness will be tested when they have to submit their accounts for scrutiny.

3. it is a very small thing that I should be judged by you or by any human court: lit. 'by a human day' (Gk *hypo anthrōpinēs hēmeras*); 'day', in the sense of 'judgment day', comes to be used for the judgment itself (by analogy, perhaps, with 'the day of the Lord', when divine judgment is executed). A trustworthy steward need not trouble greatly about the opinions of others, provided his master is satisfied with him. Members of the Corinthian church might put Paul high up or low down on their list of favourite ministers; but this was a matter of little consequence in his eyes (see note on 2.15); even his own self-assessment was ultimately immaterial, although in this as in other respects he endeavoured to preserve a good conscience.

4. I am not aware of anything against myself: the verb **I am . . . aware** (Gk *synoida*) is that from which the word for 'conscience' (Gk *syneidēsis*) is derived (cf. 8.7, etc.). The clause is strongly reminiscent of Job 27.6b, LXX, 'I am not aware (Gk *ou synoida emautō*) of having done anything wrong'.
but I am not thereby acquitted: lit. 'justified'. 'Even if . . . the "silence" of conscience can be taken to mean that a man has done nothing wrong, it can never be assumed from it that he has been accounted righteous' (C. A. Pierce, *Conscience in the NT* (1955), p. 89).
It is the Lord who judges me: he alone has the authority, because Paul is his servant; he alone has the requisite insight to appraise the true springs of action.

5. do not pronounce judgment before the time, before the Lord comes: any present judgment must be partial, premature and incompetent. How seriously Paul regarded the prospect of having his apostolic service reviewed at the parousia, the day of Christ, can be gathered repeatedly from his letters (cf. 2 C. 1.14; 5.9f.; Phil. 2.16; 1 Th. 2. 19f.).
the things now hidden in darkness: including the inner motives, of which the man concerned may himself be unconscious. Cf. 14.25.
will disclose the purposes of the heart: the heart in the Bible is the seat of the understanding and the will; cf. *OT* passages where God tests, knows, and searches the heart (e.g. Pss. 17.3; 26.2; 44.21; 139.23; Jer. 17.10; see also Ac. 1.24; 15.8; Rom. 8.27).

every man will receive his commendation from God: in accordance with his faithfulness as a servant and the quality of his service. It is noteworthy that Paul uses the positive word *epainos* ('praise'), rather than a more ambivalent word for recompense, good or bad as the case may be (as in 2 C. 5.10; Col. 3.25). The implication may be that the Lord in his omniscience will find cause for approval where another judge would find none.

THE APOSTLES AND THEIR CONVERTS 4.6–21

6. I have applied all this to myself and Apollos: lit. 'I have tranformed (transferred) all this . . .', the verb *metaschēmatizō* is used in 2 C. 11.13ff. of false teachers masquerading as apostles of Christ and of Satan disguising himself as an angel of light, and in Phil. 3.21 of the changing of the present mortal body into conformity with Christ's glorified body. Paul has used various figures of speech—agricultural workers, builders, stewards—and **applied** them to himself and Apollos. 'I have given this teaching of mine the form of an exposition concerning Apollos and myself' (Bauer–Arndt–Gingrich); if there are others to whom the lesson is suitable, then let it be applied to them too. No one who knew of the friendly relations between Paul and Apollos would suppose that any criticism of Apollos was intended here, but Paul takes care not to say anything that might be construed as criticism of Peter.

that you may learn by us to live according to scripture: lit. 'that you may learn by us the (saying) "Not beyond what is written!" ' This is a well-known crux, which has been variously explained. By an early emendation the verb *phronein* was added; hence *AV* 'not to think . . . above that which is written'. F. A. Bornemann, followed by J. M. S. Baljon and F. Blass, treated the concluding phrase as a scribal note, as though *to mē hyper ha gegraptai* were actually *to 'mē' hyper 'a' gegraptai*, 'the word *mē* ("not") is written above the letter *a*', the implication being that *mē* ('not'), the second word in the following clause, was accidentally omitted and then written in above the line, over the *a* of *hina* ('that'). This solution is more ingenious than convincing. If we take the phrase as part of the text, the absence of a verb gives it the appearance of a familiar saying, 'Not beyond what is written!' or 'Keep to the book!'—not, probably, a current proverb, but a saying well known in the Corinthian church, where some were disposed to go beyond the gospel of Christ crucified and risen, which they had received 'in accordance with the scriptures' (15.3f.), and to add to it elements more in accordance with secular wisdom (cf. M. D. Hooker, 'Beyond the things which are written', *NTS* 10 (1963–4), pp. 127ff.). Such elements might be of the nature of gnosticizing philosophy; they might also take the form of party-spirit. Either of these possibilities, and especially the latter, merited the caution: **that none of you may be puffed up in favour of one against another.** In this letter Paul repeatedly uses the verb to be puffed up (Gk. *physioomai*, 'be inflated') of attitudes or activities which smack of human pride rather than heavenly love (cf. verses 18, 19; 5.2; 8.1; 13.4).

7. who sees anything different in you?: the verb *diakrinō* means 'distinguish'; 'who concedes you any superiority?' (Bauer–Arndt–Gingrich). There is no room for pride or boasting in one's talents or attainments: these are gifts from God, and the proper attitude towards them is humble gratitude to him.

8. Already you are filled!: Paul addresses them ironically; there is no point in encouraging them to endure hardship now in view of the glory to come, for already they speak and act as though they had all that heart could wish.

Without us you have become kings: according to Paul's teaching, Christ, having been raised from the dead, was now exercising his messianic kingship in his state of glory (cf. 15.25); when his people in their turn were raised from the dead at his parousia (cf. 15.22f.), they would share his glory (cf. Col. 3.4). But as for him suffering preceded glory, so for his people the same order was prescribed: 'provided we suffer with him in order that we may also be glorified with him' (Rom. 8.17; cf. the hymn quoted in 2 Tim. 2.12, 'if we endure, we shall also reign with him'). Some of Paul's Corinthian friends, however, in terms of an 'over-realized' eschatology (cf. 15.12; 2 Th. 2.2; 2 Tim. 2.18), were speaking and acting as if they had already attained the kingdom and the glory simultaneously with the gift of the Spirit. In this, it has been suggested, they anticipated the second-century follow-ers of Prodicus, self-styled Gnostics, who claimed to be 'by nature sons of the first God' and therefore 'royal sons far above the rest of mankind' (Clement of Alexandria, *Stromateis* iii. 30). Whether there is any direct connection or not, the followers of Prodicus may have appealed to Mt. 17.25f. in support of their argument that 'for a king there is no law prescribed' and that they could therefore do as they pleased (an argument not unlike the libertarian slogan quoted in 6.12; 10.23). Paul's reaction to the Corinthians' pretensions is to say that it is a pity they are wrong because, if only they were right, he and his fellow-apostles would know that for them too suffering was a thing of the past: **would that you did reign, so that we might share the rule with you!**

9. As it is, the apostles' suffering is still very much a thing of the present: indeed, they seem to get more than their fair share of it. Not that Paul had any complaint to make on this score; on the contrary, he was eager to absorb in his own person as much as possible of what remained of 'Christ's afflictions' so that his fellow-Christians might have the less to endure (cf. 2 C. 1.4–7; 4.12; Col. 1.24). He compares the apostles' lot to that of **men sentenced to death** (Gk *epithanatioi*), condemned criminals in the amphitheatre, **exhibited . . . last of all** to fight with wild beasts (cf. 15.32) as the *grand finale* of the games, **a spectacle** (*theatron*) in the eyes of heaven and earth. A similar figure is used by Paul's contemporary Seneca when he describes the good man, the Stoic ideal, facing unfriendly fortune in such a spirit as to provide a spectacle fit for God to watch with attention and joy (*De prouidentia* ii. 9–11).

10–11. Paul piles up the antitheses between the apostles and the Corinthian Christians: the former are reckoned **fools**, albeit **for Christ's sake, . . . weak** and disreputable; they are exposed to privation of every kind in contrast to the 'fulness' and 'riches' of the latter, who (in their own estimation at least) are **wise in Christ, . . . strong** and **held in honour.**

12–13. we labour, working with our own hands: a reference more especially to Paul's own practice; cf. 9.15–18; 2 C. 11.7–11; 12.13–15; 1 Th. 2.9; 2 Th. 3.7–9; Ac. 20.34.

when reviled, we bless . . .: the teaching of Jesus to this effect, known to us from Mt. 5.39–45; Lk. 6.27–36, was familiar to the first-generation Christians; cf. Rom. 12.14–21.

we try to conciliate: Gk *parakaloumen*, 'we humbly make our appeal' (*NEB*) or 'we speak in a friendly manner' (cf. Bauer–Arndt–Gingrich). Of the wide variety of meanings covered by the verb *parakaleō*, the one to be discerned here must form a sufficient contrast to **slandered.**

as the refuse of the world: the *perikatharmata* are the impurities removed and thrown away when a vessel is cleaned, but the word was used in a derivative sense of the 'scapegoat' type of victim on to which the guilt of a community was unloaded, and this victim might be a human being. If Paul is using the word in this sense, it would fit in well with his comparison of the apostles to the condemned criminals in the ampitheatre.

the offscouring of all things: Gk *peripsēma*, that which is scraped off (*peripsaō*), has a similar meaning to *perikatharma* both primarily and derivatively, 'especially of those criminals, generally the vilest of their class, whose blood was shed to expiate the sins of the nation and to avert the wrath of the gods' (J. B. Lightfoot, on Ignatius, *Eph.* 8.1, where Ignatius calls himself the *peripsēma* of his Christian friends, their substitutionary sacrifice; cf. *Eph.* 18.1, where he calls himself the *peripsēma* of the cross, its devoted slave).

14–15. Paul assures them that if his admonitory language seems sharp, it is not intended to put them out of countenance; he writes to his **beloved children** as their **father in Christ Jesus.** Apollos and others might help them as **guides** (*paidagōgoi*) **in Christ**, but Paul alone could claim to be their **father . . . through the gospel:** they owed their spiritual life to his coming to their city and evangelizing it. The *paidagōgos* was the personal attendant who accompanied the boy, took him to school and home again, heard him recite his 'lines', taught him good manners and generally looked after him; he was entitled to respect and normally received it, but there was no comparison between his relation to the boy and that of the boy's father.

16. be imitators of me: as the father should be a model for his sons to imitate, so is Paul to his converts; see on 11.1; cf. also 1 Th. 1.6; 2 Th. 3.7ff.; Phil. 3.17; 4.9. Paul saw to it that his converts should learn the Christian way of life from his example as well as from his teaching. See W. P. De Boer, *The Imitation of Paul* (1962), especially pp. 139ff.

17. Therefore I sent to you Timothy: the aorist *epempsa* may be epistolary, in which case the proper translation would be 'I am sending' (cf. 2 C. 8.18, 22). But the absence of Timothy's name from the salutation in 1.1 (contrast 2 C. 1.1) suggests that he had already set out on his journey. There is a later reference to Timothy's visit in 16.10f. It is uncertain whether this visit of Timothy's is the same as in Ac. 19.22 and/or Phil. 2.19, 23.

my beloved and faithful child in the Lord: Timothy was one of Paul's converts on his first missionary visit to South Galatia and thenceforth one of his closest associates (Ac. 16.1–13; 1 Tim. 1.2; 2 Tim. 1.2–6). His name is associated with Paul's in the introductory salutation of six epistles (2 C. 1.1; Phil. 1.1; Col. 1.1; 1 Th. 1.1; 2 Th. 1.1; Phm. 1); for Paul's appreciation of his character and service see Phil. 2.20–22.

to remind you of my ways in Christ, as I teach them everywhere in every church: Paul's ways are the ethical principles which he practised in his life and enjoined in his teaching. This ethical use of the noun *hodos*, 'way' (cf. 12.31), may be compared with the rabbinical use of *hǎlākāh* ('rule'), and is parallel to the ethical use of the verb *peripateō*, 'walk' (cf. 3.3, etc.). Paul's concern that all his churches should exhibit the same standards of Christian practice finds expression in 7.17; 11.16; 14.33. This naturally called for a recognized tradition (*paradosis*) such as he appeals to in 11.2 (cf. 2 Th. 2.15; 3.6).

18–19. Timothy's visit will be followed shortly by a visit from Paul himself (cf. Phil. 2.23f.); on the complex question of Paul's visits to Corinth, see pp. 164ff., 250. Some members of the church, who belittled his authority, showed themselves **arrogant**, lit. 'inflated' (as he may have learned from 'Chloe's people'), suggesting that he would not dare to come and face the opposition that was mounting. He assures them all that he is determined to **come . . . soon, if the Lord wills**; then it will be seen if there is any substance in these people's confident boasting or if it will collapse like an inflated balloon when it is pricked—and this is what he expects to happen, for he has reason to believe that all this opposition and pretension to superior knowledge is so much **talk.**

20. For the kingdom of God does not consist in talk but in power: the contrast between **talk** (*logos*) and **power** (*dynamis*) has been pointed out already in 2.1–5; here, as there, it is the Holy Spirit's **power** that is meant. The form 'the kingdom of God is not X but Y' recurs in Rom. 14.17 (see also on 2 C. 1.19).

21. What do you wish?: Come he will, but it is for them to decide whether his visit will be a painful or a pleasant one, whether it will be an occasion for wielding the **rod** of apostolic discipline or for mutual **love in a spirit of gentleness.**

These references to Timothy's forthcoming visit, to be followed by one from himself, would be appropriate for the end of a letter. It is probable that Paul was indeed about to conclude this letter and despatch it by the hand of a messenger when further news from

Corinth arrived and made it necessary for him to dictate much more. This news was brought, probably, by the bearers of the letter to which he replies in 7.1ff.—possibly Stephanas, Fortunatus and Achaicus (16.17)—who supplemented the letter by word of mouth.

PAUL DEALS WITH FURTHER REPORTS 5.1–6.20

AN URGENT CALL FOR CHURCH DISCIPLINE 5.1–13

5.1. It is actually reported: the abruptness with which this subject is introduced suggests that the report has just reached Paul's ears; he deals with it immediately and peremptorily.
that there is immorality among you: the *RSV* choice of the vague word **immorality** for the quite precise Gr. *porneia* is regrettable; *porneia* means 'fornication' and is here used, in a sense occasionally attested for *'erwāh* in rabbinical Hebrew and *zᵉnût* in the Zadokite Document, of cohabitation within forbidden degrees.
and of a kind that is not found even among pagans; for a man is living with his father's wife: i.e. his step-mother (who could, of course, have been younger than himself). This was forbidden by the Torah (Lev. 18.8; Dt. 22.30; 27.20). The prohibition, with the others accompanying it, was taken over into the Church; this is probably the force of the ban on *porneia* in the Jerusalem decree (Ac. 15.20, 29; 21.25), and may also explain the reference to *porneia* in the 'exceptive' phrases of Mt. 5.32; 19.9. The traditional Greek reprobation of this particular kind of union finds expression in Euripides' *Hippolytus*; for the conventional Roman attitude to a similar relationship, cf. Cicero's *Pro Cluentio* 14, where a marriage between son-in-law and mother-in-law is denounced as 'incredible and, apart from this one instance, unheard of'. It is not clear whether the man's father was still alive; commentators who find this matter referred to later in 2 C. 7.12 naturally conclude from the mention there of 'the one who suffered the wrong' that he was, but this interpretation of 2 C. 7.12 is doubtful. Even if he was dead, the law which forbade marriage with a deceased brother's wife (except in the special case of the levirate marriage) *a fortiori* forbade marriage with a deceased father's wife. Paul does not stop to show reason why the levitical regulations in this matter should continue to be observed, when in

so many other respects they were no longer binding; had he been challenged on this point he might have considered that the coincidence of Mosaic legislation and pagan custom entitled him to silence any objection with 'Does not nature itself teach you . . .?' (cf. 11.14). Although at a later date the reckoning of a proselyte to Judaism from paganism as 'a new-born child' was held to annul all his former blood-relationships, so that he was permitted henceforth to marry any woman to whom he was akin on his father's side—even his father's wife, according to some (e.g. Rabbi Meir, TB *Y˖ḇāmôṯ* 98*b*, *Sanhedrin* 57*b*)—Paul betrays no knowledge of such a doctrine or of its applicability to a situation like this. Such a *mésalliance* would bring the Church and the gospel into public disrepute; many people were only too ready to believe the worst about Christian morality, and this would provide them with material ground for their suspicions. Besides, if news of such a thing travelled to Jerusalem (as it certainly would), misgivings about the wisdom of Paul's policy in the Gentile mission would be confirmed.

2. And you are arrogant!: lit. 'inflated' (as in 4.18, 19). This was much worse than the sexual offence itself; a significant body of opinion in the Church (cf. 6.12ff.) thought that this was rather a fine assertion of Christian liberty, of emancipation from Jewish law and Gentile convention alike. Had the Church instituted disciplinary action as soon as the illicit relation came to light, Paul would not have needed to mention it. As it is, he reproves them for cherishing a spirit of pride when they **ought . . . rather to mourn** and directs that the offender **be removed** from their midst.

3–5. The removal must take the form of a solemn act of excommunication at a special meeting of the church, convened to confirm the sentence that Paul had already pronounced **in the name of the Lord Jesus.** Although absent in body, he would be present in spirit (cf. Col. 2.5), acting along with them **with the power of the Lord Jesus**—not only his authority but the **power** (*dynamis*) to give effect to their sentence—as they carried out Paul's direction **to deliver this man to Satan for the destruction of the flesh:** the phrase **this man,** lit. 'such a one' (*RV*), is a form indicating that the man's name is to be inserted here (cf. verse 11; 2 C. 2.6f.; 10.11; 12.2f., 5). Satan has normally no power over the believer in Christ, it is implied; a deliberate act of delivery **to Satan** is

necessary. Something comparable to the discipline visited on
Ananias and Sapphira in Ac. 5.1ff. is apparently contemplated,
although Sapphira has no counterpart on this occasion (the step-
mother was probably not a Christian, and therefore one of the
'outsiders' of verse 12 who were not amenable to the Church's
censure). The language implies a severer sentence than excommunication. Delivering the offender **to Satan** (cf. 1 Tim. 1.20)
might simply mean his expulsion from the community which
confessed Jesus as Lord into the realm which was dominated by
'the god of this world' (cf. 2 C. 4.4); but delivering him **to Satan
for the destruction of the flesh** means more than this. Job
was delivered to Satan ('the adversary') for the affliction of 'his
bone and his flesh' (Job 2.5)—not by way of punishment for any
wrong he had done, but to vindicate God's good opinion of him,
that here was a man who did indeed 'fear God for naught'.
Similarly Paul's own 'thorn in the flesh' was recognized by him as
'a messenger of Satan', overruled by God for his spiritual health
(2 C. 12.7). How much more might not one who by his sin had
polluted the temple of God (cf. 3.17) endure comparable affliction
at God's hand through the instrumentality of Satan? Indeed, more
than mere affliction or sickness may be indicated by the strong
word **destruction** (Gk *olethros*); the offence was perhaps held to
be so serious that the offender's only chance of having **his spirit
. . . saved in the day of the Lord Jesus** was by suffering bodily
death here and now. But, while the church could pronounce this
solemn judgment, how could there be any certainty that sickness
or death would follow? A secret execution is not envisaged, although
J. Klausner (*From Jesus to Paul* (1944), p. 553) thought it likely.
Sickness and death in consequence of another kind of ecclesiastical
misconduct are mentioned in 11.30, and the ban of the congregation might well have been as self-fulfilling as the prophetic word in
OT. If, of course, the offender is the man referred to in 2 C. 2.5ff.,
then he recovered both health and church membership, but the
identification, as has been indicated above, is doubtful.

the day of the Lord Jesus: probably **Jesus** should be omitted,
with *P*[46] and B. The **day** is that already mentioned in 1.8; 3.13.

   6. Your boasting is not good: cf. the 'arrogance' of verse 2.
Their **boasting** (Gk *kauchēma*) is not the act of boasting but that
in which they boast; it is by no means an honourable (Gk *kalon*)
subject of boasting.

Do you not know that a little leaven leavens the whole lump?: here the question **Do you not know . . .?** does not remind them of a piece of earlier instruction (cf. 3.16) but of a popular saying, quoted again by Paul in Gal. 5.9. Leaven could be used as a metaphor either for evil influences (as in Mk 8.15) or (as in the parable of Mt. 13.33//Lk. 13.20f.) for good; here the saying is a warning of the corrupting effect of sinful practices tolerated in the community (much the same lesson is inculcated in another proverbial sentence in 15.33). The **lump** (Gk *phyrama*, 'that which is kneaded') is the batch of dough (cf. Rom. 11.16) into which leaven is put.

7. Cleanse out the old leaven that you may be a new lump: Paul's quotation of the saying about leaven reminds him of the Jewish custom of clearing out all the old leaven from the house before the Passover, so that a completely fresh start may be made with the new year's grain (Exod. 12.15; 13.6f.). The first batch of dough from which new bread is made is therefore completely unleavened, **a new lump.** That is what they should be by virtue of their turning to Christ—'a new creation' (2 C. 5.17). **as you really are unleavened:** a paradox, for the point of the admonition thus far is that they were contaminated by the 'leaven' of immorality. The paradox is involved in the tension between ideal and reality: it is a pity that *RSV* chooses **really** to add emphasis to the clause, because 'really' they were 'leavened'; only ideally, by God's calling in Christ, were they **unleavened.** Here, as elsewhere (see note on 3.1), Paul's exhortation can be summed up in the words: Be *de facto* what you are *de iure*; be really what you are ideally in the purpose of God; let your behaviour correspond to your vocation and profession. They were **unleavened** in the sense in which they were 'sanctified in Christ Jesus', set apart by God as his holy people (1.2); let them be holy in life as they were by divine calling.

For Christ, our paschal lamb, has been sacrificed: lit. 'Christ, our passover . . .' (the word 'lamb' does not occur in the Greek text here, though it is implied). The mention of the removal of leaven before the Passover leads Paul to draw an analogy from the Passover itself. It is plain that in the primitive church the sequence of events comprising the Passover, the Exodus and Israel's wilderness wanderings (which figured prominently in the recurring *OT* kerygmatic confession) provided a pictorial pattern

for the narrating of the Christian salvation-story (see especially
10.1–11). In this pattern the **paschal lamb** was the counterpart
of Jesus—the more readily so because his passion fell at Passover-
tide; indeed, in the Fourth Gospel his death coincides with the
sacrifice of the paschal lambs (between noon and sundown on
14 Nisan; compare Jn 19.14, 31 with Exod. 12.6; Dt. 16.6). Hence,
in part, the recurring references to Christ as the 'lamb' (especially
1 Pet. 1.19). The passover lamb has already been killed, Paul
implies, but the leaven has not yet been removed; make haste
therefore and remove it!

8. Let us, therefore, celebrate the festival: the Passover
meal was followed by the seven-day *ḥăgîgāh* or **festival** of
unleavened bread (Exod. 23.15; 34.18; Dt. 16.3f., etc.). Christians,
whose Passover sacrifice has been offered once for all, must thereafter live lives free from **the old leaven, the leaven of malice
and evil;** not for seven days only but for evermore their lives must
be characterized by **the unleavened bread of sincerity and
truth.** For them, 'the old has passed away, . . . the new has come'
(2 C. 5.17); sin must be a thing of the past, holiness the abiding
quality of the present and future. (Paul may well have written
this around the time of Passover and the festival of unleavened
bread; see notes on 10.1; 15.20; 16.8.)

9–10. I wrote to you in my letter: this must be a reference
to an earlier letter sent by Paul to the Corinthian church. The
aorist *egrapsa* (**I wrote**) might in itself be interpreted as an
epistolary aorist ('I am writing'; cf. 4.17), but the added phrase
in my letter (lit. 'in the letter'), together with the words that
follow, rule this interpretation out. Our certain knowledge about
the contents of this 'previous letter' is confined to what Paul here
says about its purport: **not to associate with immoral men**,
lit. 'with fornicators' (Gk *pornois*). One can agree with F. W.
Beare's criticism of the 'intolerable bowdlerism' of the *RSV*
rendering (*St. Paul and his Letters* (1962), p. 140), for Paul goes on
to specify other forms of immorality—greed, robbery and idolatry.
Whether these had been explicitly mentioned in the previous
letter is uncertain; Paul indicates that they were at least implied
there. On the relation frequently postulated between the previous
letter and 2 C. 6.14–7.1 see p. 213. Paul's directions in the previous
letter had been misunderstood or perhaps deliberately misin-
terpreted.

'**Not to associate with immoral men!** But what else can we do, in an immoral city like Corinth?' Paul corrects this mistake: **not at all meaning the immoral of this world, ... since then you would need to go out of the world.** As Bunyan puts it when he describes Vanity Fair, 'the way to the Celestial City lies through the town where this lusty fair is kept; and he that will go to the City, and yet not go through this town, must needs "go out of the world"' (*The Pilgrim's Progress*, Part I). A Corinthian Christian could not choose his butcher, his baker, or even his next-door neighbour, on the basis of his morals. 'I referred', says Paul, 'to the company one should keep inside the church.'

11. But rather I wrote to you: the variant rendering 'But now I write to you' takes the adverb *nyn* (**rather** in *RSV* text) as temporal, and the aorist *egrapsa* as epistolary. More probably, however, the adverb has adversative force ('as it is') and the aorist is a true preterite, as in verse 9. 'What I meant when I wrote that', says Paul, 'was that you should accord no man the status or privileges of a **brother** in Christ **if he is guilty of** fornication, **or greed, or is an idolater, reviler, drunkard or robber.**' We cannot be sure what moved Paul to give these directions in the previous letter. It is unlikely that he had failed to give the Corinthian church ethical instruction along these lines during his eighteen months in Corinth; possibly news had reached him early in his Ephesian ministry that some members of the Corinthian church were ignoring such instruction. It is unlikely that the previous letter was sent to inform the Corinthians of the terms of the Jerusalem decree (as suggested by J. C. Hurd, *The Origin of 1 Corinthians* (1965), pp. 259ff.), since greed, reviling, drunkenness, robbery were not contemplated in that decree; in any case, it is improbable that Paul ever thought of imposing the decree as such so far afield as Corinth. The list of vices in verse 11 amplifies that in verse 10 and is itself amplified in 6.9f.

not even to eat with such a one: table-fellowship included the Eucharist (cf. 10.16–21; 11.20ff.) but was by no means confined to it; it constituted one of the most solemn bonds of brotherhood. Within the Christian community an unwarranted breach of table-fellowship was almost tantamount to a denial of gospel truth (Gal. 2.11ff.); where it was warranted, as in the situation envisaged here, it was bound to be taken seriously and was calculated to be one of the surest ways of bringing a delinquent church

member to acknowledge the error of his ways. 'May it not be that
Paul was giving in this letter *his* idea [as contrasted with the Jewish
idea] of what constituted a "kosher" table for Christians, with all
the emphasis on the company rather than the viands?' (T. W.
Manson, *Studies in the Gospels and Epistles* (1962), p. 197).

12. For what have I to do with judging outsiders?:
General moral assessments might be made on the pagan world, as
in Rom. 1.18ff., but the pronouncing or executing of disciplinary
measures on non-Christians was not part of the apostolic office. On
the other hand, the power of binding and loosing (Mt. 16.19;
18.18), of forgiving or retaining sins (Jn 20.23), was expressly
bestowed on the apostles, to be exercised on those **inside the
church.** Not that the apostles were the only ones qualified to
exercise such judgment; members of a local church had the
responsibility of judging issues arising within their own fellowship
(cf. 6.1ff.).

13. God judges those outside: he is 'the Judge of all the
earth' (Gen. 18.25).

Drive out the wicked person from among you': this repetition of the order of verse 2b is placed between quotation-marks
because it is almost an exact quotation of the LXX version of
Dt. 17.7b; 22.24 (cf. Dt. 13.5), where idolatry and adultery are to
be purged out of the community by the most drastic means.

CHRISTIANS AND THE LAW-COURTS **6.1–11**

**6.1. does he dare go to law before the unrighteous instead
of the saints?:** the news that some members of the Corinthian
church were prosecuting others, or suing them for redress, in
the pagan courts was, in Paul's eyes, profoundly shocking. The
term **unrighteous** does not imply that the pagan judges were
unjust (in the sense of verse 9), but simply that they were, from
the Christian standpoint, 'unjustified' and unbelievers (cf. verse
6). Every Jewish community throughout the Roman Empire and
beyond its frontiers had its own *bêṯ-dîn*, its own competent machin-
ery for the administration of civil justice within its own membership; the least that could be expected of a Christian church was
that it should make similar arrangements if necessary, and not
wash its dirty linen in public. Provision for this is made in Mt.
18.15–18.

2. Do you not know . . .?: see note on 3.16.

the saints will judge the world: this expectation is based on Dan. 7.22, understood in the sense that 'judgment was given to (so *RV* as against *RSV* 'for') the saints of the Most High' (cf. also Wis. 3.8; 1 Enoch 1.38). In Christian interpretation these **saints** are the associates of the Son of Man (cf. Dan. 7.13), the appointed judge of the living and the dead (cf. Mt. 16.27; Jn 5.27; Ac. 17.31, etc.).

trivial cases: as indeed such personal disputes usually were, in comparison with the serious matter which they were urged to judge in chapter 5. Gk *kritērion* (here rendered 'case') properly means a place of judgment, a court of justice.

3. we are to judge angels: including particularly the angel-princes set over the nations (cf. Dan. 10.13, 20; Heb. 2.5, against the background of Dt. 32.8), possibly also the disobedient angels who are reserved 'in the nether gloom until the judgment of the great day' (Jude 6; cf. 1 Enoch 10.12; 12.3ff.; 22.11; 54.5f.).

4–6. If then you have such cases: lit. 'well then, if you have cases pertaining to this life' (*biōtika kritēria*).

why do you lay them before those who are least esteemed by the church?: pagan judges have no status in the church; the participle *exouthenēmenous*, if it refers to them, must mean not simply **least esteemed** but 'not esteemed at all', given no place in the church's affairs. The clause, however, may be construed not as a question (as in *RSV*) but as a command: 'lay them before those church members who are least esteemed'; they may not be qualified for the more serious responsibilities of church government, but they are perfectly competent to judge the trivial disputes that arise within the fellowship. This may sound ironical, but the irony could have been intentional, in view of Paul's statement immediately following that he says this to make them feel ashamed of themselves. To have recourse to **unbelievers** implied that none of their own company was **wise enough** to arbitrate between one Christian **brother** and another.

7. To have lawsuits at all with one another is defeat for you: if they must have their causes vindicated, let it be done within the church, as Jews did within the synagogue, but for Christians there was a more excellent way:

Why not rather suffer wrong? This was the more excellent way because it was the way of Christ, who endured injustice without seeking redress. That Christ's example was thus taken for granted

ess than 25 years after his death makes it highly implausible that
he picture of a pacific Christ should be, as has been suggested, a
replacement for the more historical reality of a militant sympathizer
with the Zealots.

Why not rather be defrauded?—or deprived of your property;
cf. Mt. 5.39–42//Lk. 6.29f. for Jesus' teaching to the same effect.
There are thus two distinct points: (*a*) Christian cases should be
ried by Christian courts . . . (*b*) There should be no cases:
Christian courts should have perpetual white gloves' (T. W.
Manson, *Studies in the Gospels and Epistles* (1962), p. 198).

8–10. That those responsible for 'wronging' and 'defrauding'
he aggrieved persons were themselves Christians made the situa-
ion the more shocking; they should be well aware **that the unrighteous will not inherit the kingdom of God,** for this was
something which they had presumably been taught already. The
unrighteous (Gk *adikoi*) are here more particularly those who
wrong' others: the cognate verb *adikeō* has been used in this sense
n the passive in verse 7 and in the active in verse 8.

Do not be deceived: an exhortation repeated in 15.33; Gal. 6.7.
The list of evildoers which follows amplifies the lists in 5.10, 11;
t bears a close resemblance to the 'works of the flesh' catalogued
n Gal. 5.19–21, where also the warning is given 'that those who
do such things shall not inherit the kingdom of God' (cf. Eph.
5.5). The fact that **the immoral** (i.e. fornicators) are mentioned
irst in the list may be a preparation for the admonition of verses
15–18. The word **homosexuals**, as the *RSV* footnote points out,
does duty for two separate Greek words here, *malakoi* and *arseno-
koitai*, denoting the passive and active rôles respectively. It is
noteworthy how regularly greed (covetousness, Gk *pleonexia*)
figures in such lists of vices; it may indicate desire for what one
should not have (as in the Tenth Commandment) or inordinate
desire for what is lawful in itself, to the point where it becomes a
form of idolatry (cf. Eph. 5.5; Col. 3.5).

11. Some of the Corinthian Christians had indeed been guilty
of these practices, but they had said a long farewell to that way of
life when they **were washed, . . . sanctified, . . . justified:**
whereas the last two verbs are in the passive voice, **were washed**
is middle (*apelousasthe*), as commonly with verbs of washing (cf.
10.2, 'were baptized'; Ac. 22.16, 'be baptized and wash away
your sins', where both verbs are in the middle voice); we migh

render 'you got yourselves washed'. They had been cleansed from
their former sins (a cleansing sacramentally signified in baptism);
they had been declared righteous by God; they had been made
his holy people.

in the name of the Lord Jesus Christ: because of their faith-
union with him 'whom God made . . . our righteousness and
sanctification and redemption' (1.30).

and in the Spirit of our God: while the Spirit's agency may
relate particularly to their being **sanctified** (cf. 2 C. 3.18), it is
also in him that they were baptized 'into one body' (1 C. 12. 13).

LIBERTY AND LICENCE 6.12–20

12. **'All things are lawful for me':** these words, occurring
twice in this place (cf. also 10.23) are rightly placed within
quotation marks; they appear to have been a slogan of the gnosticizing party in the church which was impatient of the restraints
of conventional morality. A second-century parallel may be
provided by Clement of Alexandria's description of certain
'Gnostics' mentioned above in the note on 4.8. In dealing with the
slogan, Paul adopts his regular procedure in waging his war on
two fronts, with the libertines on one hand and the ascetics on the
other: he goes along with each party as far as he can, agreeing
with its contention but adding something which neutralizes its
excesses. Here he does not contradict outright the permissive
assertion which he quotes, because in one way it might serve to
sum up his own doctrine of gospel liberty. Instead, he qualifies it
by adding, 'Yes, **but not all things are helpful':** it is not everything that is profitable or expedient for Christian life. 'Yes, **but I
will not be enslaved by anything':** if **all things are lawful**
(*exestin*) **for me**, I have authority (*exousia*) over them, but if I am
to be **enslaved** (*exousiasthēsomai*) by any of them, then *they* have
acquired authority over me, and, instead of enjoying liberty, I have
acquired a yoke of bondage.

13. **'Food is meant for the stomach and the stomach for
food':** again we should probably recognize a catchword of the
gnosticizing party which emphasized that the body and everything pertaining to it belonged to the category of religiously
indifferent things. So far as food was concerned, Paul would go
most of the way with them (cf. 8.8; Rom 14.17, 'the kingdom of
God does not mean food and drink . . .'); but he knew that for

some of them the corollary held good: 'sexual relations for the body and the body for sexual relations; lawful or illicit, such things are irrelevant to the spiritual life'. (Food and sex are bracketed together in the Jerusalem decree of Ac. 15.29 and in Rev. 2.14, 20.)

and God will destroy both one and the other: this too may have been part of the libertine argument: since food and stomach alike will pass away, why attach religious importance to either— or, for that matter, to sexual relations? Paul agreed that food and drink and the like were 'things which all perish as they are used' (Col. 2.22); in respect of them the conscience of the Christian was subject to no one's judgment (Rom. 14.3; Col. 2.16). But sexual relations were on a completely different footing; they affected the personalities of the parties involved as food did not. Jesus had contrasted food, which 'goes into a man from outside' and 'cannot defile him' with those 'evil things' which 'come from within, and . . . defile a man', and among the latter he included fornication (Mk 7.18–23). It was one thing to speak slightingly of the stomach —Paul himself could warn his converts against certain people whose 'god is the belly' (Phil. 3.19, where the same word *koilia* is used)—but **the body** falls within the scope of Christ's saving and sanctifying work: it is **for the Lord**, not for fornication. The *koilia*, related to the exigencies of this mortal life, may indeed disappear, but since **the Lord** is **for the body**, a nobler destiny lies in store for it.

14. Although some of the Corinthian Christians did not believe it (15.12), the Lord's care for the body would be finally manifested by its resurrection: **God raised the Lord and will also raise us up by his power** (cf. Rom. 6.4; 8.23). Here, as in 2 C. 4.14, Paul includes himself among those who will experience the resurrection, whereas in 1 Th. 4.15, 17, he had included himself among those who would be alive at the parousia. He makes no dogmatic affirmation either way, but, as time went on, the likelihood of his dying before the parousia increased (see notes on 2 C. 5.1ff.). As in 15.20ff., the resurrection of Christ is the pattern and precondition of his people's resurrection (cf. Rom. 8.11; Phil. 3.21). The resurrection body would be a body of a different order (15.42ff.), but sufficiently continuous with the present mortal body to demand reverence for the latter.

15. Do you not know that your bodies are members of

Christ? Again it is implied that they had learned this already. In 12.12, 27 (see notes *ad loc.*), believers are described as members (Gk *melē*) of Christ's body (i.e. the church), discharging their appropriate functions for the well-being of the community. Here, probably because of the requirements of the subject under discussion, it is more particularly their **bodies** that **are members of Christ.**

Never! This is Paul's characteristic *mē genoito*, lit. 'may it not happen!' (*AV* 'God forbid!'), with which, especially in argument, he repudiates an intolerable suggestion, usually going on to give the reason for its repudiation. To **take** (lit. 'take away', Gk *airō*) **the members of Christ and make them members of a prostitute** not only deprives the Lord of what is his, but desecrates the believer's body. Lawful sexual union involves no such deprivation or desecration because a believer's marriage is 'consecrated' even when the other party is an unbeliever (7.14); it can indeed be used as an analogy for the church's union with Christ (Eph. 5.22ff.).

16. he who joins himself: the verb is *kollaomai*, from Gen. 2.24, LXX, where the compound *proskollaomai* is used of a man's 'cleaving' to his wife.

one body: a variation on the 'one flesh' of Gen. 2.24, probably because the **body** is the explicit subject of the immediately preceding sentences. In any case, a psychosomatic union, not a merely physical one, is implied.

as it is written: lit. 'he (it) says' (Gk *phēsin*); the implied subject may be God or scripture, and either would be equally in line with Paul's thinking. For Gen. 2.24 treated as an utterance of God, cf. Mt. 19.5.

'The two shall become one': lit. 'one flesh'. This quotation from Gen. 2.24, LXX (**two,** present also in the Samaritan edition, is absent from MT), appears elsewhere in *NT* with reference to marriage (cf. Mk 10.7; Eph. 5.31). Paul's application of it to casual intercourse with a prostitute 'apparently owes nothing to any antecedent notions, and displays a psychological insight into human sexuality which is altogether exceptional by first-century standards . . . he insists that it is an act which, by reason of its very nature, engages and expresses the whole personality in such a way as to constitute an unique mode of self-disclosure and self-commitment' (D. S. Bailey, *The Man–Woman Relation in Christian Thought* (1959), p. 10).

17. he who is united to the Lord: the verb is *kollaomai*, as in verse 16.

one spirit: the believer's union with Christ is a spiritual union; the Spirit he has received is the Spirit of Christ (cf. Rom. 8.9-11). True, it is in this **one spirit** that believers become members of Christ, 'one body' in him (cf. 12.13; Rom. 12.5; Eph. 5.30); but the phrase here is in antithesis to 'one body' in verse 16.

18. Shun immorality: lit. 'flee from fornication'—an echo, perhaps, of Joseph's literal fleeing from a temptation of this kind (Gen. 39.12)?

the immoral man sins against his own body: it might be suggested that gluttony and drunkenness (the latter of which is listed in verse 10 as excluding one from the kingdom of God) are sins against the body, but they consist of excess in things which are morally neutral. Moreover, their effects can in large measure be corrected by appropriate abstinence, but the relation once established by *porneia* cannot be undone.

19. Do you not know that your body is a temple of the Holy Spirit . . .? Cf. 3.16, where the statement that the community is a temple of God is similarly introduced; but here the reference is to the individual believer's body as the sanctuary of the indwelling Spirit. In the *Testament of Joseph* 10.3 Joseph says in the same kind of context, 'Wherever the Most High dwells, even though envy or slavery or slander befall one, the Lord who dwells in him because of his chastity not only delivers him from evil but also exalts him, as he has done to me'.

which you have from God: the gift of the Spirit is mentioned in a very similar context in 1 Th. 4.8, 'whoever disregards this [the call to sexual purity] disregards not man, but God, who gives his Holy Spirit to you'.

20. you were bought with a price: repeated (with a change in the Greek word-order) in 7.23. Nowhere else does Paul use the verb *agorazō* of the Christian redemption; he may be using the language of a recognized catechesis or confession. In Rom. 3.24f.; Eph. 1.7 the redemption (there *apolytrōsis*) is procured through the blood of Christ (cf. Ac. 20.28; Heb. 9.12; 1 Pet. 1.18f.; Rev. 5.9), and this doubtless is the **price** (Gk *timē*) here.

So glorify God in your body: cf. Rom. 12.1, 'present your bodies as a living sacrifice'. The Byzantine text adds 'and in your spirit, which are God's' (cf. *AV*); J. B. Lightfoot makes the attractive

C

suggestion that these words found their way into the text from a liturgical formula in which they formed the response to the versicle, **glorify God in your body.** But their addition blunts the point of Paul's present argument.

PAUL ANSWERS THE LETTER FROM CORINTH 7.1–16.4

QUESTIONS ON MARRIAGE 7.1–40

7.1. Now concerning the matters about which you wrote: With these words Paul begins his reply to the Corinthians' letter. The **matters** which they raised can be gathered in part from Paul's introducing them successively with **now concerning** (Gk *peri de*); by this criterion they included: marriage and divorce (7.1), virginity (7.25), food offered to idols (8.1), spiritual gifts (12.1), the collection for Jerusalem (16.1), and Apollos (16.12). Probably other questions in their letter are also answered in chapters 7–16, although their treatment is not introduced with the same formula.

The transition from chapter 6 to chapter 7 illustrates the necessity Paul was under of waging a campaign on two fronts. In chapter 6 he dealt with libertines who argued that everything was permissible, and in particular that sexual licence was a matter of ethical indifference. In chapter 7 he deals with ascetics who, partly perhaps in reaction against the libertines, argued that sexual relations of every kind were to be deprecated, that Christians who were married should henceforth live as though they were unmarried, and those who were unmarried should remain so, even if they were already engaged to be married. Their outlook was summed up in the sweeping judgment, **It is well for a man not to touch a woman,** which, as Origen saw ('Origen on 1 Corinthians' §121, ed. C. Jenkins, *JTS* 9 (1907–8), pp. 500ff.), is probably an extract from the Corinthians' letter, and should therefore be placed between quotation marks like 'All things are lawful' in 6.12. The use of *anthrōpos* and not *anēr* for **a man** in the sense of a male may be explained by the consideration that the Corinthians' letter was composed from the male point of view; *anthrōpos* here is little more than the indefinite pronoun 'one' ('one is better to have nothing to do with a woman').

Advice to the married **7.2-7**

2. Again Paul goes as far as he can with the assertion to which he is replying, this time in a direction quite different from that indicated in the quotations in 6.12f., but he adds a qualification which, while it appears to concede marriage for reasons on the lowest level of prudential morality, in effect makes it completely lawful and indeed normal for Christians. 'I agree', he says 'but (adversative *de*) if only to prevent the fornication which would result from attempts by those who have not received the gift or vocation of celibacy to live as though they had received it, **each man should have his own wife and each woman her own husband'.** Paul's present treatment of this issue cannot be properly evaluated unless due regard is paid to the tensions in the situation to which he addresses himself, and his pastoral concern for those involved in this situation, together with his sense of eschatological crisis (see verse 26).

3-4. Paul does not countenance unnatural abstention by husband and wife from sexual intercourse; each should accord the other the normal **conjugal rights** (Gk *opheilēn*, 'debt' or, as *RV*, 'due'; the Byzantine text amplifies to *opheilomenēn eunoian*, whence *AV* 'due benevolence'). By the marriage vow each relinquishes the exclusive right to his or her own body and gives the other a claim to it; the verb **rule over** is *exousiazō*, denoting the exercise of *exousia* ('authority').

5. One-sided insistence on abstinence therefore amounts to robbing the other party of his or her rights; abstinence, if any, must be **by agreement** and **for a season, that you may devote yourselves to prayer:** cf. *Testament of Naphtali* 8.8, 'There is a season (*kairos*, as here) for a man to embrace his wife, and a season to abstain therefrom for his prayer' (perhaps a midrash on Ec. 3.5b). Seasons of abstention varying from a week to thirty days are permitted in Mishnah *Keṯûḇôṯ* v.6. The Byzantine text characteristically adds 'fasting' before **prayer** (cf. *AV*).
lest Satan tempt you: even well-intentioned acts of piety, if they are carried beyond the limits of natural endurance, can be exploited by the adversary to bring moral or spiritual disaster to those who practise them (cf. 2 C. 2.11).

6. by way of concession: it is the temporary abstinence, not the 'coming together again', that is permitted as a **concession;**

regular marital relations are recognized as the norm. Far from being the discourager of marriage that he is popularly supposed to be, Paul might with some justice be called, as in the title of J. M. Ford's article, 'St. Paul, the Philogamist' (*NTS* 11 (1964–5), pp. 326ff.).

7. I wish that all were as I myself am: Paul's refusal to impose even temporary abstinence **by way . . . of command** is all the more striking in view of his personal preference for the celibate life. Paul's actual status cannot be determined; he may have been unmarried or a widower, or his wife may have left him and returned to her family because of his conversion to Christianity; see J. Jeremias, 'War Paulus Witwer?' *ZNW* 25 (1926), pp. 310ff., with critique by E. Fascher, 'Zur Witwerschaft des Paulus und der Auslegung von 1 C. 7', *ZNW* 28 (1929), pp. 62ff., and reply by J. Jeremias, 'Nochmals: war Paulus Witwer?' *ZNW* 28 (1929), pp. 321ff.

each has his own special gift (*charisma*): one for marriage and parenthood, another for celibacy (cf. the 'eunuchs for the sake of the kingdom of heaven' in Mt. 19.12).

Advice to the unmarried **7.8, 9**

8. to remain single as I do: there is nothing in the Greek text corresponding to **single**; Paul may associate himself either with **the unmarried** or with **the widows** (or widowers), for both of which groups the celibate life is approved.

9. it is better to marry than to be aflame with passion: lit. 'it is better to marry than to burn', which may indeed mean 'to burn with passion', but might possibly mean 'to burn in Gehenna' because of falling into fornication (in thought if not in action), in which case the argument of verse 2 is repeated in different words. Cf. *Pirqê 'Ābôt* i.5, where the wise men say, 'Whosoever multiplies conversation with a woman . . . will in the end inherit Gehenna'; TB *Qiddûšin* 81a, where Rab says to R. Judah as they are walking along a road and see a woman walking ahead of them, 'Hurry up and get in front of Gehenna' (i.e. get in front of that woman so that, out of sight, she may also be out of mind).

Divorce prohibited **7.10, 11**

10–11. While Paul's advice to the unmarried and widows was to remain as they were, his reply to the question whether married

couples should stay together or not has the form of a commandment (**I give charge**), not of mere advice, because on this point
he can quote an explicit ruling of **the Lord, that the wife should
not separate from her husband . . . and that the husband
should not divorce his wife.** This dominical ruling is known
to us from Mk 10.2–12 and parallels. The care with which Paul,
in dealing with this whole subject, distinguishes between issues on
which he can appeal to a command of the Lord and those on
which he can give only his own considered opinion (cf. verse 25)
suggests that sayings of Jesus were not devised as freely as is sometimes alleged to settle problems which arose in the primitive church.
The parenthesis, **if she does** separate from her husband, **let
her remain single** (i.e. unmarried to any one else) **or else be
reconciled to her husband**, may be Paul's gloss on the dominical
ruling, but is in keeping with Mk 10.12.

Mixed marriages 7.12–16

12–13. To the rest: persons not covered by the straightforward
categories of verses 8 and 10, especially those finding themselves in
matrimonial difficulties as a result of conversion to Christianity.
I say, not the Lord: because Paul knows no dominical ruling
which covers the situations with which he now proceeds to deal,
those in which the one partner has become a Christian while the
other remains **an unbeliever.** The question may have been raised
in the Corinthians' letter: 'Should not the believing partner
separate from the other, rather than be "mismated" with an
unbeliever?' Paul says, 'No; if the unbeliever is content to go on
living with the believer, let the marriage continue as before'.
she should not divorce him: in contrast to Jewish law, Greek
and Roman law permitted a wife to divorce her husband.

**14. the unbelieving husband is consecrated through his
wife:** an interesting extension of the *OT* principle of holiness by
association (e.g. Exod. 29.37, 'whatever touches the altar shall
become holy'; cf. Lev. 6.18). To the question, 'Is not the believing
partner defiled by such close association with an unbeliever?' the
reply is, 'No; contrariwise, the unbeliever is to this degree (not
necessarily in the sense of 1.2; 6.11) in a state of sanctification
(perfect passive of *hagiazō*) through association with the believer,
and the same principle applies to their **children:** they **would be
unclean** if one of their parents were defiled by association with

the other, **but as it is they are holy.** In rabbinical literature the expression 'in holiness' is used of proselytes in the sense 'after conversion' (cf. Mishnah *Yᵉḇāmôṯ* xi.2). If the **children** of such mixed marriages were holy, those of two believing parents would be so *a fortiori*; this makes it less important to decide whether Paul, in saying **your children,** addresses only Christians married to non-Christians or his Christian readers in general.

15. if the unbelieving partner desires to separate, let it be so: lit. 'let him (her) separate'. It is conceivable that, in laying down what has been called the 'Pauline privilege', Paul speaks from personal experience.

is not bound: 'is not in bondage' (Gk *dedoulōtai*); the implication is that the believer **in such a case** was in a state of what amounted to widowhood. No compulsion should be exerted on **the unbelieving partner** to remain or return, and presumably remarriage would not be completely excluded for the believer.

God has called us (there is considerable authority for reading 'you') **to peace:** lit. 'in peace', i.e. those whom **God has called** should live in **peace** (cf. Rom. 12.18; 14.19), and this covers both the believer's continued cohabitation with the partner who is content to remain and refusal to force the unwilling partner to stay or return.

16. *RSV* suggests that Paul means 'Do not hold the unbelieving partner against his (her) will for **how do you know whether you will save** him (her)?' But a more optimistic interpretation is possible and indeed preferable. In *OT* 'who knows whether . . .?' (LXX *tis oiden ei* . . .) is used in the hopeful sense of 'perhaps' (cf. 2 Sam. 12.22; Est. 4.14; Jl 2.14; Jon. 3.9), and **how do you know whether** (Gk *ti oidas ei*) may have this sense here (J. Jeremias adduces a similar instance of the second singular *oidas* from Epictetus, *Diss.* II. xx. 30). The meaning then would be: 'Do not dissolve your marriage with the unbelieving partner who is willing to remain; perhaps you will be his (her) salvation' (cf. *NEB*). A mixed marriage had thus missionary potentialities; cf. J. Jeremias, 'Die missionarische Aufgabe in der Mischehe', in W. Eltester (ed.), *Neutestamentliche Studien für Rudolf Bultmann BZNW* 21 (1954), pp. 255ff., where the use of *tis oiden ei* in a comparable situation is quoted from *Joseph and Aseneth* 11.

Calling and status **7.17–24**

17. A man or woman's social status is of minor importance; what matters is the fact that one has been **called** by God into his fellowship and service (cf. 1.9). To this calling the believer should remain faithful whatever his state of life may be. Concern to change one's status could absorb energies which might be more profitably devoted to Christian life and service; Paul's **rule in all the churches** (cf. 11.16; 14.33) was that a believer should be content to remain in the state of life in which he was at the time of his conversion—married or unmarried, circumcised or uncircumcised, slave or free man.

18–19. A **circumcised** Christian should **not seek to remove the marks of circumcision:** by the operation of *epispasmos* (cf. I Mac. 1.15); neither should an **uncircumcised** Christian **seek circumcision:** lit. 'let him not be circumcised'. Timothy, as the uncircumcised son of a Jewish mother, was a special case (Ac. 16.3). Paul thinks of circumcision undertaken by Gentile Christians not only as a legal obligation, against which he set his face uncompromisingly (Gal. 5.2ff.), but for any other reason; because **neither circumcision counts for anything nor uncircumcision.** In itself, the presence or absence of this mark is religiously indifferent. What does matter supremely is **keeping the commandments of God** or, as Paul says in similar contexts in Gal. 5.6 and 6.15, 'faith working through love', the token of 'a new creation'.

20. in the state in which he was called: lit. 'in the calling with which he was called' (cf. Eph. 4.1). The 'calling' (Gk *klēsis*), as in 1.26, is the divine call from darkness to light (cf. verse 17); it is to this, not to one's social status, that **every one should remain faithful.** There is no convincing evidence for taking *klēsis* in *NT* in the later sense of 'vocation', with reference to one's employment or way of life understood as the subject of divine ordination. The man who **was called** to faith in Christ as a slave, for example, is exhorted not to **remain faithful** to his slavery but to **remain faithful** as a slave to the call which came to him in slavery. If he does that he will indeed be a faithful slave, but that is not the primary point.

21. The Christian **slave** should not chafe at this state of life, but be content in it; if, however, he **can gain** his **freedom**, he should **avail** himself **of the opportunity.** These last words in the Greek (*mallon chrēsai*, *RV* 'use it rather') are terse to the point of ambiguity, and there is a long tradition, from Chrysostom to J Héring, in favour of interpreting them to mean: 'Even **if you can gain your freedom**, make use of your present condition instead' (cf. *RSV* footnote). But the aorist imperative *chrēsai* suggests making use of a definite opportunity, and the interpretation implied in *RSV* text is supported by the context (see especially verse 23). Cf C. H. Dodd, 'Notes from Papyri', *JTS* 26 (1924–5), p. 77.

22. he who was called in the Lord as a slave: for **in the Lord** (Gk *en kyriō*) cf. verse 39, and for the whole phrase cf. 1 Pet. 5.10 ('the God . . . who has called you . . . in Christ'). Apart from the possibility of gaining emancipation from slavery, the Christian **slave** should realize that he has been blessed with a greater liberation than that: he has become **a freedman of the Lord.** The slave who was enfranchised entered into a new relationship to his former master, that of **freedman** (Gk *apeleutheros*, Lat. *libertus*) to *patronus*. The Christian **slave** who recognized that he was the Lord's **freedman** would now serve his earthly master for the Lord's sake, 'rendering service with a good will as to the Lord and not to man' as enjoined in the 'household tables' (cf. Eph. 6.5ff.; Col. 3.22ff.; 1 Pet. 2.18ff.). On the other hand, the Christian who was a free man so far as his social status was concerned, was, as Paul liked to call himself, **a slave of Christ.**

23. You were bought with a price is repeated from 6.20; here the corollary is drawn that those redeemed by Christ should **not become slaves of men.** If a man was a slave at the time of his conversion he could not help that, but otherwise a Christian should not put himself into a state of bondage; here probably Paul has in mind not only literal slavery but also spiritual bondage (cf. 2 C. 11.20; Gal. 5.1; Col. 2.20ff.).

24. in whatever state each was called: lit. 'each wherein he was called'; the rendering **state** is more permissible here than in verse 20. The injunction of verses 17 and 20 is repeated here with the added phrase **with God,** i.e. 'in the presence of God' (Gk *para theō*). While the examples adduced in verses 17–24 are circumcision or uncircumcision, slavery or freedom, the point Paul is making in the wider context is that those who were married when they were called should remain married, while those who were single should remain single.

Advice on 'virgins' **7.25–38**

25. Now concerning the unmarried: the opening words of this phrase (Gk *peri de*) suggest that this was a specific question raised in the Corinthians' letter. But the **unmarried** here are *parthenoi*, 'virgins', perhaps a more restricted group than the 'unmarried' (*agamoi*) of verse 8. It has been suggested by several exegetes, from Theodore of Mopsuestia to our own day, that persons of both sexes are included under *parthenoi* here. Paul certainly has male as well as female celibacy in view in the following discussion, but in five out of the six occurrences of the noun *parthenos* in verses 25–38 it is plainly feminine (as the form of the definite article shows). It is more likely, therefore, that it is feminine also in the present instance, where the article (genitive plural) does not indicate the gender. In verse 34 the *parthenos* (*RSV* 'girl') is distinguished from the *agamos* (*RSV* 'unmarried woman'); this suggests that a particular category of unmarried woman is denoted by *parthenos*, one (according to *RSV* of verses 36, 37, 38) who is betrothed but not yet married. The Corinthians' specific question in this regard was probably whether a betrothed girl should proceed to marriage in the normal way or remain unmarried—in a state of permanent betrothal, so to speak. The decision, whichever way it went, would involve others—her fiancé, naturally, and also perhaps her father who was responsible for giving her in marriage.

Another suggestion (cf. H. Achelis, *Virgines subintroductae: Ein Beitrag zu I Cor. VII* (1902)) is that the question concerns *virgines subintroductae*, women who lived with men in a state of virginity as their 'spiritual sisters'. This procedure, recommended by Tertullian (*Exhortation to Chastity* 12; *On Monogamy* 16) as at least preferable to remarriage for those who could not do without female companionship, but deprecated by Irenaeus (*Haer.* i. 6.3), Cyprian (*Ep.* iv. 13f.) and others (cf. Eusebius, *HE* vii. xxx. 12ff.), is not attested so early as the fifties of the 1st century A.D. and is not really implied by Paul's language here. Mention should be made also of the view of J. M. Ford ('Levirate Marriage in St. Paul', *NTS* 10 (1963–4), pp. 361ff.) that the *parthenoi* are young widows, and the question is whether their deceased husbands' next of kin should discharge the levirate obligation towards them in accordance with the law of Dt. 25.5–10. The Corinthians asked if they should observe this Jewish custom. Since the custom had fallen into general disuse among the Jews, it is unlikely that Gentile Christians would raise it, and this can hardly be said to be the obvious meaning of Paul's words.

I have no command of the Lord: cf. verse 12.

I give my opinion: Paul's reluctance to impose rules in a situation where he probably had strong feelings about the proper course to follow illustrates the strength of his libertarian principles.

one who by the Lord's mercy is trustworthy: conscious of what his stewardship required (cf. 4.2). M. Black (*The Scrolls and Christian Origins* (1952), p. 85) points out that the Syriac versions of Mt. 19.12 translate 'eunuch' by *mehaimena* (lit. 'faithful') and suggests that **trustworthy** (Gk *pistos*) has this force here: i.e. 'Paul was himself a *parthenos* in this technical sense' (of a celibate 'for the kingdom of heaven's sake').

26. in view of the impending distress: or the distress which has set in and is now 'present' (*RSV* footnote). This **distress** is the time of increasing tribulation, heralding the end of the age, of which signs had already manifested themselves; cf. the 'great distress' (Gk *anankē*, as here) of Lk. 21.23. This time would be particularly harassing for those with family responsibilities. 'The apostle writes to the Corinthians as he would do to an army about to enter on a most unequal conflict in an enemy's country, and for a protracted period' (C. Hodge). The whole discussion of marriage in this chapter is influenced by Paul's eschatological awareness in addition to his pastoral concern.

it is well: *RSV* simplifies the Greek construction, 'I think this is well in view of the impending distress, that it is well . . .'; the repetition may be due to Paul's incorporating fragmentary quotations from the Corinthians' letter in his reply.

27–28. The **impending distress** makes the advice already given on remaining in one's existing state of life doubly advantageous. It gives no occasion to a married man to **seek to be free** but it does show reason why an unmarried man should remain so. (The man who is **free from a wife** is not necessarily one whose marriage has 'been dissolved', as *NEB* has it; the perfect passive *lelysai*, lit. 'are you loosed?' is used as a counterpoise to *dedesai*, **'are you bound?'**) Nevertheless, the apostle can only advise; the responsibility lies with the persons concerned, and if they ignore his advice they **do not sin**, neither the man nor his betrothed. He thinks they are courting **worldly troubles** (lit. 'tribulation in the flesh') which they could avoid by remaining unmarried, but he has done his duty by warning them of these. A man who has no wife or children liable to suffer because of his refusal to compromise or deny his faith in face of persecution is in a stronger position than one who must consider what effect his stand will have on his dependents; Paul wants to **spare** his friends the agonizing decisions which family responsibilities impose in such a situation.

29–31. the appointed time has grown very short: and this, says Tertullian, has cancelled the primaeval command 'Increase and multiply' (*Exhortation to Chastity*, 6; *On Monogamy*, 7). It is not only a question of the impending parousia, in the light of which it is foolish to live as though one had an indefinite tenure on the present course of time; the pressures of the remaining interval will be such that the man or woman of faith must accept the discipline of iron rations and be as free as possible from the ordinary and legitimate distractions of secular life. Cf. Rom. 13.11ff.

let those who have wives live as though they had none: like men on military service. The age to come, in which 'they neither marry nor are given in marriage' (Mk 12.25), and in which other accepted priorities of the present age will be upset, already exerts its influence in this age on those whose heritage is secure in the coming age. The fourfold **as though** of these verses emphasizes this: the Christian should as far as possible live in this age **as though** the age to come were already here, regulating life by its values and not by those current among 'the sons of this age'. The values of this age are transient and relative; those of the age to come are permanent and absolute (cf. 2 C. 4.17f.).

those who mourn . . . those who rejoice: cf. the reversal of weeping and laughing in the teaching of Jesus (Lk. 6.21b, 25b).

as though they had no goods: because of the insecurity of material possessions.

those who deal with the world as though they had no dealings with it: lit. 'those who use (Gk *chrōmenoi*) the world as not using it to the full (*katachrōmenoi*)'. The **world** (*kosmos*) with its resources and its opportunities is there to be used, but it is unwise to put all one's eggs into the basket of an order whose present **form . . . is passing away** (cf. 1 Jn 2.15–17).

32–34. The conflict of interests and cares to which Christians with family responsibilities are ordinarily subject is intensified in times of 'distress', and Paul wants his readers **to be free from** such **anxieties.**

and his interests are divided: Gk *kai memeristai.* The *RSV* punctuation is best (so also *NEB*); *AV* and *RV* follow the inferior reading which begins a new sentence with *kai memeristai* and transposes to a later position the following adjective **unmarried,** without which Gk *gynē* (**woman**) is understood as 'wife' and the meaning is 'And there is a difference between the wife and the virgin'. As *RSV* text stands, **the unmarried woman** and the **girl** (Gk *parthenos*, 'virgin') must be distinguished; the latter is indeed an **unmarried woman** but one who is betrothed. Betrothal, however, probably involving no initiative on her part, does not make her **anxious about worldly affairs, how to please her husband**, as marriage would; she is still free to concentrate on undivided devotion to **the affairs of the Lord** and on the cultivation of holiness in **body and spirit.**

35. not to lay any restraint upon you: lit. 'not to put a halter on you,' and so restrict your freedom of action.

36. not behaving properly towards his betrothed: he may feel that it is unfair to keep her in a state of permanent betrothal and deny her the satisfaction to which she is entitled to look forward as wife and mother. (J. M. Ford thinks of the reproach involved in a man's refusal to consummate levirate marriage with his dead brother's childless widow.)

Levirate

if his passions are stong: lit. 'if he (she) is *hyperakmos*'. This adjective may refer to the man or his fiancée. *RSV*, relating it to the sense of *akmē* ('prime') as the height of passion, refers it to the man. If we relate it to *akmē* in the sense of the bloom of youth, it will refer to the woman, and this on the whole is preferable. He may well think it unfair to keep her waiting until the bloom of youth is past. J. M. Ford, referring the adjective to the woman, takes it in the sense of Mishnaic Hebrew *bôgeret*, lit. 'wrinkled' but actually meaning 'past her girlhood' or 'at the age when levirate marriage is incumbent on her' ('The Rabbinic background of St. Paul's use of *hyperakmos*', *JJS* 18 (1966), pp. 89ff.).

and it has to be: perhaps because of social or family pressure.

37. being under no necessity: probably from external pressure.

having his desire under control: lit. 'but has authority

(*exousia*) regarding his own will (*thelēma*)', the latter noun being
used of a man's sexual impulse, as in Jn 1.13.

to keep her as his betrothed: lit. 'to keep his own virgin'. 'If
the man followed Paul's stated ideal rather than his practical
counsel, the ultimate result would have been a situation very like
that of the *virgines subintroductae*' (H. Chadwick, 'All Things to All
Men', *NTS* 1 (1954-5), p. 268, n. 1). It would be odd if this
institution arose from an attempt to put the Pauline ideal into
practice.

38. he who marries . . . he who refrains from marriage:
in both instances the Greek verb is *gamizō*, which elsewhere in *NT*
(Mt. 22.30//Mk 12.25//Lk.20.35; Mt. 24.38//Lk. 20.35) means
'give in marriage' (hence *RV* interprets verses 36-38 of a father's
action in respect of his 'virgin daughter'). But the verb is so rare
(cf. Bauer–Arndt–Gingrich) that no conclusions about its meaning
can be based on its general usage, and the present context favours
the same sense, 'marry', as *gameō* has in verse 36. On this section
(verses 36-38), see W. G. Kümmel, 'Verlobung und Heirat bei
Paulus', in W. Eltester (ed.), *Neutestamentiche Studien für Rudolf
Bultmann .. BZNW* 21 (1954), pp. 275ff.

Advice on widows **7.39-40**

39. A wife is bound to her husband: after **is bound** some
Western authorities and the Received Text import *nomō* from
Rom. 7.2 (whence *AV* 'bound by the law'). In Rom. 7.2f. this
lifelong bond is used as an illustration of obligation to the law. The
Corinthians may have asked a supplementary question about the
remarriage of widows, calling for a more detailed answer than in
verses 8, 9.

only in the Lord: as befits one who is **in the Lord** (cf. verse 22),
in submission to the dominical rulings on this subject. It is probably
also implied that, if she exercises her freedom to remarry, she
should marry a fellow-Christian; otherwise, her choice of a second
husband is unrestricted.

40. in my judgment: cf. verse 25, where the same noun (Gk
gnōmē) is rendered 'opinion'.

she is happier if she remains as she is: substantially the same
advice as in verse 8.

I have the Spirit of God: here enabling him to speak not with
apostolic authority (an apostle cannot go beyond the directions

of the one who commissions him) but with spiritual wisdom (cf.
2.16). **I** (Gk *kagō = kai egō*, rightly rendered 'I also' in *RV*) is
emphatic: some people who laid down the law on these subjects at
Corinth claimed to be 'spiritual' men; Paul is no less so (cf. 14.37).

THE QUESTION OF IDOL MEAT 8.1–13

8.1. Now concerning food offered to idols (Gk *eidōlothyta*):
what caused the Corinthians to raise this question in their letter
cannot be determined with certainty. It was in any case one which
must have occurred sooner rather than later to Gentile Christians
in a city like Corinth. When sacrificial animals were offered in the
temples, the deity received a token portion; what the priests and
temple attendants could not use themselves would be sold to the
meat market, where it would command a ready sale among the
public, because only the best animals were acceptable for temple
sacrifices. What were Christians to do on the occasions when they
bought butcher-meat? Jews then, as now, had their own arrangements for the slaughtering of animals for food; might it not be
better for Christians to have similar arrangements? There was
always the possibility that meat bought in the meat market came
from animals which had been **offered to idols**, and there was a
feeling that the meat was somehow contaminated by this association so that any one who ate it would be infected with idolatry.
Over against those members of the church who had scruples of
this kind ('the weak', as Paul calls them) there were others who
pooh-poohed such conscientiousness and, fortified by their
knowledge that there were no such entities as idols, asserted their
freedom and right to eat. Paul's conscience was as emancipated
as theirs, and he was willing to go a long way with them, provided
(*a*) due consideration was given to the tender consciences of 'the
weak', and (*b*) the scandal of public association with idolatry
itself was avoided.

There was evidently another factor in the situation. Abstention
from 'what has been sacrificed to idols', together with avoidance
of fornication (see notes on 5.1; 6.13ff.), was urged upon Gentile
converts in the Jerusalem decree (Ac. 15.29). Paul did not invoke
this decree in dealing with the ethical problems of the Corinthian
church, perhaps because it was addressed to the church of Syrian
Antioch and her daughter-churches (see note on 5.11). Others,
however, may have tried to impose its terms on the Christians in

Corinth, and in this connection it is natural to think of the 'Peter party'. If this party was involved in such an attempt, this would have strengthened Paul's resolve to appeal to first principles and not to the Jerusalem decree. Any attempt to introduce an absolute ban on the eating of **food offered to idols** would certainly raise questions at Corinth—although when the question is raised in the apostolic or sub-apostolic church Paul is the only authority (outside Gnostic circles) who does not answer it in terms of an absolute ban. See A. Ehrhardt, 'Social Problems in the Early Church. 1: The Sunday Joint of the Christian Housewife', in *The Framework of the NT Stories* (1964), pp. 276ff.

  'all of us possess knowledge': *RSV* rightly punctuates this as a quotation from the Corinthian letter, representing one powerful viewpoint in the church. Paul agrees, but reminds them that **knowledge** (*gnōsis*) is not everything. Paul may have encouraged the Corinthians, as he encouraged the Thessalonians, to 'build one another up' (1 Th. 5.11). 'Right!' said these people. 'It is **knowledge,** of course, that "builds up" '. 'No.' says Paul. 'It is **love** that **builds up; knowledge** by itself—**knowledge** without **love—puffs up,** inflates' (a verb that Paul has already had occasion to use of some of them; cf. 4.6, 18, 19; 5.2). Those whose **knowledge** enabled them to eat idol meat with a good conscience ought to exercise an abundance of **love** towards 'the weak'; otherwise 'the weak' might suffer spiritual shipwreck through the example of the 'men of knowledge' and the church, instead of being 'built up', would be in danger of collapse.

  2–3. If any one imagines that he knows something: the perfect infinitive *egnōkenai* may be emphatic: 'any one who seems (to himself) to have attained perfect knowledge of anything' **does not yet know as he ought to know.** Paul's concern is to deflate the self-esteem of the gnosticizing party in the church. The way to true knowledge of God is love of God; **if one loves God,** then —not 'one knows him', but—**one is known** (*egnōstai*, perfect passive) **by him;** in the knowledge of God, the initiative rests with God (cf. 13.12; also Rom. 8.29, 'those whom he foreknew . . .'; Gal. 4.9, 'now that you have come to know God, or rather to be known by God . . .'). When God knows or recognizes a man in the sense of setting his choice on him and admitting him to his acquaintance, that man comes to know him in turn, but with a knowledge dependent on love (cf. 2.9).

4-6. The 'men of knowledge' took their stand on the proposi-
tions that **'an idol has no real existence'** and that **'there is no
God but one'.** True, said Paul; there are indeed **many** so-called
'gods' (*theoi*), as there are **many** so-called **'lords'** (*kyrioi*) but we
recognize none of them: **for us there is one God, the Father,
. . . and one Lord, Jesus Christ.** Here Paul may quote a
primitive 'binitarian' confession. Sometimes men or cities would
venerate a particular deity so pre-eminently as to designate him
heis theos, 'one god' *par excellence*. Paul is hardly challenging this
usage when he speaks of **one God, the Father;** he is rather
christianizing the *Shema* (Dt. 6.4). The **Father** who is confessed
as **one God** is the source of **all things** and the goal of his people's
existence; similarly **Jesus Christ,** who because of his exaltation
by God is confessed as **one Lord** (by contrast with the divinities
and cultic heroes who constituted the **many lords** of paganism
but hardly, at this early date, by contrast with the emperor), is
the one **through whom all things exist,** as his people also do—
he is the agent of God in bringing into being not only the old
creation (cf. Col. 1.16; Jn 1.3) but also the new, to which **we**
belong (cf. 1.30; Col. 1.18). Through him we come from God;
through him we return to God. The other **gods** and **lords** are
real enough in the minds of their devotees, but for those who
worship the **one God** through the **one Lord** they are only **so-
called** gods and lords. Yet Paul does not dismiss them as complete
nonentities; in so far as they exist in the minds of their worshippers they exercise power over them and must be recognized
as 'demons' (see 10.20f.).

7. The 'men of knowledge' must consider those who do not
share their standard of **knowledge.** The statement quoted in
verse 1, 'all of us possess knowledge', was too sweeping: some
Christians did not. A convert from paganism, **hitherto accustomed to idols** (although before his conversion he thought of
them as deities, not **idols**), might not be able to rid himself of the
idea that they had independent existence and potency. (For
synētheia, 'with familiarity', 'with custom', the Western and
Byzantine texts read *syneidēsei*, whence *AV* 'with conscience'.) If
such a man, encouraged by the example of a 'man of knowledge',
forced himself to eat idol meat against the voice of his conscience,
his **conscience** would be damaged. The noun *syneidēsis*, 'conscience', is related to the verb *synoida* as used as 4.4; it was a term

of Hellenistic origin but employed by Paul in a sense which borrows elements from his Jewish and Christian thought. For Gentiles it played a part comparable to that which the law played for Jews (Rom. 2.14–16) and in general it acts as an inward examiner and judge of conduct in accordance with norms which it recognizes and applies (cf. 10.25ff.). See C. A. Pierce, *Conscience in the NT* (1955); M. E. Thrall, 'The Pauline Use of *Syneidēsis*', *NTS* 14 (1967–8), pp. 118ff.

8–9. Food will not commend us to God: this may also be a quotation from the Corinthian letter, as Calvin thought (cf. J. Jeremias, 'Zur Gedankenführung in den paulinischen Briefen', in *Studia Paulina in honorem J. de Zwaan*, ed. J. N. Sevenster and W. C. van Unnik (1953), pp. 146ff., especially pp. 151f.). (Compare the quotation in 6.13, and note *ad loc.*) Jeremias takes the meaning to be 'Food will not bring us before God's judgment seat' (cf. Rom. 14.10–12), because it is an indifferent thing; **we are no worse off if we do not eat, and no better off if we do** (cf. Phil. 4.12, where the same two verbs are used in the sense of 'abundance and want'). But the corollary which Paul drew from this undoubted fact was that it was therefore better voluntarily to abstain, if by insisting on one's freedom to eat one might do harm to another's conscience. Such insistence on one's own **liberty** or 'right' (*exousia*) would **become a stumbling block to the weak** if the latter, following the example of the 'strong', were encouraged to do something of which their conscience disapproved.

10. a man of knowledge: lit. 'having knowledge'.
at table in an idol's temple: a pagan might invite his friends to a meal in a temple, as is evident from some 'invitation cards' found among the Oxyrhynchus papyri, e.g. *P. Ox.* i. 110, 'Chaeremon invites you to dine at the table of the lord Sarapis in the Sarapeion [temple of Sarapis] tomorrow, the 15th, at the 9th hour' (cf. *P. Ox.* iii. 523, xii. 1484, xiv. 1755). Such a meal would be nominally under the patronage of the deity to whom the temple was dedicated; it might even be inaugurated by a sacrifice or libation in his honour. When a leading citizen of Bononia (Bologna) built a dining-room (*cenatorium*) for Jupiter Dolichenus (Dessau, *ILS* 4313), the idea may have been that those who ate together there would constitute a cult-society with that deity's sponsorship and presence. A Christian **man of knowledge** might accept an invitation to dine in such a place with no scruples

because the deity in question meant nothing to him, but his example might prove a scandal to his more scrupulous fellow-Christian.

11–12. by your knowledge: by your acting in accordance with your *gnōsis* without considering the claims of love. **this weak man is destroyed, for whom Christ died:** cf. Rom. 14.15, in a similar context, 'Do not let what you eat cause the ruin of one for whom Christ died'. The clause **for whom Christ died** underlines the worth in God's sight of the 'weakest' believer. The *RSV* rendering of *apollymi* in Rom. 14.15 ('cause the ruin of') is preferable to its rendering of the same verb (in the passive) by **is destroyed** here. It is not the man's eternal perdition, but the stunting of his Christian life and usefulness by the 'wounding' of his **conscience when it is weak** that Paul has in mind. Such lack of consideration and charity towards fellow-Christians amounts to **sin,** not only against them but **against Christ,** who counts whatever is done to his people as done to him (Mt. 25.40, 45; Mk 9.37, 41; Lk. 10.16; Jn 13.20; Ac. 9.4).

13. Paul's own policy in this respect, always to be ready to forgo his rights if the interests of others require this, is repeated in Rom. 14.13–23. For himself, he was persuaded, in accordance with the teaching of Jesus (cf. Mk 7.19), that 'nothing is unclean in itself; but it is unclean for any one who thinks it unclean' (Rom. 14.14). 'Strong' as he was in his own conscience, and gifted with 'knowledge' beyond the Corinthian gnosticizers, he was nevertheless totally committed on the side of the 'weak', and was prepared **never** to **eat meat** (Gk *krea*, 'flesh'), if his eating it might **cause** his **brother to fall** on the way that leads to life. His attitude is completely in line with that of Jesus in Mk 9.42, where the same verb *skandalizō* is used as is twice rendered 'cause to fall' in this verse.

THE QUESTION OF APOSTOLIC FREEDOM 9.1–27

9.1–2. Am I not free? Am I not an apostle?: Readers today may be surprised by this sudden digression in which Paul turns aside to defend his apostleship before going on (in 10.1ff.) to deal with another aspect of the question about idol meat. But in the light of doubts which were ventilated in some quarters of the Corinthian church concerning Paul's apostolic authority—doubts which have already called forth his assertion of freedom from any

human tribunal (4.3ff.)—it is not so surprising. Having spoken of
his readiness to curtail his own freedom in the interests of others,
he is reminded that this very readiness of his is used by some as an
argument against the validity of his claim to be an apostle: if he
were really an apostle, said they, he would feel **free** to exercise
his rights, not forgo them. Hence the four indignant questions
with which he counters these insinuations, each of them implying
the answer 'Yes'. His apostleship is validated by two arguments:
(*a*) that he has **seen Jesus our Lord;** (*b*) that the church of
Corinth is his **workmanship in the Lord.** The former argument
points to the foundation of his apostleship, the latter to its visible
demonstration. His claim to have **seen Jesus our Lord** is a
claim to be a witness of the resurrection (cf. 15.8ff.; Gal. 1.15f.)
and refers to the Damascus road experience (cf. Ac. 22.14f.;
26.15ff.). Independent evidence that the ability to bear direct
witness to the resurrection was an indispensable qualification for
recognition as an apostle is provided in Ac. 1.21f. But this experience of Paul's was known to himself alone; he therefore appeals
to the manifest effects of his apostolic work (cf. Rom. 15.15–21)
and reminds the Corinthian Christians that the very fact of their
now being what they are is the **seal** of his **apostleship in the
Lord;** doubts might be cast on his **apostleship** elsewhere, but
they could never question it (cf. 2 C. 3.2f.; 12.11f.).

3–4. If he is challenged to say why he forgoes the **right** (*exousia*,
'authority') to eat and drink what he pleases, the **right** to claim
material support from his converts instead of earning his living
independently, his **defence** is that he certainly has all these rights
and is free to insist on them if he chooses, but that he exercises his
freedom by not insisting on them.

5. The **other apostles and the brothers of the Lord** (cf.
Mk 6.3; Jn 7.3–5; Ac. 1.14), even **Cephas** (Peter) himself (who
may perhaps be specially mentioned because his **wife** had been
with him in Corinth), claimed support not only for themselves but
for their wives by whom they were **accompanied** in their itinerant ministry. For Peter's wife, cf. Mk 1.30. It has been suggested
that in this regard James (who is not singled out as **Cephas** is) was
an exception among **the brothers of the Lord,** in view of his
asceticism (cf. Hegesippus *ap.* Euseb. *HE* II. xxiii. 4–7), and the
fact that he does not appear to have been engaged in an itinerant
ministry, but rather to have resided permanently in Jerusalem,

where he directed the affairs of the mother church (cf. Gal. 1.19; 2.9; Ac. 12.17; 15.13ff.; 21.18). If Paul did not avail himself of the same privilege, it was because he chose not to do so, not because he had no **right** to it. (For Paul's status in this respect, see note on 7.7.) The questions in verses 4 and 5, being introduced by the double negative *mē ouk* ('Perhaps we have no right . . .'), have a more ironical flavour than those in verse 1.

6. is it only Barnabas and I: Barnabas might be included in the 'we' of verses 4 and 5, or 'we' might simply be Paul's habitual use of the first person plural in reference to himself, but the practice of **working for a living** instead of being maintained by the churches evidently characterized Barnabas's ministry as well as Paul's. **Barnabas** was Paul's friend (cf. Ac. 9.27) and senior colleague in the ministry of Gentile evangelism (cf. Gal. 2.1ff.; Ac. 11.25–15.39f.); he had been a member of the Jerusalem church practically from its inception (Ac. 4.36f.), and if (as is quite likely) he was a witness of the resurrection, he would naturally be ranked by Paul along with the other apostles (cf. Ac. 14.14). For Paul's earning his living with his own hands, cf. 4.12; 1 Th. 2.9; 2 Th. 3.7ff.; Ac. 18.3; 20.34. His insistence on doing so seems to have been resented by the Corinthian Christians, who may have felt that it betokened a lack of confidence in them on his part.

7–11. His right to their support could not be questioned; it was confirmed by human analogy and divine law. The man who **serves as a soldier** receives his pay from the authorities; he does not have to fight **at his own expense** (Gk *opsōnia*; cf. 2 C. 11.8; Lk. 3.14); the labourer in the **vineyard** gets his share of the grapes or wine in due course; the herdsman is entitled to some **milk** from the **flock** which he **tends**. If these workmen receive such perquisites as a matter of course, the servants of God are not inferior to them. The principle of their maintenance is expressed in the commandment which forbids one to **muzzle an ox when it is treading out the grain** (Dt. 25.4; cf. 1 Tim. 5.18), so that the animal may eat some of the produce of its toil. It is not for the sake of the animals that God gave this commandment, says Paul; the question at the end of verse 9—**Is it for oxen that God is concerned?**—being introduced by the negative *mē*, expects the answer 'No'. His argument may clash with modern exegetical method and western sentiment, but he must be allowed to mean

what he says. The animal creation, according to Gen. 1.28, exists
for man's benefit; the commandment of Dt. 25.4 (while it was
certainly to be fulfilled literally) was accordingly given for man's
benefit, so that **plowman** and **thresher** should profit by the
crop for which they labour and, more particularly, that workers in
God's field (cf. 3.6-9) should **reap** some **material benefits** from
those among whom they **have sown spiritual good** (cf. Rom.
15.27; Gal. 6.6).

12. The man who above all others might have claimed **this
right** (*exousia*) at Corinth—Paul himself, who first preached **the
gospel** and planted the church there—refused to make **use** of it,
lest his doing so should **put an obstacle in the way of the gospel
of Christ.** If his critics were given occasion to say that he did the
work of an apostle for the material benefits he derived from it, that
he exploited his converts for his own advantage, this would be
an obstacle to the progress of **the gospel**, and sooner than give
such occasion he would **endure anything** (cf. 13.7).

13-14. A further argument for the right which he voluntarily
forgoes is provided by **the temple service**—the service of any
temple (see note on 8.1), but Paul no doubt has the Jerusalem
temple and the levitical legislation in mind—for **those who are
employed in** it, and especially those who minister **at the altar,**
get their **share in the sacrificial** flesh or cereal and so have
their **food** supplied from **the altar** (cf. Num. 18.8ff.). By an
extension of the same principle the **Lord commanded that those
who proclaim the gospel should get their living by** (Gk.
ek, 'from') **the gospel:** a reference perhaps to the logion which we
know from Lk. 10.7, 'the labourer deserves his wages' (quoted as
'scripture' alongside Dt. 25.4 in 1 Tim. 5.18). For such dominical
'commandments', cf. 7.10, 25. A collection of them was in
circulation certainly in oral and possibly already in written
form.

15-18. But Paul, while emphasizing that he is entitled to
these rights, refuses to avail himself of them, and finds in this
refusal **ground for boasting.** He finds no such **ground for
boasting** in the fact that he preaches **the gospel**, any more than
a slave would boast of his obedience to his master's commands.
The slave has no option; he knows that it will be the worse for
him if he does not obey. So Paul knows that it will be **woe** to him
if he does not **preach the gospel**; this he is compelled to do.

When he was conscripted into the service of Christ on the Damascus road, he was **entrusted with a commission** (Gk *oikonomia*, 'stewardship'). A steward (cf. 4.1f.) was a slave **entrusted with a certain commission**, and he had no option but to discharge it. If he discharged it willingly, he would to that extent reap his **reward** when it was done; but if he discharged it unwillingly, he had to discharge it nevertheless. So, says Paul, I cannot choose whether to preach the gospel or not to preach it; willingly or unwillingly, I must do it. My **ground for boasting**, my **reward**, does not lie in doing what I am bound to do; it lies in a matter in which liberty of choice is left to myself. I can exercise my right in demanding that those to whom I preach support me materially, or I can refrain from exercising it. Here I am under no constraint one way or the other, and I use my liberty of choice by preaching **the gospel free of charge**. His voluntary relinquishing of his right in this respect is on a par with his voluntary limitation of his liberty in matters of food; in either case the paramount consideration is what will best promote the interests of the gospel. (He returns to this subject in 2 C. 11.7–12.)

19. Free from all men as he is by virtue of his acceptance of the yoke of Christ (cf. 7.22), Paul has nevertheless made himself **a slave to all**, dedicated to their highest good. Such language as this, which echoes the language of Jesus (cf. Mk 10.45; Lk. 22.27), prompted the paradox with which Luther begins his *Liberty of a Christian Man*: 'A Christian man is a most free lord of all, subject to none. A Christian man is a most dutiful servant of all, subject to all.' Paul goes on to explain himself by telling how, in all indifferent things (such as the food which was at issue in chapter 8), he conforms to the customs of those with whom he is at the time, so as to put no obstacle in the way of 'winning' them for the gospel.

20. To the Jews I became as a Jew: he was already a Jew by birth and upbringing, but now that he was a Christian he continued to follow Jewish ways in Jewish company. His ready consent on his last visit to Jerusalem to take part in the discharge of a Nazirite vow in the temple (Ac. 21.23 ff.) is perfectly consistent with this statement of his policy. If he no longer felt any necessity to comply with Jewish regulations and ceremonies as matters of divine obligation, he did not go to the other extreme and regard these things as forbidden to a Christian; henceforth they ranked as morally and religiously indifferent things, to be observed or not as occasion might indicate.

to those under the law I became as one under the law: in the company of Jews who confined themselves to *kosher* meat, for example, he did the same, out of consideration for them in spite of his own persuasion that Christ had 'declared all foods clean' (Mk 7.19). Their practice was due to their being **under the law**; his conformity with their practice, although he was no longer **under the law**, was completely voluntary; his aim was to **win those under the law**. The **law** here is the Jewish law, consisting of the 613 written precepts of the Pentateuch together, probably, with their oral amplification ('the tradition of the elders'), accepted as the divinely appointed way to life (cf. Rom. 10.5, quoting Lev. 18.5), but discovered by Paul to be in practice an instrument of death (cf. 2 C. 3.6b; Rom. 7.7–13). Those who by faith have been united to Christ and live in the Spirit 'are not under law but under grace' (Rom. 6.14).

21. On the other hand, in the company of **those outside the law**, i.e. Gentiles, he lived like a Gentile, with the like aim of 'winning' Gentiles. The adjective *anomos* ('without law') is applied to Gentiles in the sense of their being **outside** the scope of the Jewish **law**; cf. Ac. 2.23, where the execution of Jesus is said to have been procured 'by the hands of lawless men (*anomoi*)'— in this case, Romans. It is not suggested that the Gentiles had no sense of any kind of law: 'When Gentiles who have not the [Jewish] law do by nature what the law requires, they are a law to themselves' (Rom. 2.14). But in the sense in which Jews were 'under the law' the Gentiles were **outside the law**, and among Gentiles Paul conformed to the Gentile way of life. Since, however, *anomos* is ambiguous, and might mean simply 'lawless' (as it does in Lk. 22.37; 2 Th. 2.8; 1 Tim. 1.9; 2 Pet. 2.8), Paul qualifies his statement that he lived **as one outside the law** by adding that he is not *anomos* in relation to **God**. He recognizes the law of God (cf. Rom. 7.22) as something more comprehensive than the law of Moses; if he is no longer **under the law** of Moses, he recognizes the will of God, comprising 'what is good and acceptable and perfect' (Rom. 12.2), as something which he is bound to obey. But this is no longer a matter of conformity to an external code, but of 'doing the will of God from the heart' (Eph. 6.6) in terms of the new covenant (2 C. 3.2–6). Paul acknowledges himself to be **under the law of Christ** (Gk *ennomos christou*), an expression which has a near parallel in Gal. 6.2, where to 'bear one another's burdens' and in general to 'walk by the Spirit' amount to fulfilling 'the law of Christ'. This **law of Christ** may be recognized in the example which Christ set his followers (cf. 1 C. 11.1) and even more explicitly in his commandments (such as those which are cited here and there in this letter). When Paul says elsewhere that 'he who loves his neighbour has fulfilled the law' (Rom. 13.8; cf. Gal. 5.14) he recalls the terms in which Jesus summed up the whole duty of man (Mk 12.28ff.; cf. Lk. 10.25ff.). But this is the spontaneous outworking of the new life in Christ by virtue of which 'the just requirements of the law' are 'fulfilled in us, who walk not according to the flesh but according to the Spirit' (Rom. 8.4). 'Certainly it would be a mistake to attempt to confine the connotation of *ho nomos tou Christou* [the law of Christ] to the comparatively restricted body of traditional Sayings of Jesus, but it appears that even for Paul, with his strong sense of the immediate governance of Christ through His Spirit in the Church, that which the Lord commanded and ordained remains the solid, historical and creative nucleus of the whole' (C. H. Dodd, 'Ennomos Christou', in *Studia Paulina in honorem J. de Zwaan*, ed. J. N. Sevenster and W. C. van Unnik (1953), p. 110; cf. his *Gospel and Law* (1950), pp. 64ff.).

22–23. To the weak I became weak (cf. 8.9): among those with scruples—even morbid scruples—Paul avoided those things which they scrupulously avoided, in order to place no stumbling-block in their way which would make it more difficult to **win** them to a better appreciation of Christian liberty. His practice, as stated in 8.13, is thus shown to be part of his wider policy.

I have become all things to all men: this adaptability and versatility probably appeared as inconsistency to Paul's critics; even today when a religious leader is said to be **all things to all men**, it is more likely to be in blame than in praise. (See H. Chadwick, 'All Things to All Men', *NTS* 1 (1954–5), pp. 261ff.) A character like Paul's cannot be measured by the standard of that 'foolish consistency' which R. W. Emerson called 'the hobgoblin of little minds, adored by little statesmen and philosophers and divines' (*Essay on Self-Reliance*). His 'inconsistency', as some thought it (cf. 2 C. 1. 17ff.), was subject to a higher consistency—

the more effective discharge of his apostolic commission, **that I might by all means save some.** He might forgo the material benefits of 'living by the gospel' (verse 14), but in pursuing this consistent policy **for the sake of the gospel** he hoped **to share in its blessings** (lit. 'that I may be a joint-partaker thereof', *RV*) on a higher level. He goes on to speak of these **blessings** by means of an athletic metaphor.

24–27. in a race all the runners compete, but only one receives the prize: the Corinthians were familiar with the rules of athletic contests, especially in the Isthmian Games which were held in their neighbourhood every two years, and at which their city had the honour of presidency. At such games only the winner of the **race** (Paul's word here is *stadion*, the course of 600 feet standard among the Greeks) received a prize, but in the Christian contest there may be more than one winner. It is necessary, however, to exercise **self-control in all things** if staying-power is to be maintained so that the spiritual **race** is run consistently to the end of the course and the coveted **prize** won. This **prize** is not a **perishable wreath** like that of pine (earlier parsley or wild celery) awarded in the Isthmian Games; it was the **imperishable** 'prize of the upward call of God in Christ Jesus', for which Paul pressed on 'toward the goal' (Phil. 3.14). This **prize,** to be awarded on the 'day of Christ', was his constant incentive to **run** straight for the tape, not **aimlessly**; or, turning from the race-course to the boxing ring, not to indulge in shadow-boxing but to get home with every punch. Only, the target of his boxing is Paul himself: **I pommel my body,** he says (lit. 'I give myself a black eye', Gk *hypōpiazō*), **and subdue it** (lit. 'lead it into slavery'), **lest after preaching** (Gk *kēryxas*, acting as *kēryx* or herald) **to others I myself should be disqualified** (Gk *adokimos*; cf. 2 C. 13.5–7), and so forfeit the prize. These vividly figurative words do not denote literal self-flagellation, but describe the moral discipline to which he constantly subjected himself, lest anything else should displace the paramount aim of his life, the proclamation of the gospel. Self-discipline involves a voluntary curtailment of one's rights and liberties, so these four verses provide a further answer to those who criticized Paul for not availing himself to the full of the freedom to which an apostle was entitled. (For the similar use of athletic language, cf. Gal. 2.2; Eph. 6.10ff.; Phil. 1.30; 2.16; 3.14; Col. 1.29; 2.1; 4.12;

1 Th. 2.2; 1 Tim. 6.12; 2 Tim. 2.3ff.; 4.7; also Ac. 20.24; Heb.
12.1ff.)

THE QUESTION OF IDOL MEAT RESUMED 10.1–11.1

In reverting to the question of idol meat, from which he has digressed to discuss the related subject of apostolic freedom, Paul
recognizes that, while over-scrupulous consciences need to be
strengthened and reassured, there are others whose attitude is due
to an inadequate perception of the evil of idolatry and to a mis-
taken idea that baptism and the Eucharist are automatic pro-
phylactics against sin and ensuing judgment. He warns them
against such a delusion, and against the peril of idolatry and
attendant forms of disobedience to God, by means of the story of the
Exodus and wilderness wanderings which, as we have seen above
(cf. 5.7), provided an analogy for Christian experience. Most of
the incidents enumerated in verses 1–10 are drawn from Exod.
13–17 and Num. 10–15, which in the second and third years of the
triennial lectionary were read in the weeks immediately following
Passover.

The example of the Israelites 10.1–13

**10.1–2. our fathers were all . . . baptized into Moses in
the cloud and in the sea:** cf. Exod. 13.19ff. The middle voice
('got themselves baptized'; cf. note on 6.11) of P^{46} and B is preferable to the passive reading of other authorities. Baptism **into
Moses** can mean only 'into his leadership', but this phrase, *eis
Mōysēn*, is patterned on the baptismal connotation of *eis Christon*
('into Christ'), for which cf. Gal. 3.27; Rom. 6.3 (see also 1 C.
12.13). The literal sense of 'baptize' (Gk *baptizō*, 'dip') cannot be
pressed here, since, while the Israelites **were all under the cloud
and all passed through the sea**, they came into direct contact
with neither. It is emphasized that **all** underwent this experience
to show that their 'baptism' did not preserve them *ex opere operato*
from premature death when they later rebelled against God, nor
guaranteed their entrance into the promised land.

3–4. Neither did the fact that **all ate** the manna and **all drank**
the water from the rock preserve them. The fact that **all** are said to
have had **the same . . . food and . . . drink** means that there was
no difference between them in this respect, so that the difference
in their fates had nothing to do with what they **ate** and **drank;**

it probably does not mean that they partook of **the same** sacrament as Christians (so Calvin, T. C. Edwards). The manna and the water are called **supernatural**—lit. 'spiritual' (Gk *pneumatikon*)—**food and . . . drink** because the material elements, like the material bread and wine of the Christian Eucharist, signified spiritual realities (cf. 'spiritual food and drink' in the eucharistic prayer of *Didache* 10.3). Paul does not elaborate the spiritual significance of the manna, but from his argument in verses 16b, 17, below, we may be sure that he would have agreed that it pointed to Christ as the 'bread of life' (cf. Jn 6.35, 48–51). Similarly, he says explicitly that the true refreshment of Israel in the wilderness came not from the material rock which Moses struck but **from the supernatural** ('spiritual') **Rock which followed them, and the Rock was Christ.** Because in the Pentateuchal narrative Moses fetches water from the rock of Meribah both at the beginning (Exod. 17.1–7) and towards the end (Num. 20.2–13) of the wilderness wanderings, Jewish legend (cf. Pseudo-Philo, *Biblical Antiquities* x. 7; Tosefta *Sukkāh* iii. 11f.) conceived the idea of a rock which travelled alongside the people throughout their forty years' journey and supplied them with water as they required it. Paul does not endorse this material fancy, but affirms that Christ accompanied his people as a spiritual source of refreshment throughout this period. This interpretation was facilitated by the use of the title 'The Rock' for Yahweh (in the Hebrew text but not in LXX) in the Song of Moses (Dt. 32.4, 15, 18, 30, 31) and elsewhere (e.g. Ps. 18.2, 31; 19.14; 28.1; 62.2; 78.35; 89.26; 144.1; Isa. 26.4), and by the identification of Christ before his incarnation with the angel of Yahweh's presence who accompanied Israel in the wilderness (Exod. 14.19; 23.20ff.; 32.34; 33.2, 14ff.; cf. Ac. 7.30, 38), if not indeed with 'the Lord' (LXX *kyrios*) who went before his people, rescued them from their enemies and healed them in the wilderness (Exod. 13.21; 14.30; 15.26). This goes far beyond the conception of the Messiah as a second Moses, supplying his people with bread and water (cf. Jn 6.14; 7.37–41a). A comparable interpretation appears in Philo, for whom 'the flinty rock is the wisdom of God' (cf. 1.24), while the manna is the word of God (*Leg. alleg.* ii. 86, iii. 169f.; *The Worse attacks the Better* 115). It is hazardous to try to establish a connection between **rock** (Gk *petra*) here and in Mt. 16.18 (see note on 3.11).

5. with most of them God was not pleased: in fact, with the entire generation of military age, twenty years old and upward, that came out of Egypt (apart from Caleb and Joshua); they all perished **in the wilderness** (Num. 14.20–24, 28–35; Dt. 1.34–40).

6. these things are warnings (*typoi*) **for us:** they serve as salutary examples of the consequences of disobedience against God. Some biblical theologians go farther and hold that these and other *OT* events were (not merely in retrospect but in original intention, though this could not be appreciated until the coming of Christ) 'pointers' prefiguring the *NT* consummation (cf. G. von Rad, *OT Theology*, II (1965), pp. 383f.). All that Paul implies, however, is that, just as their 'baptism' and partaking of spiritual food and drink did not protect the Israelites against the consequences of their misdeeds, neither will Christian baptism and the eucharistic partaking of Christ protect **us** or *ipso facto* ensure our entry into final bliss, if we **desire evil as they did**; cf. Num. 11.4–34, where the Israelites who sinned thus were buried in Kibroth-hattaavah ('graves of craving').

7. Do not be idolaters: Paul thinks especially of the narrative of the golden calf, from which he makes an explicit quotation, **'The people sat down to eat and drink and rose up to dance'** (Exod. 32.6), which in his mind may have been an apt summary of what happened at the idol feasts which some of the Corinthian Christians were happy to attend.

8. We must not indulge in immorality: lit. 'fornication' (cf. 5.1, 9ff.; 6.9, 13ff.); here Paul thinks especially of the apostasy of Peor, in which Israel 'began to play the harlot with the daughters of Moab' when the latter 'invited the people to the sacrifices of their gods, and the people ate, and bowed down to their gods' (Num. 25.1f.). The relevance of this episode to the Corinthian situation called for no emphasizing. The figure of **twenty-three thousand** is a variant on the 24,000 who 'died by the plague' according to the text and versions of Num. 25.9; attempts to explain the difference by insisting that Paul's 23,000 **fell in a single day** (which is not said of the 24,000 of Numbers) savour of harmonistic pilpulism.

9. We must not put the Lord to the test: i.e. see how far his patience will stretch or question if he means what he says (cf. Exod. 17.3, 7; Ps. 95.8f.). The variant 'Christ' is read in place of

the Lord by *P*[46] and the Western authorities and may well be original; in view of verse 4 it is not inconsistent with the following clause **as some of them did.**

and were destroyed by serpents: cf. Num. 21.4–9 (Jn 3.14).

10. nor grumble: a recurrent practice in the record of the wilderness wanderings; cf. Exod. 15.24; 16.2ff.; 17.3; Num. 11.1; 14.2ff.; 16.11, 41; Dt. 1.27 (Ps. 106.25).

were destroyed by the Destroyer (Gk *olothreutēs*): a reference perhaps to the 'fire of Yahweh' which broke out as a sequel to the murmuring of Num. 11.1, but the word denotes the angel of destruction ('the destroyer', LXX *olethreuōn*) of Exod. 12.23 (cf. Heb. 11.28), where his activity in Egypt during Passover night is described.

11. these things happened to them as a warning (Gk *typikōs*): i.e. as a warning for us; see note on verse 6. The pattern of divine revelation, human disobedience and divine judgment manifested in the Israelites' experience from Egypt to Canaan is reproduced in the *NT* era.

they were written down for our instruction: had they not been **written down** they might have been forgotten, and so would not have served **for our instruction.**

upon whom the end of the ages has come: lit. 'the ends of the ages (*ta telē tōn aiōnōn*) have met', the number of the former noun having been attracted to that of the latter. The **ages** whose 'ends' have 'met' on the believers of the apostolic age (cf. 7.29–31) are the ages past in their totality; the plural 'ends' does not suggest the terminal point of 'this age' and the beginning of 'the age to come', for the beginning of the new age is not its *telos*. Cf. Heb. 9.26; 1 Pet. 1.20 for similar expressions to the present one used in the same sense: the *NT* era was the time of fulfilment of all that the prophets had spoken (cf. Mk 1.15; Lk. 10.23f.; 24.25ff.; Ac. 2.16).

12–13. The record of the wilderness wanderings should be a warning against over-confidence, to which it is likely the 'spiritual' members of the Corinthian church were specially prone. The privations of the wilderness were designed by God to test his people, to bring out their true character (Dt. 8.2); the temptations of Corinth could serve the same purpose for the Christians of that city. They might count on God, however, not to expose them to trials and temptations beyond human ability to resist and overcome: with each **temptation** he would **also provide the way of**

escape, to enable them **to endure it.** But if they deliberately put themselves in the way of temptations to idolatry and its associated evils, they were ignoring the proffered **way of escape** and need not be surprised if they 'fell'.

The sanctity of the Lord's table 10.14-22

14. shun the worship of idols: lit. 'flee from idolatry'. For a parallel injunction, cf. 6.18a.

15. judge for yourselves what I say: turning from *OT* analogy, he is now about to present them with an argument based on their everyday experience, the force of which, as **sensible men**, they will readily recognize. This argument is based on the analogy between the Christian Eucharist and an idol feast.

16. The cup of blessing (Gk *eulogia*) may precede **the bread which we break** for the simple reason that Paul intends to develop the significance of the bread, and so mentions it after the cup. In the shorter Lukan account of the institution (Lk. 22.17–19a) and in the *Didache* (9.2ff.), however, the thanksgiving for the bread follows that for the cup. The designation of the cup as **the cup of blessing** (a common Jewish expression for the cup of wine taken at the end of a meal) is amplified by the clause **which we bless** (Gk *eulogoumen*), i.e. for which we bless God, in such words as 'Blessed art thou, O Lord our God, King of the universe, who createst the fruit of the vine'. At the Passover feast the third cup (out of four in all) is distinctively called 'the cup of blessing' because when it is poured the blessing ('grace after meat') is said over the meal (Mishnah, *Pesāḥîm* x.7). Cf. Joseph's prayer for Aseneth: 'let her eat thy bread of life and drink thy cup of blessing' (*Joseph and Aseneth* 8.11). At the Eucharist the blessing over the cup may have been cast in more explicitly Christian terms; cf. the form in the *Didache*: 'We give thee thanks, our Father, for the holy vine of David thy servant, which thou hast made known to us through Jesus thy Servant; thine be the glory for ever' (9.2). Paul's statement that the cup is **a participation** (*koinōnia*, 'communion') **in the blood of Christ** amplifies and interprets the dominical words of institution (cf. 11.25) as his description of **the bread which we break** as **a participation in the body of Christ** amplifies and interprets the words of institution spoken over the bread (cf. 11.24). Neither the **blood** nor the **body** has a material sense here; the point is that in the

Eucharist the communicants partake jointly of the life of Christ, yet not in such a way as to be immunized against divine judgment, regardless of their subsequent behaviour.

17. Eating together of the **one bread**—the 1946 and 1952 editions of *RSV* have 'one loaf'—symbolizes the fact that all participants, however **many** they may be, constitute **one body.** For this portrayal of the church as a **body** see the fuller statement in 12.14–27, with notes *ad loc.* The eucharistic 'communion in the body of Christ' is the sacrament of Christian unity, proclaiming the communicants' common membership in the **one body.** The words of institution, 'This is my body', are thus given a further reference (cf. 11.29). The contrast between the one and the many appears also in the thanksgiving for the eucharistic bread in the *Didache*, without mention of 'the body': 'As this broken bread was scattered upon the mountains, but was brought together and became one, so let thy church be brought together from the ends of the earth into thy kingdom; for thine is the glory and the power through Jesus Christ for ever' (9.4).

18. Consider the practice of Israel: lit. 'look at Israel according to the flesh', i.e. the earthly Israel, still observing the levitical ritual. A contrast is implied with the 'spiritual Israel' (cf. Gal. 6.16; Phil. 3.3). According to the ancient prescriptions, which were still followed in the Jerusalem temple, those who ate the sacrificial flesh—the priests and Levites especially (cf. Lev. 10.12ff.; Num. 18.8ff.; Dt. 18. 1ff.) in the discharge of their sacred ministry (cf. 9.13), but also the lay worshippers (cf. Lev. 7.11ff.; Dt. 12.5ff.; 1 Sam. 1.4; 9.19ff.; 16.2ff.)—were by that act **partners in the altar**, an expression occurring in Philo, according to whom such a 'partner in the altar' is also 'sharer in a common table' (*Spec. Leg.* i. 221; cf. verse 21b below).

19. 'Sensible men' must by now have seen the drift of Paul's argument. If those who ate of the eucharistic bread were partakers of Christ and those who ate of the Jewish sacrifices were 'partners in the altar', then those who ate the flesh of animals which had been offered to idols were partners in the pagan altar and partakers of the false god. 'But', the sensible men would have protested, 'you have already agreed with us that "an idol has no real existence" and that "there is no God but one". How can we be partakers of a nonentity?' 'I know', Paul replies; 'I am not saying that **food offered to idols is anything, or that an idol**

is anything'. (The last six words are absent from several ancient authorities, such as *P*⁴⁶ Aleph* A C*; but this is simply explained by the close similarity of this series of words to the preceding series.)

20. 'What I do mean is this', he goes on: **'what pagans sacrifice they offer to demons and not to God.'** There is an echo here of the Song of Moses: 'They sacrificed to demons which were no gods' (Dt. 32.17, reproduced in Bar. 4.7). In view of the analogy with the wilderness wanderings in verses 1–11, this quotation is apposite. (A more remote parallel is provided by the mention of sacrifice 'to non-existent demons' at the end of Isa 65.3 in the LXX version.) The *Didache*, which is not over-restrictive in regard to food-laws ('Concerning food, bear what you can') draws the line at idol meat: 'but keep strictly from what has been offered to idols, for it is the worship of dead gods' (6.3), an allusion perhaps to the psalmist's description of the idolatrous feasts of Peor as eating 'sacrifices offered to the dead' (Ps. 106.28).

In what sense does Paul regard those who share in such sacrificial feasts as **partners with demons**? It is plain that he does not think in this way of eating idol meat as such, whether it is bought in the market or served up in a neighbour's house (verses 25, 27) He is thinking of feasts which are explicitly under the patronage of a pagan deity, involving in some degree the acknowledgment and even worship of that deity. Those who shared such a feast under the patronage, for example, of Sarapis (see note on 8.10), whether in his temple or in a private house, were considered to have 'perfect sacrificial communion' with him (Aristides, *Concerning Sarapis*, 8) Pagan deities had no objective existence, but they were real and powerful as concepts in the minds of their devotees, whose lives might be profoundly affected by the values which these deitie represented. The **demons**, for Paul, were probably not personal beings but impersonal forces, which exerted a powerful influence over unregenerate men. Christ, by his victory on the cross over 'principalities and powers', had disabled these demonic forces and liberated his people from their influence; but his people might foolishly put themselves in situations where this influence was still potent. Paul knew that at social, and especially religious, festivities an atmosphere of enthusiasm was generated which carried the participants along with it (cf. 12.2). When the festivities were avowedly pagan in character and sponsorship, this atmosphere was bound to have an adverse effect on a Christian guest, no matter how firm his purpose might have been to maintain an attitude of reserve and not be carried away; and in the cool light of next morning he might well realize that he had joined in words or practices totally at variance with his Christian profession: for all his assurance that 'an idol has no real existence', he had been the victim of a demonic force associated with the worship of the 'idol'. If he were a gnosticizer of the type in view in 6.12–20, he might argue that his participation in the feast and even in such sexual licence as might have followed it were religiously indifferent; and if he had joined with his companions in using language inconsistent with the requirements of the gospel, there was a convenient tag from Euripides: 'the tongue has sworn; the heart remains unsworn'. But a Christian with a conscience about these matters would for long rue the day he had accepted such an invitation and unintentionally found himself participating in demonic fellowship.

21–22. What **the Lord** stood for and what **demons** stood for were so incompatible that it was impossible consistently to **drink the cup** of both or **partake of the table** of both (cf. Isa. 65.11). For **the cup of the Lord** cf. 11.27; **the cup of demons** may have reference to the libation poured at the end of a meal in honour of the sponsoring deity. The solemn warning in Mal. 1.7, 12 against 'thinking that the LORD's table may be despised' was probably in Paul's mind as one of those things which 'were written down for our instruction'. 'Sensible men' surely could not suppose it possible to have fellowship both with **the Lord** in the Eucharist and with **demons** at idol feasts. When the Israelites in the wilderness tried to combine idolatrous worship with the worship of Yahweh, then, as the Song of Moses says, 'they stirred him to jealousy with strange gods' and incurred his fiery anger (Dt. 32.17, 21f.). This 'happened to them as a warning': **Shall we provoke the Lord to jealousy** in spite of that example? Only if **we** were **stronger than he** could such an attempt be made with impunity; as it is, it is madness to act in such a way as deliberately to court the wrath of the Almighty.

Liberty and charity 10.23–11.1

23–24. '**All things are lawful**': see the note on the earlier quotations of this libertarian slogan in 6.12. Here, as there, Paul's first qualifying addition is **but not all things are helpful;** this

D

second on this occasion is **but not all things build up**: i.e. it is not everything that builds up a strong Christian character in myself or in my neighbour who may be influenced by my example, and it is not everything that builds up the Christian community as a whole (cf. 3.16f.). To attend a feast in a pagan temple under the auspices of the deity worshipped there would not, in Paul's judgment, be to the spiritual advantage of the participant, his fellow-Christian, or the community to which they belong. As in the earlier discussion of idol meat (8.7ff.), the wellbeing of one's neighbour is of paramount importance. The maxim of verse 24 is paralleled in Rom. 15.2 and Phil. 2.4; in both these places the example of Christ is adduced as the conclusive argument for the loving consideration of others and promotion of their highest interests.

25. In this new paragraph Paul makes it plainer than ever that there is no harm in eating idol meat. It was unnecessary to enquire scrupulously **in the meat market** whether an otherwise suitable joint of meat came from a sacrificed animal or not. Observant Jews were not likely to buy their butcher-meat in the ordinary market, if an orthodox slaughterer were available; but if there was none (e.g. because the Jewish community was too small), then, together with Jewish Christians who still preferred their food *kosher*, or Gentile Christians who wished to conform as strictly as possible to the Jerusalem decree, they would be most careful **on the ground of conscience** to ask just such a **question** as this before buying the joint. Paul assures his readers that they need have no qualms on this score. Even if the meat did come from a sacrificed animal, they are not going to eat it as part of an idolatrous feast or in company where they risk becoming 'partners with demons'.

The **meat market** (Gk *makellon*, a loanword from Latin *macellum*) is mentioned on a fragmentary Latin inscription found near the Lechaeum road, north of the city *agora*; see H. J. Cadbury, 'The Macellum of Corinth', *JBL* 53 (1934), pp. 134ff. Another fragmentary inscription in the vicinity suggests that fish as well as meat was sold there: it might indeed have been a general food market. In any case, that Paul should give Christians *carte blanche* to **eat whatever is sold** in a pagan market shows how completely emancipated he was from Jewish obligations in the matter of food and how loosely he sat to the food-restrictions of the Jerusalem decree. Cf. 1 Tim. 4.3–5 where, however, the assertion that 'every-

hing created by God is good and nothing is to be rejected if it is
received with thanksgiving' is more probably a *riposte* to asceticism
of a gnostic type.

26. The principle that any food for which one thanks God (cf.
verse 30) is thus rendered *kosher* is probably implied in the quotation from Ps. 24.1, **'the earth is the Lord's and everything in
it'**. In Tosefta *Beraḵôṯ* iv.1 this text is quoted as the justification for
saying grace at mealtimes; cf. E. Lohse, 'Zu 1 Cor. 10.26, 31',
ZNW 47 (1956), pp. 277–80.

27. If one of the unbelievers invites you to dinner: the
words **to dinner** are not expressed in the most reliable Greek
texts, but they are certainly implied. 'In that case', a scrupulous
observer of food-laws would say, 'it is better not to accept the
invitation, for you never know what kind of food might be set
before you.' The strict Jewish attitude to eating with Gentiles is
illustrated by Peter's words to Cornelius in Ac. 10.28 and the
circumcision party's criticism of Peter for visiting Cornelius and
his household and eating with them (Ac. 11.2f.). Even after the
Gentile mission began, table-fellowship between Jewish and
Gentile Christians was a delicate question, as appears from Peter's
discontinuance of this practice at Antioch because of representa-
tions made by visitors from Jerusalem (Gal. 2.11ff.). It was probably to facilitate such fellowship that the food-restrictions of the
Jerusalem decree were promulgated. But table-fellowship with
non-Christian Gentiles would have been deprecated in the strongest
terms by many church leaders. Paul, however, who has already
made it plain that his prohibition of table-fellowship with 'immoral
men' had in view immoral church members, not men of the world
(5.9–12), now tells his readers that if they **are disposed to go** to
an unbeliever's house in response to his invitation, they may freely
do so and **eat whatever is set before** them (cf. Lk. 10.8) **without
raising any question on the ground of conscience.** This
permission goes even farther than that of verse 25; food which a
Christian bought in the market would at least be eaten in the
atmosphere of a Christian home, but now no hindrance is put in
the way of his sharing a meal in a pagan home.

28–29a. There is one *caveat* attached to this permission; *RSV*
rightly treats it as a parenthesis. Someone may draw your attention to the fact that a particular course **has been offered in
sacrifice**—here the Greek term is not Paul's usual *eidōlothyton*,

which treats the deity as an 'idol', but *hierothyton*, 'sacrificed in ·
temple', which would be more appropriate on pagan lips or, eve·
if used by a fellow-Christian, in pagan company. If in this way ·
test is made of your faith or principles, then it would be best not t·
eat it. A present-day analogy may be imagined if someone wit·
strong principles on total abstention from alcohol were the guest ·
friends who did not share these principles. He would be we·
advised not to enquire too carefully about the ingredients of som·
specially palatable sauce or trifle, but if someone said to him point·
edly, 'There is alcohol in this, you know', he might feel that he wa·
being put on the spot and could reasonably ask to be excused fron·
having any of it. In the persecutions of Jews under Antiochus I·
(cf. 2 Mac. 6.7ff.), and possibly of Christians under the Roma·
Empire, the eating or refusal of 'forbidden' food was made a tes·
of faith: if eating was publicly identified with apostasy, then ·
confessor would refuse. At the table of a pagan neighbour such ·
polite refusal might be made **out of consideration for the ma·
who informed you**, whether he were the host or a fellow-guest·
because he might think abstention from idol meat to be essentia·
to Christianity, or **for conscience' sake**—not the conscience ·
the Christian to whom this advice is being given, for he is pre·
sumably a 'strong' Christian whose conscience is as fully emanci·
pated as Paul's, but the conscience of someone else, whether tha·
someone else be his informant (who might be a 'weaker' fellow·
Christian) or another guest or even the host. On the whole, th·
language is best satisfied by the first of these three possibilities·
especially if the informant is a Christian fellow-guest with con·
scientious scruples. The essential point is that Christian libert·
should be modified (only, but certainly) by Christian charity.

29b–30. The force of the question, **For why should m·
liberty be determined by another man's scruples?** is bes·
understood if the conjunction **for** links it with the permission ·
verse 27, not with the parenthesis of verses 28–29a. Paul associate·
himself with the man who is disposed to accept his pagan neigh·
bour's invitation: he says, in effect, 'If I were disposed to accep·
such an invitation, I would eat whatever was set before me withou·
raising any question on the ground of conscience, **for** to wha·
purpose (Gk *hina ti*) is **my liberty** judged **by another** conscienc·
(Gk *hypo allēs syneidēseōs*)?' The following question leads on fron·
this one: the Christian whose conscience is 'strong' says grace ove·

his food (silent grace, perhaps, at someone else's table) and thus renders it *kosher*; **'why'**, he asks, **'am I denounced because of that for which I give thanks?'** He will, as the parenthetic *caveat* urges, limit his liberty voluntarily out of regard for another man's scruples, but he will not allow others to sit in judgment on his exercise of his liberty or to make their conscience the standard by which his liberty must be regulated (cf. Col. 2.16).

If these two questions arose directly from the *caveat* of verses 28–29a, they might be interpreted as the interjection of an indignant 'man of knowledge' (cf. 8.10) who objects to having his liberty to eat what he likes in a neighbour's house curtailed by the scruples of a fellow-guest; but in that case the objection would be introduced by 'but', not **for**; and Paul would have given it some kind of answer.

31. The **glory of God**, not the observance of food-laws, nor the satisfaction of one's natural appetite, nor even the assertion of one's personal liberty, is the main object of Christian life and action —eating, drinking, or anything else (cf. Col. 3.17). And **the glory of God** is signally served when the conscience of his people is sympathetically treated and their general wellbeing is promoted.

32. **Give no offence to Jews or to Greeks or to the church of God:** put no obstacle in their way which would hinder **Jews or Greeks** from accepting the gospel or hinder members of **the church of God** from making progress in Christian maturity. The **church of God** is neither Jewish nor Gentile; it is a new society comprising former Jews and Gentiles alike (cf. 12.13), a 'new race' (*Epistle to Diognetus*, 1) or a 'third race' (*Preaching of Peter*, quoted by Clement, *Stromateis* VI. v. 39), as later Christian writers liked to call it.

33. The positive counterpart to 'giving no offence' is the policy which Paul lays down for himself in 9.19–23 and repeats here: **I try to please all men in everything I do.** This is formally at variance with his rejection of the charge of 'men-pleasing' in Gal. 1.10, but there is no real contradiction. The charge in Gal. 1.10 is that he trimmed the truth of the gospel to suit his company for the time being; here, as in 9.22f., the purpose of his endeavour **to please all men in everything** is to allow no attitudes or practices of his own to stand between the truth of the gospel and those whom he seeks to win. We can easily understand, however, that his critics might be unwilling or unable to distinguish between 'men-pleasing' of the right and the wrong kind. **not seeking my own advantage** (cf. verse 24), **but that of many**: lit. 'the many', the mass of mankind (cf. Rom. 5.15, 19, where there is an echo of 'the many' of Isa. 53.11 who are 'accounted righteous' because of the Servant of Yahweh).

that they may be saved: cf. 9.22, 'that I might by all means save some'.

11.1. In this, as in other respects, he presents his own course to them as an example to follow (see note on 4.16). He, in turn, set Christ before him as his exemplar in this and other respects; 'for Christ did not please himself' (Rom. 15.3) but made himself the servant of all (cf. Mk 10.45; Lk. 22.27). It is not the example of the Lord in present exaltation that Paul has in mind but the example he set when 'he emptied himself, taking the form of a servant' (Phil. 2.7; see also note on 2 C. 8.9). It is instructive to compare the qualities which Paul recommends to his readers when he urges them, in one form of words or another, to be **imitators . . . of Christ** with those which characterize Jesus in the Gospels (see notes on 13.4–7; 2 C. 10.1).

COMMENDATION AND CRITICISM **11.2–34**

The veiling of women **11.2–16**

2. I commend you: From this point to 11.34 Paul seems not to be answering questions raised in the Corinthians' letter, but rather commenting on a statement which they had made in it: 'we **remember** you **in everything and maintain the traditions even as** you have **delivered them to** us.' 'That is fine', says Paul; **'I commend you'.** The **traditions** (Gk *paradoseis*) were the instructions, relating to matters of doctrine and practice alike, which he delivered to his churches on the authority of Christ. They might be delivered either 'by word of mouth or by letter' (2 Th. 2.15); those to which the Corinthians refer were probably delivered orally. Two traditions which Paul delivered to the Corinthians are elaborated later (11.23ff.; 15.1ff.); with regard to them he says that he himself had 'received' them as the Corinthians in turn 'received' them from him. But it is not necessary to confine all the Pauline **traditions** to things which he himself first 'received' from those who were in Christ before him. Tradition must start somewhere, and while the bulk of apostolic tradition may indeed have stemmed 'from the Lord' (cf. verse 23), Christian *paradosis* in *NT* is not invariably a synonym for *kyrios* ('Lord'). The 'tradition' of earning one's own living and not becoming a burden on others, to which Paul refers in 2 Th. 3.6ff., was one that was based chiefly on his own example. So the particular 'tradition' which he goes on to emphasize in verses 3–16—his instruction about propriety in regard to the veiled and unveiled head—probably does not go back beyond his own teaching (which he imparted, of course, as one who had 'the mind of Christ').

3. Paul, it appears, had taught the Corinthians (as he taught his other converts) that in meetings of the church women should have their heads veiled when they prayed. But this piece of instruction was being ignored in Corinth. What difference did it make in the sight of God (it was probably asked) whether they prayed with or without veils? Learning of this attitude either from the Corinthians' letter or from his three visitors, Paul deals with the matter in a variety of ways, appealing (*a*) to the order of creation, (*b*) to a common sense of seemliness, (*c*) to the teaching of 'nature', (*d*) to the general practice of the churches.

As for the order of creation, there is a hierarchy of the order: **God–Christ–man–woman.** Each of the first three members of this hierarchy is the **head** of the member following. By **head** in this context we are probably to understand not, as has frequently been suggested, 'chief' or 'ruler' but rather 'source' or 'origin'— a sense well attested for Gk *kephalē* (cf. S. Bedale, 'The Meaning of κεφαλή in the Pauline Epistles', *JTS* n.s. 5 (1954), pp. 211ff.). In the light of the account of the formation of Eve from **her husband** (Gen. 2.21–23), man is the source of woman's existence ('she shall be called Woman, because she was taken out of Man'). Since it is not true of married couples in general that **the head of a woman is her husband** (*RSV*) in this sense of **head**, it is better to translate with *NEB* (cf. *RV*), 'woman's head is man' (and so also in Eph. 5.23, even if there the principle is applied more particularly to the husband–wife relation than here). Again, **Christ** is the source of man's existence because he is the archetypal Man (but cf. 15.46–49) and also because he is the agent in the creation of all things (8.6; cf. Col. 1.16), **every man** included— and it is **man** in the sense of 'male' (Gk *anēr*) that is relevant at this point in Paul's argument. Lastly, it is from **God** the Father that **Christ**, as Son, derives his eternal being (cf. 3.23; 8.6).

4–6. We now mark a transition from the sense of **head** in verse 3 to its literal sense, and thenceforth an oscillation between the two senses. **Any man who prays or prophesies with his head covered dishonours his head:** that is, in the sense of verse 3, he **dishonours** Christ. Perhaps synagogue practice in the apostolic age was more flexible in this regard than it is today, when the covered head for men is a matter of orthodox obligation; but what Paul has in mind is a veil which covers the whole head and in particular conceals all the hair; something worn on top of the head like a present-day cap or hat does not really come within the scope of his argument. A man **dishonours his head** if he **prays or prophesies** 'with (something hanging) down from his head' (Gk *kata kephalēs echōn*): he should worship 'with unveiled face' (an expression used in a different context in 2 C. 3.18). He **dishonours his head** because he is practically abdicating the sovereignty and dignity with which the Creator has invested him. It is improbable that Christian men were actually veiling their heads in Corinth; the reference to their (hypothetically) doing so is necessary to complete the argument: if such a practice would (by common consent) be a denial of man's status in the order of creation, so it is equally a denial of woman's status in that order if she **prays or prophesies with her head unveiled.** That there was liberty in the church (for it is church order, not private or domestic devotion, that is in view here) for women to pray or prophesy is necessarily implied by Paul's argument: he does not suggest that there is anything undesirable about their doing so (whatever the injunction of 14.34f. means, it cannot be understood thus), but requires them to do so with their heads covered. Their praying might be participation in congregational prayer, but prophesying was an individual charismatic exercise (cf. 14.1ff., and especially 14.31, 'one by one'). The church experienced the fulfilment of the promise of Jl 2.28 that in the new age not only 'your sons' but also 'your daughters shall prophesy' (cf. Ac. 2.17; 21.9). So then, says Paul, a woman **dishonours her head** if she **prays or prophesies with her head unveiled,** because this is tantamount to a denial of her relation to man by the ordinance of creation, and also because it is a disgrace for **her head** in the literal sense—as **disgraceful** as it would be, by general consent, for her to have her hair shaved or cropped close (the principle of 'following nature', which is hinted at here, is expressed more clearly in verse 15b). That the shaving

of the head of a woman who had undertaken a Nazirite vow
involved public, though voluntary and permissible, humiliation
is evident from the case of Bernice (Josephus *BJ* II. 313f.); but it
is hardly likely that Paul has this in mind. If, on the other hand,
he knew that pagan prophetesses in the Graeco-Roman world
prophesied with uncovered and dishevelled heads, this would be
a further argument in his eyes against Christian women doing so.

**7–9. a man ought not to cover his head, since he is the
image and glory of God:** in Gen. 1.26f. it is mankind (Hebrew
ʾāḏām, Gk *anthrōpos*), comprising male and female, not the male
only (Gk *anēr*, as here), that is created in the image of God. Paul
does not deny that woman also bears the image of God; indeed, he
implies that she does by carefully avoiding complete parallelism
in the following statement, **woman is the glory of man**. He
does not say she is his 'image and glory' (as the **man** is God's); it
is Seth, not Eve, that bore Adam's image (Gen. 5.3). Reading Gen.
1.26ff. in the light of Gen. 2.18ff., to which he refers in verses 8 and
9, Paul probably concluded that it was in the form of the male
that man was first created in God's image with dominion over the
earth; 'male and female he created them' must mean (when
interpreted by Gen. 2.22) 'first male and later female'—the
woman being formed subsequently **from man** and for the sake
of man 'to be a helper fit for him' (Gen. 2.18, 20). The man, that
is to say, was created directly for God, to bear his image and reflect
(or even share) his glory. Of the man is implied here what is said
in Isa. 43.7 of Israel: 'whom I created for my glory, whom I
formed and made' (cf. Rom. 3.23, where 'the glory of God' is the
appointed standard or goal from which all—all mankind—'fall
short'). The glory of God is manifested pre-eminently 'in the face of
Christ' who is 'the likeness (*eikōn*, image) of God' (2 C. 4.4ff.);
here (as in verse 3) Christ is to be understood as the middle term
between God and man, in reference to the old creation (cf. Col.
1.15–17) as to the new (cf. Col. 1.18–20). Woman, on the other
hand, was made **for man**, to reflect (or share) *his* glory. Even if
the order of the old creation has been transcended in Christ by the
order of the new creation, yet, so long as the former order survives,
those who are in Christ must show respect for it by their appearance and demeanour. The glory of God should not be veiled in the
presence of God (that would be an acted contradiction in terms);
by the same token the glory of man *should* be veiled in the presence

of God. So Paul's argument may be paraphrased, but now he goes on to transcend it.

10. That is why a woman ought to have a veil on her head: *RSV* **veil** obscures the point of the argument. As the marginal note states, the Greek word (*exousia*) means 'authority'. The **veil** is no doubt 'a symbol of this' (as the marginal note goes on to say), but in a letter in which 'authority' is a key-word its presence here should be indicated in the translation. Here, as elsewhere in this letter, 'authority' is probably to be understood in an active sense: the **veil** is not a sign of the woman's submission to her husband's authority (cf. F. Godet, C. Hodge) nor even of her social dignity (cf. *NEB* margin) and immunity from molestation (cf. W. M. Ramsay, *The Cities of St. Paul* (1907), pp. 202ff.); it is a sign of her authority. In the synagogue service a woman could play no significant part: her presence would not even suffice to make up the requisite quorum of ten (all ten must be males). In Christ she received equality of status with man: she might pray or prophesy at meetings of the church, and her **veil** was a sign of this new authority (cf. M. D. Hooker, 'Authority on her head: an examination of 1 Cor. XI. 10', *NTS* 10 (1963-4), pp. 410ff.). Its ordinary social significance was thus transcended. As man in public worship manifests his authority by leaving his head unveiled, so woman manifests hers by wearing a **veil**. Her status in Christ does not mean that the creation ordinances are already things of the past: she should keep her head covered **because of the angels**, who are guardians of the created order (cf. G. B. Caird, *Principalities and Powers* (1956), pp. 17-22, especially p. 18). By discarding the **veil** Corinthian women were ignoring the tension set up by existence in Christ at a time when 'the form of this world' has not yet passed away completely (cf. 7.26-31). It is a far-fetched exegesis of this reference to **the angels** to understand it in terms of the angels of Gen. 6.1-4 who were captivated by the beauty of the 'daughters of men' (cf. Jude 6), as Tertullian did (*On the veiling of virgins*, 7). The appeal to **angels** as an argument for propriety in gatherings of the people of God is paralleled in the Qumran texts, where they are said to be present, e.g., at meetings of the congregation (1 QSa ii.8f.) and in the camo of the 'sons of light' (1 QM vii.6).

11-12. Nothing that has been said on the subject thus far must detract from the interdependence of man and woman. If, in the story of the formation of Eve, **woman was made from man**

(see verse 8), it is true that, ever since, **man is now born of woman**. Their mutual dependence, which is sufficiently evident in ordinary life, is specially manifest **in the Lord**, in the new creation, where, as Paul says elsewhere, 'there is . . . neither male nor female' in the sense that, since they are 'one in Christ Jesus' (Gal. 3.28), neither has higher dignity than the other before God, the author of **all things**. The covering or uncovering of the head is neither here nor there **in the Lord**, but Christians, living in the period when the two ages overlap, should as far as possible respect the ordinances of both, 'giving no offence' (cf. 10.32). (We may compare the christianization of the accepted codes of domestic conduct by the repetition of 'in the Lord' in Col. 3.18ff.; Eph. 5.21ff.)

13. For (secondly), in addition to the creation ordinances, public propriety or social convention calls for some respect. The standards of propriety and convention change from time to time and from place to place; in the cultural milieux with which Paul was most familiar (both Jewish and Tarsian) it was not normally reckoned **proper** or seemly for a woman to flout these standards and appear in public **with her head uncovered**, still less to **pray to God** in public thus; this is something which he invites his readers to **judge for** themselves. There is nothing frivolous about such an appeal to public conventions of seemliness. To be followers of the crucified Jesus was in itself unconventional enough, but needless breaches of convention were to be discouraged. A few decades later, if not as early as this, people were ready to believe the most scandalous rumours of what went on at Christian meetings; unnecessary breaches of customary propriety would be regarded as confirmation of such rumours. It was far better to give the lie to them by scrupulous maintenance of social decorum. Though the application of this principle may vary widely, the principle itself remains valid, especially where the public reputation of the believing community is likely to depend on such externalities.

14–15. Paul's third argument is an appeal to what **nature itself** can be seen to **teach**, and recalls the Stoic ideal of 'living agreeably to nature' (*homologoumenōs zēn*). But appeals to **nature** (Gk *physis*) were commonplace, and it is unnecessary to postulate a Stoic source for Paul's present reference to patent physical facts. In the world which he and his readers knew **nature** gave a lead by endowing **man** with shorter hair than **woman**, so that long hair in **a man** was regarded as effeminate, whereas in **a woman** it was **her pride. For her hair is given to her for a covering:** or, with the omission of the variously located **to her** (Gk *autē*), for which we have the authority of P^{46} and the Western manuscripts D and G, 'hair has been given for a covering'. This is a general statement, from which an analogical inference is drawn: since hair is intended to serve as a covering (Gk *peribolaion*, a different term from those used in the preceding verses for 'cover' or 'veil'), then nature, which has given woman (Mediterranean woman) an abundant supply of this covering, manifestly intends her to be covered. However readily the opposite conclusion might be drawn from Paul's premise here—since hair is given in lieu of a covering, woman, whose head is amply covered with hair, needs no other head-covering—the preceding arguments make it plain that this is not Paul's conclusion.

16. Paul's fourth argument is an appeal to general Christian practice; this was his last word to **any one** who was **disposed to be contentious** about this subject or to deny the validity of his previous arguments: **we** (that is Paul and his fellow-apostles, or Paul and his associates in the Gentile mission, if indeed **we** does not mean 'I', as it often does in his letters) **recognize no other practice** than the one recommended in the preceding verses, **nor do the churches of God**—including possibly the church of Jerusalem and her daughter-churches as well as those planted by Paul and his colleagues. A tendency on the part of the Corinthian church to be a law to itself, without reference to Christian procedure elsewhere, is implied below in 14.36.

The Lord's Supper 11.17–34

17–18. Paul has commended them for maintaining the 'traditions' which he delivered to them, but his commendation is not unqualified. **In the following instructions** is a doubtful interpretation of the Greek, which *RV* translates more literally 'in giving you this charge'; the particular pronoun rendered 'this' (Gk *touto*) usually refers to what precedes. 'In giving you this charge', says Paul, **'I do not commend you,** and more especially because there is something in your meetings more serious than any deviation in respect of a head-covering—something that turns them into positively harmful occasions instead of the blessing they ought to be. This is the class-distinction that manifests itself **when you come together.'** **In the first place** (Gk *prōton men*) is not formally caught up by such a companion phrase as 'in the next place', unless we so regard verse 34b, 'About the other things . . .' (Gk *ta de loipa*). **when you assemble as a church:** Gk *en ekklēsia* (so also 14.19, 28, 35), with reference perhaps to occasions when the whole church of Corinth meets together (cf. 14.23). That it met thus in the house of Gaius (cf. 1.14) may be inferred from Rom. 16.23, where Gaius is called 'host . . . to the whole church'. **I hear that there are divisions among you:** these **divisions** (Gk *schismata*) are not those of 1.10ff., which were manifestations of party-spirit, but appear to have been largely social, involving in practice discrimination against the poorer members of the fellowship. Paul's informants may have been 'Chloe's people' (as in 1.11) or his more recent visitors from Corinth (cf. 16.17). His comment, **I partly believe it,** does not suggest that he thought their report exaggerated, but that he was already prepared in some degree for news of this kind by the conviction that such developments must be expected before the end.

19. there must be factions: Gk *haireseis,* but as the *schismata* of verse 18 are not 'schisms' in the later sense, neither are these *haireseis* 'heresies' in the later sense. The two terms are here used synonymously. A similar logion is ascribed to Jesus by Justin Martyr (*Dialogue* xxxv.3) and the *Didascalia* (vi.5): 'There will be divisions (*schismata*) and factions (*haireseis*)'. (See J. Jeremias, *Unknown Sayings of Jesus*³, E.T., 1964, pp. 76-77.) Whether Paul knew this logion or not, he means that in a mixed community divisions are inevitable, so that the **genuine** (*dokimoi*) may be distinguished from the counterfeit (*adokimoi,* as in 2 C. 13.5). Such divisions anticipate the final division of the judgment-day, which is probably in view in the dominical logion.

20. The factions which manifested themselves at meetings of the Corinthian church, however, were such that they could not **eat the Lord's supper,** the fellowship meal in the course of which they were accustomed to take the Eucharist. The adjective *kyriakos,* here translated **Lord's** (as in Rev. 1.10, its only other *NT* occurrence, where it is used of the first day of the week as 'the Lord's day'), is found in contemporary Greek in the sense 'imperial', where the *kyrios* to which it refers is the emperor. Here it means 'belonging to the *kyrios Iēsous*' (as he is called in verse 23).

It was no more possible for the **Lord's supper** to be eaten in an atmosphere of social discrimination than it was for the same people to 'partake of the table of the Lord and the table of demons' (10.21). The Eucharist could be profaned by faction as certainly as by idolatry.

21–22. The Eucharist, then, was evidently taken in the course of a communal meal, at which the proper procedure would be for the food and drink brought by members of the church to be shared among all. Instead of this, the various individuals and groups in the Corinthian church were eating and drinking what they themselves brought, so that the rich had more than enough and the poor were not only unsatisfied but embarrassed and humiliated. A meal marked by such an affront to Christian fellowship was not **the Lord's supper**; on the contrary, it was a case of each going **ahead with his own** supper. If that was what they wanted to do, says Paul, it should be done in their own houses; as it was, such conduct was an insult to **the church of God**, and was liable to incur the retribution of 3.17. Their unbrotherly behaviour in this regard could receive no praise, but outright condemnation (cf. verses 27, 29).

23. **For I received from the Lord what I also delivered to you:** the verbs 'receive' (*paralambanō*) and 'deliver' (*paradidōmi*) are those appropriate to the transmission of tradition (see note on verse 2), corresponding respectively to Hebrew *qibbēl* and *māsar* (cf. also 15.3). Here the tradition goes back to **the Lord**. Too much weight should not be laid on the fact that the preposition rendered **from** is *apo*, not *para* (although *para* is the reading of the Western codex D), as though *para* would denote communication from the Lord without intermediaries whereas *apo* means simply that the tradition derives originally from him. It is the context (including the two significant verbs), not the single preposition, that indicates a process of transmission; moreover, **the Lord** is not only the originator of the chain of tradition but the one who, exalted in glory, maintains and confirms the tradition by his Spirit (cf. O. Cullmann, '*Kyrios* as Designation for the Oral Tradition concerning Jesus', *SJT* 3 (1950), pp. 180ff.).

In endeavouring to correct the abuses at the Corinthian Eucharist, Paul reminds his readers of the circumstances and purpose of its institution, as he had **delivered** it to them when he was with them, and thus provides us with the earliest account of the institution. Even so, the Markan account appears to have preserved some more archaic features than this one, as its Aramaisms suggest (see also notes on verse 25). Since Paul's account proper begins with the statement **that the Lord Jesus . . . took bread**, instead of 'he . . . took bread', where 'he' would refer back to **the Lord**, it may be inferred that he is quoting more or less verbatim what he had **received**, from **the Lord Jesus** to the second **in remembrance of me** (verse 25).

on the night when he was betrayed: this is primarily a reference to Judas Iscariot's treachery, but the same verb (*paradidōmi*) is also used of Jesus' being 'delivered up for our trespasses' (Rom. 4.25 (*RV*), probably reflecting Isa. 53.12, LXX; cf. Rom. 8.32; Gal. 2.20), and this idea may not be entirely absent from the present passage.

took bread: or 'a loaf' (see note on 10.17); cf. Mk 14.22 (Mt. 26.26); Lk. 22.19.

24. and when he had given thanks: Gk *eucharistēsas*; from the verb *eucharisteō* (the commonest Gk word meaning 'I thank' or 'Thank you') as used in this context comes the term 'Eucharist' as a synonym for the Holy Communion. Lk. 22.19 has the same verb; Mk 14.22 (followed by Mt. 26.26) has the synonymous *eulogēsas* (cf. 10.16). The common Jewish form of thanksgiving for bread was 'Blessed art thou, O Lord our God, King of the universe, who bringest forth bread from the earth'; it may be, however, that Jesus used a distinctive form of his own.

he broke it: so all three Synoptic records. From this action the Holy Communion came to be known also as 'the breaking of bread'. **'This is my body which is for you':** Aleph G and the majority of later witnesses ineptly add the participle 'broken'. Behind **my body** (Gk *mou . . . to sōma*) may be discerned Aramaic *biśrī*, lit. 'my flesh', perhaps meaning 'I myself'. In Mk 14.22 **This is my body** is preceded by the imperative 'Take' (Mt. 26.26 has 'Take, eat'). Neither Mark, Matthew, nor the shorter Lukan text has the adjective clause **which is for you**; the longer Lukan text (22.19) has it in the amplified form 'which is given for you' and follows it, as Paul's account does, with the command: **Do this in remembrance of me.** In the biblical sense **remembrance** is more than a mental exercise; it involves a realization of what is remembered. At the Passover feast the participants are one with their ancestors of the Exodus; at the Eucharist Christians experience the real presence of their Lord. As the Passover meal was, in the words of the paschal liturgy, 'a memorial of the departure from Egypt' (cf. Exod. 12.12; 13.3, 9; Dt. 16.3), so this breaking of bread was to be a memorial of Jesus after 'his departure (Gk *exodos*), which he was to accomplish at Jerusalem' (Lk. 9.31). It is improbable that he meant 'Do this in order that God may remember me by bringing about my parousia and consummating his kingdom', as J. Jeremias argues (*The Eucharistic Words of Jesus*, E. T. (1958), pp. 159ff.), although the memorial was certainly to be observed in the presence of God and had an eschatological reference (see verse 26).

25. In the same way also the cup, after supper: these words appear, with a minor change in order, in the longer Lukan text (Lk. 22.20). **In the same way** (Gk *hōsautōs*) means that as he had taken the bread and given thanks for it, so he took the cup and gave thanks for it: the verb of thanksgiving is not expressly repeated by Paul, as it is by Mark (14.23, *eucharistēsas*; cf. Mt. 26.27). Since Jesus took **the cup after** the Passover **supper**, the reference may be to the 'cup of blessing' drunk when grace after meat was said (cf. 10.16). The drinking of wine at the Passover meal was obligatory, and it was customarily red wine, which lent itself the better to Jesus' interpretation of it as **the new covenant in my blood**. Probably the oldest form of this word of institution is the Markan: 'This is my blood of the covenant (my covenant-blood), which is poured out for many' (Mk 14.24). This form is reproduced in Mt. 26.28 practically without alteration, except for the epexegetic supplement 'for the forgiveness of sins'; the longer Lukan text replaces 'for many' (which may echo Isa. 53.12) by 'for you' (Lk. 22.20), probably a liturgical adaptation applying the language directly to the congregation (cf. 'which is for you' in verse 24). The 'blood of the covenant' is (perhaps deliberately) reminiscent of Exod. 24.8, 'Behold the blood of the covenant which the LORD has made with you . . .' (where, however, it was real sacrificial blood that was poured); cf. also Zech. 9.11. The addition of the adjective **new** before **covenant** makes explicit what was in any case implied: the new covenant foretold by Jeremiah is about to be ratified (cf. the antithesis between the new covenant of Jer. 31.31–34 and the old one of Exod. 24.6–8 in Heb. 8.8ff.; 9.18ff.). Quite apart from the presence or absence of the adjective, **the new covenant in my blood** (so also Lk.

22.20) probably represents a smoothing of 'my blood of the covenant'; both stylistically and in the matter of content the latter is
the harder saying and so the more likely to be original. But there
is no essential difference in meaning: the cup is not identical
either with the covenant or with the blood which seals it; it
symbolizes both the sacrifice which ratifies the covenant and the
covenant so ratified.

The repeated command after the institution of the cup, **Do this,
as often as you drink it, in remembrance of me,** is peculiar
to Paul; its absence from the longer Lukan text (together with that
text's qualification of 'the cup' by the phrase 'which is poured out
for you') should make us hesitate to explain the latter as simply
due to the influence of 1 Cor. 11.24f. The longer Lukan text more
probably combines an independent 'short' tradition with the
tradition which Paul for his part reproduces here (for a fuller discussion, cf. E. E. Ellis, *The Gospel according to Luke*, Century Bible
(1966), *ad loc.*). The clause **as often as you drink it** anticipates
verse 26.

26. In the Passover service each element is explained in terms
of the Exodus narrative; for example, at an early stage in the
service the head of the household says of the unleavened bread:
'This is the bread of affliction [cf. Dt. 16.3] which our fathers ate
in the land of Egypt; let all who are hungry come and eat' (it is
not certain if these precise words were used at the beginning of
the Christian era). So, in the course of the passion Passover, Jesus
gave a new explanation to some of the bread and wine on the
table: the one and the other set forth his life, about to be given in
sacrifice for his people, and by eating and drinking them they
sacramentally appropriate that sacrifice with its saving benefits
(cf. 10.16). The addition of the command to **do this** repeatedly
as his memorial does not mark a change or reinterpretation of the
original intention of the Jerusalem rite (so H. Lietzmann, *Mass
and Lord's Supper*, E.T. (1953), pp. 204ff.); it brings out that intention more clearly, because (Paul continues) **as often as you eat
this bread and drink the cup, you proclaim the Lord's
death until he comes.** This may be Paul's interpretation of the
words **Do this in remembrance of me.** The memorial act is
indeed a 'visible word', an acted affirmation of the communicants'
interest in the Saviour's blood; but the verb **you proclaim** (Gk
katangellete) cannot be satisfied by anything less than a public

narration of the death of Christ as the *haggadah* or *hieros logos* which explained the act. The Eucharist, like the preaching of the gospel, in which 'Jesus Christ was publicly portrayed as crucified' (Gal. 3.1), was thus a powerful factor in the early crystallizing of the passion story in a form recognizable in all four gospels. Martin Kähler exaggerated when he called the gospels 'passion narratives with extended introductions' (*The So-called Historical Jesus and the Historic Biblical Christ*, E.T. (1964), p. 80), but he exaggerated a real situation.

The clause **until he comes** retains the eschatological emphasis which was present from the beginning, as in Jesus' words about never again drinking the fruit of the vine until the day when he drinks it 'new in the kingdom of God' (Mk 14.25; Lk. 22.18), or never eating the Passover again 'until it is fulfilled in the kingdom of God' (Lk. 22.16). The survival of the Aramaic invocation *Marana-tha*, 'Our Lord, come' (see note on 16.22), as part of the Eucharistic liturgy even in Greek-speaking churches (*Didache* x.6) shows how firmly embedded this element was from early days. What is from one point of view a memorial act is from another point of view an act of anticipation. As in some strands of Jewish expectation the messianic redemption was associated with the Passover—'in this night they were redeemed', said Rabbi Joshua ben Hananiah (*c.* A.D. 90), 'and in this night they shall be redeemed' (*Mᵉkiltâ* on Exod. 12.42)—so at the Eucharist the partition between here and hereafter became transparent; the parousia came as near as possible to being realized. There may be a suggestion of purpose in **until he comes**, in addition to the primary temporal sense; the eating and drinking would in that case constitute a 'prophetic action' helping to ensure the fulfilment of the prayer *Marana-tha*. O. Hofius compares the final force of 'until' in Isa. 62.1, 6f. ('Bis dass er kommt', *NTS* 14 (1967–8), pp. 439ff.).

27–28. Since the bread and the cup betokened Christ's body and blood, to eat or drink **in an unworthy manner**—a just assessment of the discourtesy described in verse 21—was to **be guilty of . . . the body and blood of the Lord.** There is no word in the Greek text corresponding to **profaning**; this is added in *RSV* to make the sense clearer in English. (Without such an addition Paul's language might be taken by an English reader to denote responsibility for the death of Christ; this is not his meaning.) Such 'unworthy' eating or drinking was possible only for

Christian whose behaviour belied his profession; pagan parti-ipation is not in view here. This is the first instance in Christian terature of 'fencing the table'—ensuring that only those com-municate who are in a fit moral and spiritual condition to do so. o, several decades later, the *Didache* enjoins: 'let none who has a uarrel with his fellow join in your meeting until they are re-onciled, lest your sacrifice be defiled' (xiv.2, perhaps alluding to 1t. 5.23f.). The Christian who is about to communicate should **xamine himself** to make sure that he is 'genuine' (verse 19) and a a fit state to **eat of the bread and drink of the cup**; then he 1ay properly take the holy supper. The context implies that his :lf-examination will be specially directed to ascertaining whether r not he is living and acting 'in love and charity' with his eighbours.

29. Paul now makes plain what eating or drinking 'in an un-orthy manner' means by adding that **any one who eats and rinks without discerning the body eats and drinks judg-ment upon himself**. The Western additions (from verse 27), nworthily' after **eats and drinks** and 'of the Lord' after **body**, re epexegetic in intention. In the word of institution 'This is my ody' he sees a reference not merely—perhaps not even primarily -to Jesus' 'body of flesh' (cf. Col. 1.22), but to the corporate nity of all who share his life: 'we who are many are one body, for e all partake of the one bread' (10.17). But for certain members the church to eat and drink their fill, in unbrotherly disregard their poorer fellow-Christians, as some were doing at Corinth, as to eat and drink **without discerning the body**, without any onsideration for the most elementary implications of their llowship in Christ. Such conduct was as serious a profanation the holy supper as was the table-segregation between Jewish 1d Gentile Christians in Syrian Antioch, which Paul condemns Gal. 2.11ff.; it was not surprising that those guilty of it should cur divine **judgment**.

30–32. The **judgment** took the form of sickness and death, hich were rife in the community. That such could be the con-quences of violating the sanctity of the Christian fellowship has ready been indicated in 5.5. 'The fact that an idea is foreign us does not mean that it was an alien and intrusive element early Christianity' (A. D. Nock, *Early Gentile Christianity and Hellenistic Background* (1964), p. 131). **But if we** examined

ourselves, and **judged ourselves truly** (the *RSV* addition **truly**
attempts to convey the force of the prefix *dia* in *diakrinō*, the verb
translated 'discern' in verse 29), we should amend our ways and
so not fall under the judgment of God. Nevertheless, as in 5.5 the
'destruction of the flesh' had the salvation of the spirit as its
purpose, so here the judgment of **the Lord** is a disciplinary
chastisement to preserve believers from being overwhelmed in the
condemnation pronounced on the godless **world** (cf. Exod
15.26). This is suggested by Paul's statement that 'some have
fallen asleep' (so, literally, *RSV* margin for **some have died** of
the text); he reserves this terminology for the death of Christians
(cf. 15.6, 20; 1 Th. 4.13ff.). In Wis. 11.10 the author, addressing
God, says of the Israelites in the wilderness: 'thou didst test them
as a father does in warning, but thou didst examine the ungodly
as a stern king does in condemnation'. So here the fact that the
people warned **are chastened** is a token of their being true
children of God; we may compare the argument of Heb. 12.5–11
except that there (as in Job) the chastisement is not the result of
any antecedent misdemeanour. It is reading too much into our
present text to suppose that, at this early date, the death of
Christians before the parousia was felt to be so unnatural that
some special explanation was called for (cf. 1 Th. 4.13ff., where no
explanation is offered for some Christians' having 'fallen asleep'.

**33–34a. when you come together to eat, wait for one
another:** instead of each 'going ahead with his own meal' (vers
21), the food and drink brought should first be shared out and due
consideration given to those who could not bring much. If some
were so **hungry** that they could not wait, they should **eat at
home**; then whatever they took at the meeting of the church
would be for fellowship instead of an unedifying display of selfishness and gluttony. Their meetings would thus be a means of grace
and not of condemnation.

34b. Whatever else had to be regulated in this regard could
wait until Paul's next visit (cf. 4.18ff.; 16.2f., 5ff.).

THE QUESTION OF SPIRITUAL GIFTS **12.1–14.40**

Discerning spiritual utterances **12.1–3**

12.1–2. Now concerning spiritual gifts: more probably
'spiritual persons', i.e. persons endowed with **spiritual gifts** (

in 2.15; 3.1); the genitive plural *pneumatikōn* may be masculine or neuter. These words take up a new issue raised in the Corinthians' letter, but Paul (not for the first time) shows himself in command of more precise knowledge about the situation in Corinth than could have been derived from a question in a letter.

This section of 1 Corinthians goes on to 14.40, and the inclusion in it of the exhortation to love (13.1–13) is essential to Paul's argument. The argument of 12.1–14.40 might be summed up thus in one sentence: 'The primary token of the indwelling Spirit, the indispensable evidence that one is truly "spiritual", is not glossolalia, but love.'

The Corinthians' question on this subject, then, had been framed in such a way as to imply that the surest sign of the presence and power of the Spirit was glossolalia—utterance in languages not normally used by the speakers, as a result of appropriate stimulation of what since 1861 has been known as 'Broca's area', the centre for articulate speech in the third frontal convolution of the dominant cerebral hemisphere. Glossolalia differs from 'prophecy', which was also current in the Corinthian church, in that the latter was uttered in the speaker's habitual tongue; moreover, Paul attaches much more value to prophecy stimulated by the Holy Spirit than he does to glossolalia. His first point in replying to the Corinthians' question is that it is the source and content of an utterance that are all-important, not the fact of its 'inspiration'. He knew that the phenomena of glossolalia and prophecy could be paralleled in paganism: **You know**, he says, **that when you were heathen, you were led astray to dumb idols, however you may have been moved.** The **idols** might be **dumb**, unlike the living God who speaks, but the 'demons' which they represented exercised malign power over the worshippers of the **idols** (see note on 10.20). In classical literature, Apollo was particularly renowned as the source of ecstatic utterances, as on the lips of Cassandra of Troy, the priestess of Delphi or the Sibyl of Cumae (whose frenzy as she prophesied under the god's control is vividly described by Virgil); at a humbler level the fortune-telling slave-girl of Ac. 16.16 was dominated by the same kind of 'pythonic' spirit. Paul does not suggest that any prophecy or glossolalia at Corinth proceeded from such a source; he simply reminds his readers that there are 'inspired' utterances other than those produced by the Spirit of God.

3. Ecstasy or enthusiasm is no criterion of spirituality: attention must be paid to the words spoken. In particular, their testimony to Jesus is of supreme importance. It is not necessary to suppose that the utterance **'Jesus be cursed!'** (*anathema Iēsous*) had ever been heard in the church of Corinth (see p. 21)—it was the kind of thing that persecutors of Christians tried to make them say (cf. Ac. 26.11), and such affirmations were allegedly required later of candidates for admission to the Ophite sect (Origen *Celsus* vi.28)—but Paul insists, by means of this extreme example adduced for the sake of the argument, that no false or unworthy witness to Jesus can ever be attributed to **the Spirit of God**, just as contrariwise **no one can say 'Jesus is Lord' except by the Holy Spirit**. Ecstatic utterance can be produced by a variety of stimuli, and the character of the stimulus must be inferred from the substance of the utterance, but the confession of **Jesus as Lord** (cf. Rom. 10.9; Phil. 2.11), whether in ecstasy or not, is an unmistakable sign of the Holy Spirit's working. Every true Christian, in short, is a 'spiritual person'. (We may compare the test of prophetic utterances prescribed in 1 Jn 4.1–3, where the Spirit-inspired confession of Jesus is worded in such a way as to exclude the docetic denial of his true manhood.)

Varieties of spiritual gifts 12.4–11

4–6. Paul will return to this question of glossolalia and deal with it in more detail (14.2ff.); first, however, he states some general principles about spiritual gifts (Gk *charismata*). The Spirit does not confer the same gifts on each believer: the **Spirit** is one but the 'distributions' (Gk *diaireseis*, *RSV* **varieties**) of his gifts are manifold (cf. Rom. 12.6), just as the **Lord** is one, although he distributes various commissions for **service** (*diakonia*) among his people, and **God** is one, although he distributes the operation (*energēmata*) of his power variously in his children's lives. **Gifts** **service** and **working** are not distinct categories. The correlation of the **Spirit**, the **Lord** and **God** is a notable adumbration of later trinitarian formulae (cf. Eph. 4.4–6, in a passage which perhaps draws upon this one; also 2 C. 13.14).

7. Each member of the church, then, receives some spiritual gift which is a **manifestation of the Spirit**; there is no warrant for saying that one such gift manifests his presence more than another. Some gifts may be more extraordinary and spectacular than others, but it does not follow on that account that those who receive them are more spiritual than others. And however various in character the gifts may be, all are given **for the common good**—a point illustrated later by means of the figure of the body (verses 12–27).

8–10. Nine forms of spiritual 'manifestation' are enumerated, probably in descending order of value—(*a*) **the utterance of wisdom**; (*b*) **the utterance of knowledge** (Paul presumably intends some distinction between *sophia* (**wisdom**) and *gnōsis* (**knowledge**), but the distinction is not clear to us; the former, however, calls for special qualities of maturity and insight; cf. 2.6–13; 14.6); (*c*) **faith**, not the saving faith which is basic to all Christian life, but a special endowment of faith for a special service (cf. 13.2b); (*d*) **gifts of healing** (distinguished from ordinary medical skill), such as are amply documented in the Gospels and Acts; (*e*) **the working of miracles** (*dynameis*, mighty works) which, like those in the Gospels and Acts (cf. Ac. 2.22, 43), were 'signs' of the new age (cf. Gal. 3.5; Heb. 2.4a); (*f*) **prophecy**, the gift possessed, among others, by Agabus (Ac. 11.28; 21.10f.) and Philip's daughters (Ac. 21.9); (*g*) **the ability to distinguish between spirits**—that gift of spiritual discernment by which, in particular, genuine and counterfeit 'prophecy' could be recognized for what they were; (*h*) **various kinds of tongues**, including those intelligible to some hearers, though not normally commanded by the speakers, as in Ac. 2.6ff., and those which could not be understood by speakers or hearers, unless someone present could exercise the ninth and last gift in this series, (*i*) **the interpretation of tongues**. (Compare the eightfold list in verse 28 below.)

11. Each of these gifts was a work of **one and the same Spirit** of God, who allotted them to one and another as he saw fit (cf. Heb. 2.4b). The list is not intended to be exhaustive; some gifts might be known in one area and not in another, and the possibility is not excluded that new gifts might subsequently be bestowed to meet changing needs for which some of the gifts mentioned here made no adequate provision.

The body and its members 12.12–26

12. The exercise of the various gifts of the Spirit by members of the church 'for the common good' is now compared to the functioning of the various parts of **the body** for the health of the whole. This comparison was in Paul's mind before he came to the present section of his letter; it finds passing expression in the two quite different contexts of 6.15 and 10.17; 11.29. But this is the first place in his extant correspondence where he elaborates the comparison: **as the body is one and has many members,** so also Christ is one and has many members; as **all the members of the body, though many, are one body,** so the members of the church, though many, are 'one body in Christ, and individually members one of another' (Rom. 12.5, in a context which reproduces in abbreviated form the exposition of this passage). It is not particularly helpful to try to determine the source of Paul's conception of the church as the body of Christ; it could have come to him independently. Something of the sort is implied in the words 'why do you persecute me?' which he heard on the Damascus road (Ac. 9.4; 22.7; 26.14); the state (*polis*) or the world-state (*cosmopolis*) was compared by Stoics to a body, each citizen having his part to play; the Hebrew tendency to think in terms of corporate personality would also help. Paul, moreover, thought of believers in Christ as sharing his risen life; they were 'in Christ' as Christ lived in them. He could thus the more readily think of them as members of 'Christ corporate'. The thought, similarly expressed in Rom. 12.4–8, is further developed in Colossians and Ephesians (cf. Col. 1.18; 2.19; Eph. 1.22; 4.15; 5.23). But here and in Romans the emphasis is laid on the co-operation of the individual members for the well-being of the total community.

13. It is through baptism in the Spirit that believers in Christ— **we** (*hēmeis*, emphatic) **all,** Paul and his converts alike—have become members of his body. This is the one place in *NT* outside the Gospels and Acts where the baptism of the Spirit is mentioned. The prediction of John that, while he baptized with water, the Coming One whose way he was preparing would baptize 'with the Holy Spirit' (Mk 1.8), is interpreted in Acts as fulfilled at Pentecost when Jesus, as the exalted Christ, 'poured out' the promised Spirit on his followers (Ac. 2.33; cf. 1.5; 11.16), and thus inaugurated the church as the people of God of the new age. Paul expresses much the same thought here: the preposition **by** (Gk *en*) in the phrase **by one Spirit** does not point to the Spirit as the baptizer, but as the one in whom **we were all baptized**—not an exclusive élite of 'spiritual persons'—at a particular point of

ime. Faith-union with Christ brought his people into membership
of the Spirit-baptized community, procuring for them the benefits
of the once-for-all outpouring of the Spirit at the dawn of the
new age, while baptism in water was retained as the outward and
visible sign of their incorporation 'into Christ' (cf. Gal. 3.27).
And as it was in **one Spirit** that they **were all baptized**, therefore it was **into one body** that they **were all baptized**. Whatever
racial or social differences might have separated them before—
Jews or Greeks, slaves or free—disappeared in this new
unity of the Spirit' (Eph. 4.3). The same outpouring of the
Spirit by the exalted Christ is indicated in different language in
the following clause: **and all were made to drink of one
Spirit.** This language is reminiscent of Jn 7.37–39, where Jesus'
invitation to the thirsty to come to him and drink is interpreted of
the Spirit, which those who believed in him were to receive'; the
supernatural (lit. spiritual) drink' of 10.4 also comes to mind, but
the aorist (*epotisthēmen*), apart from any other consideration, makes
it unlikely that the reference here is to the Eucharist. Both aorists,
we were . . . baptized and **were made to drink**, refer to an
initiatory experience. The verb *potizō* is used of watering plants or
irrigating the ground as well as of causing men or animals to
drink (its primary sense), and here it denotes the refreshment
and life which reception of the Spirit imparts: 'we were all
watered with one Spirit'.

14–26. The analogy of the one body and its **many** members is
applied in various ways. No member is less a part of the body than
any other member: all are necessary. Variety of organs, limbs and
functions is of the essence of bodily life. No one organ could
establish a monopoly in the body by taking over the functions of
the others. A body consisting of **a single organ** would be a
monstrosity: the rule is **many parts, yet one body.** No limb or
organ can regard another as dispensable, **nor again** can **the head
say to the feet, 'I have no need of you'**; such language would
be inappropriate in Colossians and Ephesians, where Christ himself is the head of the body (whether in the physiological sense or in
that of 1 C. 11.3). When, in Menenius Agrippa's fable, the more
active members of the body agreed to starve the belly because, as
they thought, it did no work in return for the labour which they
expended on feeding it, they soon discovered how dependent they
were on its being regularly fed. The **weaker** parts, says Paul,

are indispensable, and must receive special care; those part
which (as nature itself teaches, he implies) are less **presentabl**
are provided with special covering which the parts fit for publi
display **do not require**. All this bespeaks the providence with
which God has arranged the various parts of the body and
adjusted their functions and relations so that they are all inter
dependent. If there is **discord** (Gk *schisma*) between the members
that is a sign that **the body** is in an unhealthy state; a fragment o
Empedocles says similarly that there is 'no dissension or un
seemly strife among the members' of the cosmos. The suffering o
one member means the suffering of all; the wellbeing of on
means the wellbeing of all.

The exercise of spiritual gifts 12.27–31

27. What is true of the human body is applicable to the church
you (*hymeis*, emphatic) **are the body of Christ and indi
vidually members of it.** It is a mistake to argue that, sinc
body lacks the definite article, the translation should be 'you ar
a body of Christ', as though each local church was a separate bod
of his. (We are dealing here with an instance of 'Apollonius'
canon', according to which nouns in *regimen*, i.e. one nou
governing another in the genitive case, must have the article pre
fixed to both of them or to neither—as here, *sōma christou*—withou
any necessary difference in meaning between the two construc
tions.) The Church, wherever it is found, in Corinth or in an
other place, is Christ's body, and the men and women who mak
up the Church are **individually members of** that body, eacl
with a distinctive contribution to make for the benefit of the whole

28. Eight kinds of members with special functions are no
enumerated. The list has several points of contact with the list c
nine spiritual 'manifestations' in verses 8–10, but the two lists d
not completely correspond; probably neither is intended to b
exhaustive.
**God has appointed in the church first apostles, secon
prophets, third teachers:** the explicit **first . . ., second . .**
third mark these out as exercising, in Paul's estimation, the thre
most important ministries. In Eph. 4.11 these are also enumerated
together with evangelists, in the order (*a*) apostles, (*b*) prophets
(*c*) evangelists, (*d*) pastors and teachers, as given by the ascende
Lord to equip the people of God 'for the work of ministry, fo

building up the body of Christ'. Apostles and prophets are singled
out also in Eph. 2.20 as constituting the foundation on which the
new, spiritual temple is based (cf. Rev. 21.14). **Apostles**, like
Paul himself, were doubly qualified for their ministry by having
seen the risen Christ (cf. 9.1; 15.5–10) and having been specifically
called by him to this service (cf. 1.1). **Prophets** declared the
mind of God in the power of the Spirit; their importance was not
comparable to that of the great prophets of Israel, for their
ministry was directed in the main to the requirements of the
moment rather than to the enunciation of permanent principles;
but Paul places a high value on this gift and urges his readers to
seek it earnestly (14.1). **Teachers** had as their special business the
instruction of their fellow-members in Christian faith and
practice; the content of this instruction was based on the teaching
of Jesus himself (cf. Rom. 12.9–13.14 for a sample of Paul's own
teaching ministry). Two, or even all three, of these ministries
might be exercised exceptionally by one man; the five leaders of
the church of Syrian Antioch, including Barnabas and Paul, are
described as 'prophets and teachers' in Ac. 13.1.

As for **workers of miracles** (lit. 'mighty works', as in verse
10) and **healers** (lit. 'gifts of healings', as in verse 9), these have
appeared in the earlier list. **Helpers** (lit. 'helps') may have been
those who were specially deputed to attend to the poor, weak or
sick members; **administrators** (Gk *kybernēseis*) were the 'helms-
men' of the church, who directed its life and action. It is not by
accident that **speakers in various kinds of tongues** come last
in this list, as, together with interpreters of 'tongues', they do also
in the list of verses 8–10. Interpreters of 'tongues' are not included
separately in this list, but they are mentioned in verse 30.

29–30. The seven questions from **Are all apostles?** to **Do all
interpret?**—amounting to a third list of spiritual gifts in descending order of value—are each introduced by the Greek negative
mē, implying the answer 'No'. 'It would be as preposterous', says
Paul, 'for all to have one and the same gift as for all the parts of the
body to perform one and the same function.' Once more he
inculcates the principle of diversity in unity, and incidentally
explodes any tendency to claim that all spiritual persons must
manifest glossolalia.

31. But earnestly desire the higher gifts: the 'greater' ones
(*meizona*), perhaps those which come near the head of the lists in

verses 8–10, 28 and 29f. Apostleship, in the nature of the case, was not open to them; but they should cultivate an ambition for the other leading gifts, especially prophecy (14.1).

And I will show you a still more excellent way: this transition to chapter 13 may be rendered: 'And yet beyond all this I am showing you a way' (a way to reach the highest goal, to achieve the noblest ambition), or, if we adopt the Western reading (*ei ti*, 'if anything', for *eti*, 'yet'): 'if there is anything beyond all this, I am showing you a (the) way'. This Western reading is supported in part by P^{46}, but, as P^{46} is mutilated here, its precise wording (which, had it been extant, might have solved the textual problem of this sentence) is inaccessible to us.

The supremacy of love 13.1–13

It may be that the lofty exhortation to love of which chapter 13 consists—'one of the most strikingly original things St. Paul ever wrote' (A. D. Nock, *Early Gentile Christianity* (1964), p. 96)—was an independent composition of Paul's, introduced here because of its relevance to the situation with which he was dealing, and attached to its new context by the transitional clauses in 12.31b and 14.1a. But it is so integral to the course of Paul's present argument that, had it not lain ready to hand, he must have composed something along the same lines to complete his demonstration that love surpasses the richest spiritual endowments. The gifts or manifestations of the Spirit repeatedly enumerated in chapter 12 are variously apportioned; no one Christian has them all, and some Christians may not have any of those expressly named. More important than the gifts of the Spirit is 'the fruit of the Spirit' (Gal. 5.22f.), the harmony of nine graces which make up a mature Christian character and provide conclusive evidence of the Spirit's indwelling presence. First among these graces is love—the divine love which 'has been poured into our hearts through the Holy Spirit which has been given to us' (Rom. 5.5), God's love for men displayed in Christ (cf. Rom. 5.8) and now reproduced in their attitude towards him and towards one another. It is not the Greek word *agapē* in itself that has this force; it is the fact that the love described is divine love. A Christian community can make shift somehow if the 'gifts' of chapter 12 be lacking: it will die if love is absent. The most lavish exercise of spiritual gifts cannot compensate for lack of love.

13.1. If I speak in the tongues of men and of angels: this is not a reference so much to natural eloquence as to a supernatural endowment with glossolalia. The speech **of angels** is mentioned here and there in the pseudepigrapha and in rabbinical literature: Job's daughters are said to have used it in praising God (*Testament of Job* 48–50) and Yoḥanan ben Zakkai to have been granted the ability to understand it (TB *Babâ Baṭrâ* 143*a*; *Sukkāh* 28*a*). We need not infer that the power to speak with angels' tongues was actually claimed in the Corinthian church. 'Yet', says Paul, 'even if I command this power **but have not love,** I am no better than **a noisy gong or a clanging cymbal'**, such as were used in various well-known cults, producing much sound but little sense.

2. if I have prophetic powers: lit. 'if I have prophecy', which is a higher gift than glossolalia (cf. 14.5), but which nevertheless is valueless without love.

and understand all mysteries and all knowledge: so as to have insight into the mind and purpose of God. The 'secret and hidden wisdom of God' of 2.7 transcends all other forms of mystery and knowledge precisely because it is an unfolding of the love of God: 'Wisdom in a mystery / Of bleeding love unfold' (C. Wesley). **if I have all faith, so as to remove mountains:** a reminiscence, probably, of the saying of Jesus preserved in Mk 11.23 or Mt. 17.20 // Lk. 17.6; this **faith** would be the special sort mentioned in 12.9, but even with such a gift as this, if I **have not love, I am nothing**.

3. If I give away all I have: lit. 'if I turn all my property into morsels of food'; the verb translated **give away** is *psōmizō* (translated 'feed' in Rom. 12.20), from *psōmion* (used of the 'morsel' at the Last Supper in Jn 13.26f., 30). *AV* 'though I bestow all my goods to feed the poor' expresses the sense well enough, and reminds us that what is called 'charity' today is no substitute for 'charity' in the *AV* sense.

if I deliver my body to be burned: like the three Hebrews who 'yielded up their bodies' (Dan. 3.28) and the martyrs under Antiochus of whom similar language is used (2 Mac. 7.37; 4 Mac. 18.3). In the light of these precedents, it is not really necessary to adduce such examples as that of the Indian holy man Zarmanochegas, who burnt himself alive at Athens while on an embassy to Augustus and whose tomb was one of the sights shown to visitors

(Nicolaus of Damascus in Strabo, *Geog.* xv.i.73; Dio Cassius, *Hist.* liv.9; Plutarch, *Life of Alexander* 69), although J. B. Lightfoot found in this incident the explanation of Paul's remark (*Colossians* (1879), p. 395). The charitable disposal of one's property or the acceptance of martyrdom might indeed spring from love, but Paul implies that if such actions spring from any other motive, even that of religious obligation, they are valueless in God's sight and bring no **gain** to those who perform them. For **to be burned** (Gk *hina kauthēsomai*) there is an early and strongly attested variant 'that I may glory' (Gk *hina kauchēsōmai*) in P^{46} Aleph A B 1739. If, in spite of this weighty testimony, **to be burned** is preferred, it is on grounds of intrinsic probability: it is certainly by far the more forceful of the two readings.

4–5. Love is patient and kind: the number of negative clauses in verses 4–7 has suggested to some expositors that this paragraph has been modelled on the 'negative confession' pattern; cf. G. von Rad, 'The Early History of the Form Category of I Corinthians XIII. 4–7' in *The Problem of the Hexateuch and Other Essays*, E.T. (1966), pp. 301ff., where parallels are adduced from the *Testaments of the Twelve Patriarchs*. More important than the form is the content: what is predicated of **love** in these four verses describes a character which is ruled by love. It is a commonplace to say that the character of Christ is here portrayed; we may go farther and say that God is here portrayed, since God is love (cf. J. T. Sanders, 'First Corinthians 13', *Interpretation* 20 (1966), pp. 159ff., esp. p. 187). Naturally, then, these statements must be true of those of whose hearts the love of God has taken possession. The 'patience' and 'kindness' of which Paul speaks are included along with 'love' in the 'fruit of the Spirit' in Gal. 5.22.

love is not jealous or boastful: this last word, *perpereuesthai*, occurring here only in *NT*, denotes empty bragging; it is not so different from the 'arrogance' which is mentioned next as incompatible with **love**—that 'inflated' spirit which Paul has had occasion to criticize earlier in this letter (cf. 4.6, 18f.; 5.2; 8.1).

love is not . . . rude: the verb (*aschēmonein*) is that rendered 'not behaving properly' in 7.36. P^{46} reads the antonym *euschēmonein*; this can only mean 'love does not behave in an affected manner' (assuming a fine outward appearance which does not express the inward reality).

Love does not insist on its own way: or seek its own interests (cf. Phil. 2.4); the inferior reading of P^{46} and B, 'does not seek what is *not* its own' (i.e., is not covetous), represents the standard of bare justice rather than of divine love.

is not irritable: i.e. 'is not provoked to anger' (Gk *paroxynetai*); compare the 'contention' (*paroxysmos*) of Ac. 15.39, and contrast the exhortation 'to stir up one another (*paroxysmos* again) to love and good works' of Heb. 10.24.

or resentful: lit. 'does not reckon up evil' with a view to paying the offender back in his own coin (the Gk phrase is a quotation of Zech. 8.17a, LXX, where the idea seems to be rather that of plotting evil); cf. Rom. 12.17ff.

6. it does not rejoice at wrong: in true love there can be no room for *Schadenfreude*.

but rejoices in the right: lit. 'in the truth'. The second occurrence of **rejoices** is a more intensive form (Gk *synchairein*) than the previous one (*chairein*).

7. Love bears (*stegein*) **all things:** this presumably means something different from **endures** (*hypomenein*) **all things** at the end of the verse, although *stegein* often means 'endure', as in 9.12. Perhaps the first clause means that love *covers* all things unworthy instead of exposing them or blazing them abroad, in the sense of I Pet. 4.8 (cf. Jas. 5.20), although there a different verb is used.

believes all things, hopes all things: love is always eager to believe the best and put the most favourable construction on ambiguous actions; it **hopes** against hope, and is always ready to give an offender a second chance and to forgive him 'seventy times seven' (Mt. 18.22).

8. Love never ends: lit. 'never falls', but *RSV* gives the true interpretation: **love** does not belong to this age only, but reigns in the eternal order. The parallel statement in *Pirqê ʾAbôt* v.16 is only a verbal parallel, lacking Paul's eschatological orientation: 'All love that depends on a material factor passes away with the passing of that factor; love that has no such dependence never passes away.' The gifts of the Spirit—**prophecies . . ., tongues . . ., knowledge . . .—will pass away** for they are but temporary manifestations: the fruit of the Spirit abides. The **knowledge** (*gnōsis*) which **will pass away** is a special kind of knowledge, a manifestation of the Spirit designed for the present requirements of church life (cf. 1.5; 12.8), in which the Corinthians were prone to take undue pride (8.1) and which was useless in isolation from love (13.2). The highest knowledge, the knowledge of God in Christ, far from passing away, would attain transcendent perfection in the age to come (13.12).

9–10. In this present age which is soon to be superseded **our knowledge is imperfect and our prophecy is imperfect** (Gk *ek merous*, 'in part'), by contrast with the fulness of revelation that lies in store for those who love God (cf. 2.9); **but when the perfect comes** at the parousia of Christ and the consummation is realized for which the sons of God at present long eagerly (Rom. 8.23), **the imperfect will pass away.** The Spirit is the pledge of the eternal heritage into which believers will enter at resurrection (cf. 2 C. 1.22; 5.5) and his gifts belong to the present, anticipatory stage of his ministry: they are **imperfect** in comparison with the coming perfection. The eschatological emphasis of verses 8–13 must not be overlooked if Paul's argument and point of view are to be properly appreciated.

11. The present phase of our existence is to that coming perfection as childhood is to maturity. The mind and practice which are appropriate to childhood are inappropriate for maturity: a grown man has given up **childish ways.** The Corinthians must recognize that the things to which they attached paramount importance were the transient concerns of spiritual immaturity and learn to set the highest value on the things that endure for ever. This kind of contrast between childhood and maturity was a common figure in Hellenistic rhetoric.

12. Another figure pointing the contrast between present and future knowledge is the contrast between seeing a dim and distorted reflection in a metal **mirror** (Gk *esoptron*) and seeing the direct reality. Although the figure of the **mirror** serves a different purpose here from that in 2 C. 3.18, the analogy of Moses is present in both places—here by implication and there expressly. In Num. 12.8 Yahweh says of Moses: 'With him I speak mouth to mouth, clearly, and not in dark speech, and he beholds the form of the LORD'. Some strands of rabbinical exegesis interpreted 'the form (Hebrew *mar'eh*) of the LORD' as referring to a *clear* mirror in which Moses beheld him (*Leviticus Rabba* i.14). The LXX rendering of the phrase 'in dark speech' (*di' ainigmatōn*, 'through riddles') is similar to the phrase rendered **dimly** in our present passage (*en ainigmati*, 'in a riddle'). The reflection in a metal mirror might be so dim or distorted that one would have to guess

(Gk *ainittesthai*) what the reality was like, **but then**, says Paul, we shall see **face to face** (cf. also the reference in Dt. 34.10 to 'Moses, whom the LORD knew face to face').

Finally, leaving figures of speech behind, Paul declares that his present partial and imperfect knowledge will give way at the parousia to knowledge so perfect that **then I shall understand fully, even as I have been fully understood**. The *RSV* change from **know** to **understand** reflects Paul's transition from the simple verb *ginōskein* to the compound *epiginōskein* which here at any rate has intensive force, denoting the fulness of knowledge which comes with the unimpeded vision of God which, says Philo, 'is both seeing and being seen' (*On Dreams* ii.226). Here and now, 'if one loves God, one is known (*ginōskein*) by him' (8.3), but not until then can our knowledge of God hope to approach his knowledge of us.

13. So faith, hope, love abide, these three: this is the best-known instance of a triad which appears elsewhere in the Pauline corpus (cf. Rom. 5.1–5; Gal. 5.5f.; Eph. 4.2–5; 1 Th. 1.3; 5.8) and other early Christian literature (cf. Heb. 6.10–12; 10.22–24; 1 Pet. 1.3–8, 21f.; Barnabas 1.4; 11.8; Polycarp 3.2f.), and which may belong to the common stock of primitive Christianity, in which case 1 C. 13.13 presents Paul's exegesis of the triad (cf. A. M. Hunter, *Paul and his Predecessors* (1961²), pp. 33ff.). **Faith, hope** and **love** were added in Christian ethics to the four Platonic virtues (wisdom, courage, temperance, justice) to make up the traditional seven cardinal virtues. **So** is the *RSV* rendering of *nyni de* (lit. 'and now', 'but now') which is thus understood as resumptive (or even adversative), not temporal. **So**, in distinction from the things which pass away, **faith, hope, love abide**. **Faith** here is not the special gift of 12.9; 13.2, but the common response of all the people of God to his saving grace. Paul's argument would have been satisfied with the conclusion that **love** abides; his inclusion of **faith** and **hope** suggests that we have here a quotation familiar in the early Church. But when he has quoted it, he makes a distinction within the three. Whatever form faith and hope may take in the resurrection age, when faith as we now know it gives place to open vision (cf. 2 C. 5.7) and hope is swallowed up in realization (cf. Rom. 8.24f.), love remains unchanged in its nature even when it attains perfection; therefore **the greatest of these is love**.

E

Prophecy preferable to 'tongues' **14.1–12**

14.1. Make love your aim: this sums up the exhortation
to love, and provides a transition to the resumed discussion o
spiritual gifts.
earnestly desire the spiritual gifts: a near-repetition o
12.31a, the encouragement there to aim at 'the higher gifts' takin
the form here of a special encouragement to **prophesy**. O
several counts prophecy is recommended as superior to glossolalia

2–4. Glossolalia edifies no one but the speaker; unintelligibl
language cannot convey any benefit to those who hear it. If a ma
uses glossolalia in his private devotions—if it brings him more int
the presence of God—good and well: God reads his mind, but s
far as others are concerned, **he utters mysteries** (riddles wit
no solution) **in the Spirit** (on the assumption that his glossolali
is prompted by the Spirit of God). Prophecy, on the other hand
edifies the church: when Christians assembled together hear th
mind of God cogently declared in a language they can understand
this promotes **their upbuilding and encouragement an
consolation.**

5. Paul recognizes **tongues** as a spiritual gift, and does no
condemn or forbid it; but he is eager that his converts should hav
a proper sense of values. **'I want you all to speak wth tongues'**
he says, **'but even more to prophesy'.** As in other matter
(asceticism, libertarianism), so in regard to glossolalia he goes a
far as he can with those whom he criticizes before interposing
caveat. 'The entire drift of the argument of I Cor. xii–xiv is such
as to pour a douche of ice-cold water over the whole practice. Bu
Paul could hardly have denied that the gift of tongues was
genuine supernatural *charisma* without putting a fatal barrie
between himself and the Corinthian enthusiasts' (H. Chadwick,
'All Things to All Men', *NTS* 1 (1954–5), p. 268). The building
up of the church is the purpose for which spiritual gifts have bee
given, but **tongues** cannot achieve this purpose unless a trustworthy interpreter be available; prophesying in the power of the
Spirit, on the other hand, cannot fail to achieve it. **He who
prophesies is** for this reason **greater than he who speaks in
tongues.**

6–12. It is the content of the utterance that is important,
whether that content takes the form of **revelation or knowledge**

or prophecy or teaching. In the light of 12.8, the revelation may be related to 'the utterance of wisdom' mentioned there. The important point is that the utterance must be intelligible to be profitable. Even with inanimate instruments this is true; soldiers must recognize whether the bugle note is a signal for advance or retreat if it is to be of any use. A man might as well speak into the air as address a company of his fellows in a tongue they do not understand. This is true of ordinary languages as well as of glossolalia; a non-Greek was a foreigner (Gk *barbaros*, an onomatopoeic word signifying that his speech was gibberish) to a Greek, and equally the language of a Greek was 'Greek' to anyone who did not understand it. Paul's remark in verse 11 recalls Ovid's self-pitying complaint in exile at Tomi on the Black Sea: 'I am a barbarian here because no one understands me, and the stupid Getae laugh at my Latin speech' (*Tristia* v. x. 37f.). 'If, then,' he adds, 'you are so eager for manifestations of the Spirit (Gk *pneumatōn*, lit. 'spirits'), cultivate the most useful ones, and so excel in building up the church' (cf. verses 4f.).

'Tongues' must be interpreted 14.13–19

13–17. But what if a man has received the gift of tongues and wishes to use it for general profit? He should pray for the power to interpret the glossolalia into language which the church understands; then, if what he says is Spirit-inspired, the whole company will benefit. What if my gift of tongues expresses itself in prayer? Then my spirit (i.e. whatever part of me exercises this spiritual gift) prays but my mind is unfruitful; I may have a sense of religious exaltation (as is experienced in present-day glossolalia) but my prayer is not intelligent, because I do not understand what I am saying. (This is hardly the same phenomenon as the 'sighs too deep for words' with which, according to Rom. 8.26, 'the Spirit himself intercedes' for the people of God.) Let my prayer and praise be Spirit-inspired, indeed, but let it be intelligent too. This is specially important in meetings of the church: uninterpreted glossolalia may edify someone in his personal prayer-life (cf. verse 4) but in the church the one who leads in prayer or thanksgiving does so on behalf of the others present, who signify their assent by adding their 'Amen' to what is said. But how can any one in the position of an outsider (Gk *idiōtēs*, here of the 'uninitiated' person who cannot interpret the words of thanksgiving) **say the 'Amen'** intelligently? God no doubt understands the sense perfectly, **but the other man is not edified**.

18–19. I thank God that I speak in tongues more than you all: if the Corinthian enthusiasts were disposed to maintain that no one who lacked the gift of glossolalia could rightly claim to have received the Spirit or to be able to discern spiritual realities, Paul makes it plain that they cannot object to his argument on this score. It was no doubt true that in the ordinary sense he was linguistically better equipped than any of them, but the context requires us to understand him to claim a richer endowment of glossolalia than theirs (an endowment of doubtful relation to the experience described in 2 C. 12.3f.). We should certainly never have guessed this had Paul not had occasion to say so in the course of the present argument, so careful is he not to encourage the irrational element in religion. 'No stronger assertion of his belief in the validity of this gift of the Spirit could be made; and in the context it is a master-touch which leaves the enthusiasts completely outclassed and outmanœuvred on their own ground' (H. Chadwick, *NTS* 1, p. 269). If he claims the gift here, it is to depreciate it immediately: **in church** (cf. 11.18) **I would rather speak five words with my mind**—i.e. intelligently (and therefore intelligibly)—**in order to instruct others, than ten thousand words in a tongue** which the others could not follow. Instruction, in Paul's view, was indispensable for the building up of the church.

A sign for unbelievers 14.20–25

20. Over-concentration on glossolalia is a mark of immaturity. There is indeed a right way for Christians to be childlike—in their freedom from guile (the **evil** (Gk *kakia*) more particularly in view here)—but in their intelligence they ought to be **mature.**

21–25. In the law (here used of the whole *OT*) there is a divine oracle suitable to the Corinthian situation. When Isaiah warned his fellow-citizens of the folly of their ways, they mocked him for using baby-talk: *ṣaw lā-ṣāw, qaw lā-qāw* (Isa. 28.10). (These terms have been variously explained as names of letters of the alphabet recited by children when learning their ABC, or as imitations of glossolalic utterance.) Accordingly he assured them that, since they would not listen to Yahweh's lesson when it was communicated in elementary Hebrew, they would learn it from the foreign speech of Assyrian invaders, 'by men of strange lips

and with an alien tongue' (Isa. 28.11). In this sense the message
of God conveyed in unfamiliar language was **a sign ... for
unbelievers**, a sign of divine judgment. Paul quotes neither MT
nor LXX; his future construction **and even then they will not
listen to me** (from Isa. 28.12b, where MT and LXX have 'they
refused to listen', implying a refusal preceding the foreign incur-
sion) is said by Origen (*Philocalia* 9) to resemble Aquila's version.
From the clause **says the Lord** with which Paul concludes his
quotation, J. M. P. Sweet, following E. E. Ellis (*Paul's Use of the
OT* (1957), pp. 107ff.), infers that Paul may be adapting to his
present purpose a piece of early Christian anti-Jewish polemic
('A Sign for Unbelievers', *NTS* 13 (1966-7), pp. 240ff., esp. pp.
243f.). Paul's point is that a divine communication in strange
tongues addressed to the deliberately disobedient will but confirm
them in their disobedience: they will remain all the more **unbelievers**. (This has no bearing on the narrative of Acts 2.4ff.,
where the hearers were disposed to listen to the apostles' preaching
'because each one heard them speaking in his own language', not
in a strange tongue. See, however, J. G. Davies, 'Pentecost and
Glossolalia', *JTS* n.s. 3 (1952), pp. 228ff.)

Thus, if **unbelievers** enter a meeting of the church and hear
the members **all** speaking what sounds like confused gibberish,
they will not be favourably impressed; they will conclude that
everybody is **mad**. The picture of **the whole church** assembling
(cf. 11.18) suggests that at Corinth glossolalia was not so likely to
be a feature of private devotion as a manifestation of group fervour
—an experience which at the time may be intensely meaningful to
those caught up in it but which leaves the detached spectator cold,
if not contemptuous. The **outsiders** here (*idiōtai*) differ from those
in verse 16, who were simply members of the congregation un-
versed in glossolalia; in verses 23f. they are evidently non-Christians.

By contrast with glossolalia, **prophecy is** a sign **for believers**
in the sense that it produces believers; the **unbeliever or outsider**
who would be put off by an outburst of tongues will be impressed
if, on entering a church meeting, he hears **all** the members speaking
words in a language he knows, which pierce direct to his heart and
conscience, expose his inmost secrets, and convict him of sin. This,
he will say, is God's message for me; **and so, falling on his face,
he will worship God and declare that God is really among
you**: a quotation from Isa. 45.14.

Edification and orderliness are paramount **14.26–33a**

26. The upshot of all this is that, when the church meets, it is perfectly proper for each member to contribute to the worship, provided that **all things be done for edification.**
a lesson: Gk *didachē* ('teaching'); cf. the listing of 'teachers' alongside prophets in 12.28f. The **revelation** here would naturally be the contribution of a prophet.

27–28. If edification is to be the aim, then there must be orderliness and balance. The rule for the exercise of glossolalia—**only two** speakers **or at most three, and each in turn**—would prevent it from getting out of hand, especially as the utterances have to be interpreted one by one. And since the church will not be edified by language it does not understand, those who are endowed with the gift of tongues must not exercise it in church **if there is no one to interpret**, but reserve it for private devotion, when each can **speak to himself and to God** (cf. verses 2, 4a).

29. Even prophecy must be orderly; it will be sufficient if **two or three prophets speak**, and while they speak, **the others** should **weigh what is said** (lit. 'discern' or 'distinguish' it (cf. 12.10), or, just possibly, 'discuss' it), so as to ascertain its direct relevance. Grammatically **the others** might mean 'the other prophets', but in 12.10 'the ability to distinguish between spirits' is given to others than prophets, so **the others** here are more probably the hearers in general.

30–31. A prophet must be prepared to give way to **another** who has **a revelation** to impart and to listen to it in silence. The natural sense of verse 31 is that the ability to **prophesy**, at least on occasion, is open to most, indeed to all, members of the Church, although only a few may exercise it at any one meeting, speaking **one by one, so that all may learn and all be encouraged.** In 11.4f. prophesying appears to be as common an exercise as praying, and that on the part of men and women alike, so real and pervasive was the sense of the Spirit's presence and power in meetings of the church.

32–33a. There is no thought here of prophesying under an uncontrollable impulse; the prophets' rational mind is expected to be in command, even in moments of inspiration, so that they can speak or refrain from speaking at will, whichever may be more expedient. The **spirits of prophets** are their 'spiritual gifts' or

manifestations of the Spirit', as in verse 12; the Spirit of wisdom
operates through men's higher faculties rather than their irra-
ional drives. Since **God is . . . a God . . . of peace** (cf. Rom.
5.33; 2 C. 13.11; Phil. 4.9), anything like **confusion** or disorder
s alien to his nature and will.

The rôle of women 14.33b–36

33b. As in all the churches of the saints: whether this
phrase belongs to what precedes or what follows is debatable. One
argument against its close association with what follows is the
stylistic inelegance of **in all the churches** and **in the churches**
coming so close together in one sentence, although the latter
phrase means 'in all meetings of the church of Corinth', whereas
the former means that the order prescribed for the church of
Corinth is that followed by other churches, especially in Paul's
mission field (cf. 11.16, where 'the churches of God' has the same
force as **the churches of the saints,** i.e. of the people of God, in
his passage).

34–35. After the recognition in 11.5ff. of women's 'authority' to
pray and prophesy, the imposition of silence on them here is
strange. We must, of course, beware of accommodating Paul's
views to ours, but here the difficulty lies in accommodating the
views expressed in these two verses to Paul's clear teaching earlier
in this letter. Some commentators have solved the problem by
observing that verses 34–35 come after verse 40 in the Western
text, and concluding therefore that they are in origin a marginal
gloss (based perhaps on 1 Tim. 2.11f.), which was later copied
into the text. G. Zuntz considers that this intrusion 'interrupts the
evident connexion between vv. 33a and 36' and regards the
Western position as 'an unsuccessful attempt at removing the
hitch' which 'witnesses to the early existence of the insertion'
The Text of the Epistles (1953), p. 17).

If we regard these two verses as integral to the text (or even as
a Pauline fragment out of context), the imposition of **silence** on
women may be explained by verse 35 as forbidding them to inter-
rupt proceedings by asking questions which could more properly
be put to **their husbands at home,** or by taking part with more
ardour than intelligence in the discussion of prophetic messages. (It is doubtful, however, whether such expressions as **they
are not permitted to speak** and **it is shameful for a woman**

to speak in church can be understood to mean no more tha this.)

as even the law says: on the reasonable assumption that **th law** is the Pentateuch (as in 9.8) rather than the whole Hebre Bible (as in verse 21), Gen. 3.16 has commonly been regarded a the authority for the statement that women **should be sub ordinate**. This is unlikely, since in MT and LXX Gen. 3.1 speaks of the woman's instinctive inclination or passionate desir (Hebrew *tᵉšûqāh*, Gk *apostrophē*) towards her husband, of which h takes advantage so as to dominate her. The reference is mor probably to the creation narratives of Gen. 1.26ff.; 2.21ff., o which Paul has based the argument of 11.3ff. (a different argumer from the present one).

36. The Corinthians must not be a law to themselves, as thoug it was from Corinth that **the word of God** first went forth, c only to Corinth that it came. Some regard must be had to churc practice elsewhere (cf. 11.16; 14.33b), including places which wer evangelized before Corinth. Besides, there may be an implicatio that, in fulfilment of the prophecy of Isa. 2.3//Mic. 4.2, it is fror Jerusalem (as in Rom. 15.19) that the word goes forth (cf. I Gerhardsson, *Memory and Manuscript* (1961), pp. 273 ff.).

Summing up **14.37-40**

37. If any one thinks that he is a prophet, or spiritual: a many a Corinthian Christian did (cf. 2.15; 3.1ff.; 12.1ff.). Ho should such a person prove the validity of his claim? 'Not b speaking with tongues,' says Paul, 'but by acknowledging **tha what I am writing to you is a command of the Lord**.' Her it is not a question of appealing to something laid down by Jesu in the course of his ministry (as in 7.10, 25), but of the dominic authority by which the apostle speaks. The noun **command** (G *entolē*), coming at the end of the sentence, appears in the plural i later texts, and is absent from the Western text, which here pr bably preserves the original reading: 'My ruling on this subject c spiritual gifts', says Paul, 'is not mine, but the Lord's; and the ma of the Spirit, the man with the gift of prophecy, will show h quality by recognizing this to be true.'

38. Any one who does not **recognize** that the apostle's injunc tions are vested with the authority of the exalted Lord **is no recognized**: i.e., as a 'spiritual' man. The variant 'let him n recognize it' (Gk *agnoeitō* for *agnoeitai*), i.e. 'let him remain in his ignorance', is attested as early as P^{46}, which suggests that the severity of the 'harder' reading was toned down by some second-century scribe or editor.

39. Prophecy, then, is heartily encouraged; speaking with **tongues** is permitted. The latter is indeed one of the manifestations of the Spirit, but the least important and helpful of them all. Paul's concern is to divert the Corinthians' zeal into more profitable channels.

Prophets were active in many of the churches until well into the second century. The *Didache* gives them an honoured place; Ignatius was subject to prophetic ecstasy; the *Shepherd* of Hermas, itself the composition of a Christian prophet, indicates that prophets were known in the Roman church, and Justin Martyr, towards the middle of the century, can claim that 'prophetic gifts remain with us even today' (*Dialogue* lxxxii. 1). But prophecy in this sense was dying out about mid-century, when its vigorous and unconventional resurgence among the Montanists produced a strong catholic reaction against 'enthusiasm' in general.

40. Much of the teaching in this chapter is relevant only to such exceptional circumstances as prevailed in the church of Corinth. But two principles are emphasized throughout which have permanent and universal validity for Church life: all things should help to build up the Church (verse 26) and **all things should be done decently** (Gk *euschēmonōs*, 'in a seemly manner') **and in order** (cf. verse 33).

THE QUESTION OF RESURRECTION **15.1-58**

The Apostolic Gospel **15.1-11**

It is not clear that the subject of resurrection was included among the questions in the Corinthians' letter to Paul: Paul does not introduce it with 'Now concerning . . .'. But, learning that some members of the Corinthian church were denying the doctrine of resurrection as he had taught it to them, he deals with the subject in some detail, first reminding them of the gospel which they had heard and believed at the beginning of their Christian career, in order to impress upon them that resurrection is integral to the way of salvation.

15.1. in which you stand: i.e. by which you have your standing in Christ (cf. Rom. 5.2; 11.20).

2. if you hold it fast: lit. 'if you hold fast (in mind) in what language I told you the good news'.

unless you believed in vain: not that Paul really entertains this as a serious possibility, but if their denial of resurrection were carried to its logical conclusion, the denial of the gospel itself, then indeed it would be shown that their belief was fruitless, perhaps because it was exercised superficially and 'at random' (Gk *eikē*).

3. For I delivered to you as of first importance what I also received: Paul uses the same two Greek verbs appropriate to the transmitting of tradition (*paradidōmi* and *paralambanō*) as in 11.23; this implies that the outline of the Christian message which follows was imparted to him by others. How then can such a statement be reconciled with Gal. 1.11f., where he solemnly affirms of the gospel which he preached: 'I did not receive it (*paralambanō*, as here) from man, nor was I taught it, but it came through a revelation of Jesus Christ'? He must have distinguished in his own mind the sense in which the gospel came to him by direct revelation from that in which it came to him by tradition. The contradiction is apparent, not real: both senses were equally true to his experience, but the apologetic or polemic requirements of the moment might lead him at times to emphasize the one to the seeming exclusion of the other. His explanation might be that the essence of the gospel, 'Jesus is the risen Lord', was communicated to him from heaven on the Damascus road: it was no human testimony that moved him to accept it. His own account agrees with Luke's, that as soon as he received this revelation he began to declare it publicly (Gal. 1.15–17; cf. Ac. 9.20–22). But the historical details of the teaching of Jesus, the events of Holy Week, the resurrection appearances and so forth were related to him by those who had first-hand experience of them. The things **of first importance** are four in number: (*a*) **Christ died,** (*b*) **he was buried,** (*c*) **he was raised,** (*d*) **he appeared** in resurrection to many. Whatever differences there might be in primitive Christian faith and preaching, there was evidently unanimity on these fundamental data.

Christ died for our sins in accordance with the scriptures: to the event itself three points of interpretation are added: (*a*) the person who **died** was the **Christ;** (*b*) he **died for** his people's sins; (*c*) his death took place **in accordance with the** Old Testament **scriptures**. For a pagan (like Tacitus) to say **Christ died** would involve no expression of opinion about the person in question; for one of Paul's Jewish upbringing to say so involved the acknowledgement that the person in question was the Messiah of Israel. That he **died for our sins** (cf. 2 C. 5.21; Rom. 3.24–26; 4.25; Gal. 1.4) probably implies that Jesus was further identified with the suffering Servant of Isa. 53.12 who 'bore the sin of many'; this would account also for the phrase **in accordance with the scriptures**. The identification of Jesus with the Servant of the Lord is made repeatedly in the earlier speeches of Acts (cf. Ac. 3.13ff.; 8.32ff.), although they do not explicitly emphasize the Servant's bearing of sin. The insistence that the death of Jesus was something 'written' concerning him pervades the gospel tradition (cf. Mk 9.12; 14.21, 49; Mt. 26.54, 56; Lk. 18.31; 22.37; 24.44, 46; Jn 19.28).

4. that he was buried: this is not said to be 'in accordance with the scriptures', but if it is implied that it is, then Isa. 53.9a comes to mind. Separate mention is made of his burial because (*a*) burial emphasizes the finality of death (cf. Ac. 2.29 concerning David: 'he both died and was buried, and his tomb is with us to this day'); (*b*) burial in the present instance emphasizes the reality of the resurrection which followed, as a divine act which reversed the act of men (cf. Ac. 13.29f.). The clause bespeaks belief in the empty tomb.

and that he was raised on the third day: unlike the aorists in the two previous clauses, this is a perfect tense (*RV* 'hath been raised'), perhaps indicating that, having been **raised** from death by God, he is alive for evermore. The apostles' proclamation was from the beginning, above all else, their witness to the fact that Christ was risen: that his resurrection took place **on the third day**, by inclusive reckoning (i.e. on the Sunday morning following Good Friday), was a matter of history (not in the sense that anyone saw him rise, but that was the day on which they first saw him risen). Expressions like 'after three days' have their life-setting in the period preceding the resurrection (cf. Mk 8.31; 9.31; 10.33; Mt. 27.62); in the post-resurrection period **the third day** is constant.

in accordance with the scriptures: if these words refer simply to the statement **that he was raised**, as they well may, a number

of *testimonia* come into consideration, e.g., Ps. 16.10 (cf. Ac. 2.25-32; 13.35–37); Isa. 53.10b, 11; if they refer to his being **raised o**
the third day, the range of likely *OT* passages is more restricted
Hos. 6.2 (quoted in rabbinical tradition as a prophecy of the fina
resurrection) is frequently adduced; the use of Jon. 1.17 is attestec
in Mt. 12.40; but in the light of verses 20, 23 below Paul is mor
likely to have thought of Lev. 23.10ff., where the presentation o
the firstfruits of the new harvest is prescribed for 'the morrow
after the sabbath', i.e. for the Sunday following Passover.

5. and that he appeared to Cephas: independent evidenc
for an early and personal appearance of the risen Lord to Peter i
provided by Lk. 24.34 (cf. Mk 16.7, 'and Peter'). The choice of th
term **appeared** there and in the present context (Gk *ōphthē*, usec
as the passive of *horaō*, 'see') marks the experience out as one i
which Christ takes the initiative. Peter and the others saw him ir
resurrection because he manifested himself to them or, in the sens
of the Hebrew 'tolerative Niph'al', he 'let himself be seen' by
them. As in the speeches of Acts, so here the eyewitness evidenc
for the resurrection is stressed: such evidence was as important i
the immediate context of the apostolic preaching as it was i
Roman law. The testimony of the women, of which much is mad
in the resurrection narratives of the Gospels, is not mentionec
here, probably because it was not formally admissible as publi
evidence and if so used would in the minds of many have dis
credited the resurrection (cf. Origen, *Celsus* ii. 55). Peter's primacy
as a witness to the risen Lord had no doubt much to do with hi
status in the primitive church.

then to the twelve: not necessarily to be taken with numerica
strictness (cf. such occasions as Mt. 28.16f.; Lk. 24.33ff.). Matthia
was indeed a witness to the resurrection (Ac. 1.22) but clearly no
in circumstances which would in themselves have aligned hin
distinctively with the eleven.

The clauses in verses 3b–5 ('that Christ died . . . then to th
twelve'), each introduced by 'that' (*hoti recitantis*), are probably a
quotation from a pre-Pauline summary of Christian belief (cf. E
Schweizer, 'Two *NT* Creeds Compared', *Current Issues in NT
Interpretation*, ed. W. Klassen and G. F. Snyder (1962), pp. 166ff.)
confirmation of its origin in the Aramaic-speaking church ha
been found in indications of a Semitic substratum (cf. J. Jeremias
The Eucharistic Words of Jesus, E.T. (1955), pp. 129ff.; B. Klappert

'Zur Frage des Urtextes von 1 Kor. xv. 3–5', *NTS* 13 (1966–7),
pp. 168ff.). If it be asked where and when Paul is most likely to
have 'received' it, he himself supplies the answer: at Jerusalem,
when he 'went up' there 'to visit Cephas' (better, 'to inquire of
Cephas' or 'to gain information from Cephas') three years after his
conversion (Gal. 1.18).

**6. Then he appeared to more than five hundred brethren
at one time:** Paul adds further information about resurrection
appearances, culled from various sources, to what he had ascer-
tained during those fifteen days in Jerusalem. The occasion mentioned here is not referred to in any other *NT* document: there is
no good reason for regarding it as a variant account of the
Pentecostal event of Ac. 2.1–41. Since not more than a quarter of
a century had elapsed, it is not surprising that **most of** them were
still alive to bear witness to what they had seen, **though some**
had **fallen asleep** (for this expression see note on 11.30).

7. Then he appeared to James: i.e. the brother of Jesus. An
elaboration of this incident is given in the *Gospel according to the
Hebrews* (quoted by Jerome, *On illustrious men*, 2; cf. *NT Apocrypha*,
ed. E. Hennecke, W. Schneemelcher, R. McL. Wilson, i (1963),
p. 165). This experience accounts for the fact that James who, with
the other members of Jesus' family, was not one of his followers
before his crucifixion (cf. Mk 3.21, 31ff.; Jn 7.5), quickly emerges
as leader in the Jerusalem church. If Paul's information about the
appearance to Cephas was acquired from that apostle, his information about the appearance to James may equally well have been
acquired direct during the same Jerusalem visit when, as he says, 'I
saw none of the other apostles except James the Lord's brother'
(Gal. 1.19).

then to all the apostles: evidently a larger company than 'the
twelve' of verse 5; as 'the twelve' included Peter, so **all the apostles**
include James, who did not belong to 'the twelve'. A. Harnack
(*Sitzungsberichte der preussischen Akademie der Wissenschaften* (1922),
pp. 62ff.) and B. W. Bacon (*The Apostolic Message* (1925), pp.
132ff.) regarded the appearances of verses 5–7 as falling into two
series, each introduced by the name of the individual with whose
authority it is associated; this may be accepted, apart from the
incident of verse 6 which, in part at least, is related in Paul's own
terms. It is going too far to distinguish with Bacon a Galilaean
tradition exalting Peter's claims to primacy and a Jerusalem one

maintaining James's claims in opposition to Peter's; Paul probably received both 'traditions' in Jerusalem very early in his
Christian life.

8. Last of all: in Paul's reckoning, his Damascus road experience was of the same order as the appearances he has just listed.
This is his personal addition to the testimony which he had 'received': as the apostleship of Peter, James and their colleagues was
validated by the fact that they saw the risen Lord, his own apostleship was validated on identical grounds (cf. 9.1), even if the earlier
appearances belonged to the 'third day' and the period immediately following, while the appearance granted to him took place
after the lapse of a considerable interval. All those to whom the
risen Christ appeared were believers; even if, like James and Paul,
they were not believers up to that moment, their encounter with
Christ immediately brought faith to life within them; it was thus
in no merely detached sense that thenceforth they were 'witnesses'
to his resurrection. To Paul's knowledge, no such appearance had
been granted to anyone else after his own experience; hence he was
last of all among those entitled to be called apostles.

as to one untimely born: lit. 'as if to the abortion' (Gk *hōsperei
tō ektrōmati*). Whatever the point of this disparaging comparison may
be, it cannot be based on the prematurity of an abortion: Paul has
just emphasized that his commission was belated, not premature.
The best explanation is that some of his detractors called him an
'abortion' of an apostle, implying that he was as much an ugly
parody of a true apostle as an abortion is of a healthy infant born
at the proper time. Yet Paul does not altogether repudiate the
insulting designation; when he remembers his past record, he
recognizes that it is not entirely undeserved. (Cf. A. Fridrichsen,
'Paulus abortivus', in *Symbolae philologicae O. A. Danielsson dicatae*
(1932), pp. 79ff.; G. Björck, 'Nochmals Paulus abortivus',
Coniectanea Neotestamentica 3 (1938), pp. 3ff.; J. Munck, 'Paulus
tanquam abortivus', in *NT Essays . . . in Memory of T. W. Manson*,
ed. A. J. B. Higgins (1959), pp. 180ff.)

he appeared also to me: if Paul uses the same language of his
own experience as of the experience of Peter and the others, it is
to suggest not that their experience was as 'visionary' as his but
that his was as objective as theirs. (Cf. S. H. Hooke, *The Resurrection of Christ as History and Experience* (1967), pp. 54ff.)

9. For I am the least of the apostles: the conjunction for may indicate that the following words explain Paul's partial acceptance of the disparaging term 'abortion'. When he thinks of his career as a persecutor of **the church of God** in Jerusalem and Judaea (cf. Gal. 1.13, 22f.; Phil. 3.6a), he acknowledges that he is **unfit to be called an apostle** at all; to be **the least of the apostles** is too high an honour for him, and it is a signal token of divine grace that he should be entitled to be so described.

10. Nevertheless, latecomer as he was to the apostolate, he strove to make up for lost time, and the sum-total of his achievements thus far surpassed the record of those who had been called earlier. The extent of these achievements is impressive enough, even if we go no farther back than the six or seven years immediately preceding the writing of this letter: he had evangelized the provinces of Galatia, Macedonia and Achaia, and was now actively engaged in evangelizing proconsular Asia, and two or three years later he would be able to treat his task in the Aegean lands as finished (Rom. 15.19, 23). Yet all the credit is ascribed to **the grace of God** which called him from his persecuting course to be the Gentiles' apostle (cf. Gal. 1.15f.) and made him what he was; his apostolic record was proof enough that he had not received that grace **in vain** (cf. 2 C. 6.1). It was not superfluous to point this out to a community which was inclined at times to compare him with others to his disadvantage.

11. To revert to the main point which he is concerned to make, Paul insists that the basic outline of saving events which he has reproduced is common ground to himself, Peter, James and the other apostles. This was important for the Corinthian Christians because it showed that the resurrection was not a doctrine proclaimed by Paul alone; it is important for readers of later date because it shows that Paul and the others mentioned were in agreement on the basic facts of the gospel, however much they might differ on the interpretation and practical corollaries of the facts. He does not suggest that the gospel to the Jews entrusted to Peter differed in content from the gospel to the Gentiles entrusted to himself (Gal. 2.7f.), nor does he imply that Peter and his associates were guilty of preaching the 'different gospel' of which he disapproves (cf. 2 C. 11.4; Gal. 1.6–9).

No resurrection, no salvation **15.12–19**

12. In the gospel, then, no matter who the preacher is, **Christ is preached as raised from the dead.** But if, as some members of the Corinthian church hold, **there is no resurrection of the dead,** then Christ was not raised, as the gospel says he was. It is not quite clear what form their denial of resurrection took. Conceivably they thought that the respectable Greek belief in the immortality of the soul (see on 1.13) was perfectly adequate, and that the idea of the resurrection of the body was an embarrassing Jewish handicap to the progress of the gospel in the Gentile world: it stood to reason that (in the words which Aeschylus puts into the mouth of Apollo) 'when the earth has drunk up a man's blood, once he is dead, there is no resurrection' (*Eumenides* 647f.). Some kind of assumption into glory at death or at the parousia might be envisaged, but certainly not the reanimation of corpses. Perhaps they maintained a more sophisticated view, like Hymenaeus and Philetus at a later date, who held 'that the resurrection is past already' (2 Tim. 2.17): since Paul himself taught that believers in Christ had been raised from death with him, why should they think of any further resurrection? This point of view would be in line with the gnosticizing 'over-realized eschatology' implied in 4.8.

13–14. Paul refuses to admit the logic of such an argument, or of such a corollary from his own teaching: the resurrection of Christ is not an isolated phenomenon but integral to God's work of raising the dead; so much so that **if there is no resurrection of the dead** in general, then Christ cannot have **been raised,** and in that case the apostles' **preaching** is an empty sham, as is also the **faith** of those who have believed it. The word **faith** here is probably subjective, referring to their belief in the preaching; it might possibly be regarded as objective, referring to what they believed, but this has been taken care of in the previous clause.

15. The consideration that the preachers of resurrection would be guilty of **misrepresenting God** (lit. would be found 'false witnesses' against him) **if** in fact **the dead** were **not raised** might be thought to be a rhetorical emphasizing of the argument, were it not that in Paul's eyes such misrepresentation would be a most serious offence, aggravating what would otherwise be a sad mistake.

16–18. The argument of verses 12–14 is repeated in different terms: **if Christ has not been raised**, if he is still dead (which Paul would regard as the only alternative to his resurrection), then the **faith** reposed in him **is futile** and, far from procuring salvation, leaves the believers **still in** their **sins**, without any hope of forgiveness or eternal life; those who had died in this ill-founded faith (for **fallen asleep** see 11.30; 15.6) were dead indeed; they had **perished** irretrievably, being eternally cut off from God (for Paul's use of the verb 'perish' see 1.18).

19. If hope **in Christ** is limited to **this life, we are of all men most to be pitied:** not that the gospel brings no benefits for the present life (cf. 1 Tim. 4.8), but Christian hope rests in a risen and living Christ, and if he is neither risen nor living, then 'hopes were dupes' indeed. Paul himself had 'suffered the loss of all things' for the sake of the Christ who had appeared to him (Phil. 3.8); what a fool he had been if Christ after all had never left the tomb! His regulating his life and work by the prospect of the Lord's assessment at the parousia (4.4f.), his striving to win an imperishable wreath (9.25), would be but a hollow mockery. Not that he entertains such a possibility for a moment: he aims to show how preposterous the denial of resurrection is.

Firstfruits and Harvest **15.20–28**

20. But in fact (Gk *nyni de*, lit. 'but now', as in 13.13) **Christ has been raised:** there is no need to contemplate further what would be involved in his not being raised; since the evidence for his resurrection is incontrovertible, it is more profitable to contemplate what is involved in that. Since he was raised, his people will be raised: as surely as **the first fruits** guarantee the coming harvest, so surely does his resurrection guarantee theirs. This analogy may have come the more readily to Paul's mind if he was writing between Passover (5.7f.) and Pentecost (16.8): the presentation of the first fruits soon after Passover inaugurated the seven weeks which terminated at Pentecost (Lev. 23.15ff.; cf. verse 4 above).

21–22. Paul now draws an analogy between two uniquely representative men: **Adam**, head of the old creation, in whom **all die**, and **Christ**, head of the new creation, 'the first-born from the dead' (Col. 1.18; cf. Rev. 1.5), in whom **all** are to **be made alive** in resurrection.

To Paul, Adam was no doubt a historical individual, the first man from whom all other men are descended. But he was more: he was what his Hebrew name signifies—'mankind'. The whole of mankind is viewed as originally existing in Adam. Because of his disobedience, however, Adam is mankind in alienation from God, under sentence of death. The details of the fall narrative (Gen. 3) are viewed by Paul as re-enacted in the life of the human race (Rom. 1.18ff.) and of the human individual (Rom. 7.7ff.). Because of his familiarity with the Hebrew concept of corporate personality his thought could oscillate freely, on the one hand, between Adam and alienated mankind and, on the other hand, between Christ and mankind reconciled to God in him. He envisages two kinds of solidarity—the old solidarity of death **in Adam** and the new solidarity of life **in Christ** by which the old solidarity is now being broken up and replaced (cf. Rom. 5.12–19).

as by a man came death: cf. Gen. 2.17; 3.22–24; Rom. 5.12. **by a man has come also the resurrection of the dead:** cf. Rom. 5.18. That the power of death should be broken by a man is set forth as both proper and necessary in Heb. 2.14f. The resurrection of the wicked (cf. Ac. 24.15) is not expressly dealt with here; only the resurrection of the just is, strictly speaking, a resurrection to life (Dan. 12.2; Jn 5.29). Paul might have agreed that even the resurrection of the wicked depends in some sense on the resurrection of Christ, but his present concern is to show that the resurrection of 'the dead in Christ' (cf. 1 Th. 4.16), i.e. those who have 'fallen asleep', is ensured by Christ's resurrection.

23. But each in his own order (Gk *tagma*, 'rank', a military term): first comes the resurrection of **Christ the first fruits, then** (Gk *epeita*, next in order) **at his coming** (Gk *parousia*) that of **those who belong to Christ.** It is unwarranted to infer from this that Paul allows no further development of salvation-history between Easter and the parousia; it is because he is concerned with resurrection here that he says nothing of what may take place between these two points (see Rom. 11.11–27 for the completion of the Gentile mission and consequent salvation of all Israel in this interval).

24–26. Then (Gk *eita*, next after that) **comes the end:** i.e. the end of this age or world-order, to be followed by the resurrection age (the age to come). Since there is no verb in this clause in the Greek text, some commentators have argued that **the end** (Gk *to telos*) should be taken in the sense 'the rest (of the dead)', who would thus constitute the third *tagma* ('rank'), as in Rev. 20.5

(where, however, the word rendered 'rest' is not *telos*). This sense of *telos* is but rarely and doubtfully attested in Greek literature; and there is no reason for not understanding the word here in the eschatological sense it commonly has in *NT*. The temporal adverb *eita* implies an interval of indeterminate duration between the parousia and the **end,** when Christ hands his dominion back to God; the context suggests that the interval is short. Earlier in this letter Paul has indicated that in the final phase of Christ's kingship his people will share it with him (4.8) and judge the world (6.2). When this has been accomplished, the present age comes to an **end.** The kingship of Christ, the age of the Messiah, began with his exaltation to 'the right hand of God'; Paul envisages him as reigning from that position of supremacy, in terms of Ps. 110.1, **until** God **has put all his enemies under his feet.** The opening words of the oracle, 'Sit at my right hand', are one of the commonest messianic *testimonia* in the early church; but this is the only place in *NT* where the relevance of the following **until** clause is drawn out. The **enemies** are hostile principalities and powers, all the forces that endeavour to oppose and hinder the fulfilment of God's saving purpose in the world. The resurrection harvest marks the destruction of death, **the last enemy,** and not the least formidable of the principalities and powers (cf. Heb. 2.14f.; Rev. 20.14a). If elsewhere the principalities and powers (Col. 2.15; 1 Pet. 3.22), including death itself (2 Tim. 1.10), are viewed as already disarmed, subjugated and indeed 'abolished', that is because the death and resurrection of Christ constitute the decisive battle in the war that ends victoriously with the resurrection of his people (cf. O. Cullmann, *Christ and Time*, E.T. (1951), p. 141).

27. '**God has put all things in subjection under his feet**': a quotation from Ps. 8.6, which here, as in Heb. 2.5ff., is brought into close association with Ps. 110.1 (because of the common term **under his feet**). In Ps. 8.5–8, which reflects the creation narrative of Gen. 1.26–30, it is man that is vested with dominion over **all things,** but Paul, like the writer to the Hebrews, applies the psalmist's language to Christ as the last Adam, the 'son of man' who retrieved the situation which the first Adam lost. God's man as the fulfiller of God's purpose is a recurrent biblical theme: when one man fails in the fulfilment of that purpose, God raises up another man to take his place. But Adam's place could be taken only by one who was competent to undo the mortal effect of Adam's disobedience and become the founder and representative of a new humanity. To Christ, who has proved his competence in this respect, **all things are put in subjection**—except God himself, of course, **who put all things under him.**

28. When this subjection is completed and the last enemy destroyed, Christ has fully accomplished his mediatorial ministry. He has brought the whole estranged creation back into harmony with God; now he 'delivers the kingdom to God the Father' **that God may be everything to everyone**, or more literally, and more accurately, 'that God may be all in all' (cf. Rom. 11.36). The kingdom of Christ comes to an end in its present phase, but only to merge in the eternal kingdom of God, so there is no failure of the prophetic promise that Messiah's kingdom will know no end (Isa. 9.7; Lk. 1.33). His mediatorial kingship is the means for the consummation of the kingdom of God, which was inaugurated by his work on earth. The humble submissiveness to his Father's will which characterized him then will continue to characterize him to the consummation, when **the Son himself will also be subjected** (or 'will subject himself') **to him who put all things under him.** But since the Son is the image and revelation of the Father, 'Father and Son are really one in this activity' (O. Cullmann, *The Christology of the NT*, E.T. (1959), p. 293).

Practical Arguments 15.29–34

29. If there is no resurrection, **what do people mean by being** (lit. 'what will they do who are') **baptized on behalf of the dead?** The *prima facie* meaning of these words points to a practice of baptism by proxy. If some disciples in Corinth (conceivably in an epidemic) died before they could get themselves baptized (cf. 6.11), did some of their friends undergo baptism vicariously in their name? We could not easily envisage Paul referring without disapproval to a practice of vicarious baptism on behalf of *unbelieving* friends (which is not attested until much later, and only among the Marcionites and some other gnostic groups), but such an action on behalf of believing but unbaptized friends might be mentioned by him in passing in an *ad hominem* argument with neither praise nor blame. The reference has been explained by analogy with the practice of praying for the dead, commended in 2 Mac. 12.39-45 (cf. E. Stauffer, *NT Theology*, E.T. (1965), p. 299); but the analogy is too distant to be convincing. Still less convincing is A. Schweitzer's view that the dead on whose behalf others underwent baptism were expected in consequence to rise at the parousia instead of waiting till the end of Christ's messianic reign (*The Mysticism of Paul the Apostle*, E.T. (1931), pp. 283ff.). The only serious alternative interpretation to one which involves some form of proxy baptism is that propounded by M. Raeder ('Vikariastaufe in 1 Cor.15, 29?' *ZNW* 46 (1955), pp. 258ff.), which contemplates some people accepting baptism in order to be reunited with their departed Christian friends in the life to come. It is just possible to understand **on behalf of the dead** in this way, which is free from the theological difficulties attaching to proxy baptism. Whether **the dead** are those on whose behalf others are vicariously baptized, or departed Christians with whom their friends desire to be reunited, the baptism is pointless, says Paul, **if the dead are not raised at all**: in the former contingency, vicarious baptism can do the dead no good; in the latter, there is no hope of reunion in any case—for Paul does not think of immortality or survival after death apart from resurrection.

30-31. For another practical argument, Paul appeals to his own experience: why should he endure so many hardships and dangers in his apostolic service if there is no resurrection? **by my pride in you which I have in Christ Jesus our Lord:** this is a better rendering of an ambiguous expression than 'by the praise (renown) which I have among you' (i.e. because you are the fruit of my ministry). His language takes the form of an oath, introduced by the Greek particle *nē*. Paul might criticize and scold his converts when addressing them directly, but when speaking about them to others, he boasted of them (cf. 2 C. 1.14; 7.4, 14; 8.24; 9.2f.; 1 Th. 2.19f.); here he makes this boasting the basis of a solemn asseveration that he looks death in the face every day (cf. 4.9; 2 C. 4.10-12; 11.23; Rom. 8.35f.). If his readiness to do so does not prove the objective validity of the resurrection hope, it certainly bears witness to his firm grasp of that hope.

32. One outstanding instance of his facing death is mentioned— the occasion when he **fought with wild beasts at Ephesus**. This is figurative language, as the phrase **humanly speaking** (Gk *kata anthrōpon*) shows (Roman citizens, moreover, were exempt by law from such treatment), but it refers to some mortal peril of which the Corinthians presumably had heard. Whether it had to do with the Demetrius riot (Ac. 19.23ff.) or some other threat to his life, probably at the hands of an infuriated mob, we have no means of knowing. A century later the Asian presbyter who composed the fictitious *Acts of Paul* took the reference literally, and told a remarkable story of the apostle's encounter with a lion in the Ephesian theatre (see *NT Apocrypha* ii, ed. E. Hennecke, W. Schneemelcher, and R. McL. Wilson, E.T. (1965), pp. 370-3).

Even such a feat as this (figurative or literal) would bring no advantage **if the dead are not raised.** Paul speaks in the spirit of the martyrs under Antiochus Epiphanes, who witnessed a good confession and readily endured outrageous torture because of the resurrection hope (2 Mac. 7.9ff.; cf. Heb. 11.35b). But if there is no ground for such hope, **'Let us eat and drink, for tomorrow we die':** the quotation is taken *verbatim* from Isa. 22.13, but the thought is that of Ec. 2.24a where, in the absence of any hope of life beyond the grave, the Preacher affirms that 'there is nothing better for a man than that he should eat and drink, and find enjoyment in his toil' (cf. Ec. 9.7-10).

33. The quotation **'Bad company ruins good morals'** is an iambic trimeter from Menander's comedy *Thais*; it had probably become a proverbial saying, and Paul need no more have been consciously quoting Menander than people today who quote Shakespearean or biblical tags (including the *AV* rendering of this quotation) are always aware of their source. The Corinthian Christians who rejected the doctrine of resurrection may have been those who took a libertine line in morals (cf. 6.12ff.); hence the relevance of the quotation.

34. Come to your right mind (lit. 'sober up properly'), **and sin no more:** the first imperative is in the aorist, the second in the present ('don't go on sinning'). The admonition amplifies the force of the Menander quotation. That Paul has the gnosticizing party in view is further indicated by his following words, **some have no knowledge of God:** lit. 'some have ignorance (*agnōsia*) of God'—not knowledge (*gnōsis*), as these people claimed they had. **I say this to your shame:** for those who boasted of their knowledge, the charge of ignorance would be felt as a disgrace: Paul's aim is not to humiliate them (so he names no names) but to bring them to a better frame of mind.

The Nature of the Resurrection **15.35-49**

35-36. But someone will ask: a supposed objection, introduced in accordance with the current rhetorical style of the
diatribe. The questions **'How are the dead raised? With what
kind of body do they come?'** are envisaged not as genuine
requests for information but as arguments against the doctrine of
resurrection: hence the sharp retort, **'You foolish man!'** (Gk
aphrōn)—another rhetorical feature. All kinds of things might
happen to the material of which dead bodies were made; if
resurrection meant (as many imagined) the reanimation of precisely the same materials as were buried or otherwise disposed of,
this was so manifestly impossible as to rule the whole doctrine out
of court. Paul dismisses such an idea of resurrection as foolish;
personal identity does not require such material reconstitution.
He uses the analogy of the seed that is sown and the ears of grain
that spring up from it.
What you sow does not come to life unless it dies: cf.
Jn 12.24. But Paul is not necessarily quoting Jesus; the analogy
was common form in discussing resurrection, as rabbinical usage
indicates.

37-38. The **kernel** that is sown is different from the plant that
springs up, for all the continuity of life; whatever variety of **seed**
be sown, God provides it with its appropriate **body,** in which the
full-grown plant is 'clothed'. All that is necessary for the analogy
is the combination of identity with difference; that the seed does
not 'die' as the mortal body does is neither here nor there.

39-41. There are many different kinds of **flesh,** and that of
men is different from that of **animals** (i.e. quadrupeds), **birds**
and **fish,** above all in that God plans to replace it by something
imperishable. In addition to these **terrestrial bodies** there are
celestial bodies, each vested with its appropriate **glory** or
degree of brightness—**the sun** has one, **the moon** has another,
and **star differs from star in glory.** All this is designed to
emphasize the infinite variety that reigns in the world which God
created: why then should it be supposed that there can be only
one kind of human body, the one with which we are familiar in
this life?

42-43. In fact, the resurrection body is as different from this
mortal body as the plant that grows is different from the seed that

is sown. **What is sown is perishable**, marked by **dishonour** (Gk *atimia*, not here positive disgrace, but absence of glory) and **weakness**; **what is raised is imperishable**, marked by **glory** (cf. Rom. 6.4; 8.17) and **power**—the power of God, which has already raised Jesus from the dead (cf. 6.14; Eph. 1.19f.; Phil. 3.21). The 'sowing' need not be restricted to the act of burial; this mortal life may itself be the sowing that is followed by the harvest of resurrection life, but Paul does not draw out all the details of his metaphor.

44–45. It is sown a physical body: Gk *sōma psychikon*, a 'soulish' body (cf. 2.14), a statement which Paul bases on Gen. 2.7, where the first man is said to have become **a living being** or 'a living soul' (Hebrew *lᵉnepeš ḥayyāh*; Gk *eis psychēn zōsan*). It is difficult for any English version to indicate the close relation between the adjective translated **physical** and the substantive translated **being**. But such is the variety in the universe that **if there is a physical body, there is also a spiritual body**, one that partakes of the nature of Christ, **the last Adam**, who in resurrection **became a life-giving spirit** (this is no quotation, but Paul's own antithesis to Gen. 2.7). Plainly Paul envisages a radical change from the body of Jesus which was laid in the tomb to the form in which he rose—'his glorious body', as it is called in Phil. 3.21, into the likeness of which 'our lowly body' is to be changed. While he speaks of **a life-giving spirit** here, he does not exclude by that phrase the fact that Jesus has a resurrection body: the form in which Jesus rose from the dead was one in which he could be seen (9.1). But his present existence is in the spiritual realm (1 Tim. 3.16; 1 Pet. 3.18); his resurrection body, like that which his people are to receive, is 'a totality taken up into the life of the Spirit himself, . . . so controlled and possessed by the Spirit that it shares his life-giving powers' (M. E. Dahl, *The Resurrection of the Body* (1962), pp. 81f.). Cf. also 2 C. 3.17a. The life-giving potency of the Spirit (cf. Jn 6.63) is viewed by Paul in a later letter as operating already in the believer's life: 'If the Spirit of him who raised Jesus from the dead dwells in you, he who raised Christ Jesus from the dead will give life to your mortal bodies also through his Spirit which dwells in you' (Rom. 8.11). The present body is animated by 'soul' and is therefore mortal; the resurrection body is animated entirely by immortal and **life-giving spirit**, and is therefore called **a spiritual body**.

46. The point of Paul's emphasis that **the physical** precedes **the spiritual** is probably that Philo had said the opposite. In Philo's Platonizing interpretation the man created in God's image in Gen. 1.26ff. is the ideal, incorruptible, heavenly man, of whom the man of earth in Gen. 2.7 is a material copy (*Opif. mundi* 134; *Leg. alleg.* i. 31). Paul reverses this order; he is here thinking of Christ not as the Eternal Wisdom 'through whom are all things' (8.6) and who as such is necessarily antecedent to Adam, but as the one who in resurrection is 'the second man', the head of the new creation as the earthly Adam was of the old.

47–49. The first man was from the earth, a man of dust (as is said expressly in Gen. 2.7); **the second man** (the risen Lord) **is from heaven:** this does not refer to his heavenly pre-existence (as in Jn 3.13, etc.) but to his resurrection life; cf. the description of the resurrection body in 2 C. 5.1f. as a 'heavenly dwelling'. The thought may be influenced by the apocalyptic portrayal of a human figure ('one like a son of man') coming 'with the clouds of heaven' (Dan. 7.13; cf. Mk 13.26; 14.62; Rev. 1.12ff.; 1 Enoch 46.1ff.; 2 Esd. 13.1ff.). At present, in mortal body, men—even men 'in Christ'—bear **the image of the man of dust** (and so 'in Adam all die'); at the resurrection they will **bear the image of the man of heaven**—which indeed is already being reproduced in them inwardly by the Spirit (cf. 2 C. 3.18). There is a variant 'let us bear' (Gk *phoresōmen*, aorist subjunctive), attested by *P*[46] Aleph and the Western text, in place of **we shall . . . bear** (Gk *phoresomen*, future indicative), but the context requires a statement of what is to take place, not an exhortation. The Creator's purpose, that man should be made in his image (Gen. 1.26) is seen to be realized when the heirs of the new creation **bear the image of the man of heaven**, who is himself the image of God (2 C. 4.4); cf. Rom. 8.29, where those whom God foreknew are 'predestined to be conformed to the image of his Son'.

A *New Revelation* 15.50–57

50. I tell you this: or 'What I mean is this'. **Flesh and blood** means this mortal body, and may denote the living rather than the dead, to whom **the perishable** perhaps refers more particularly (so J. Jeremias, 'Flesh and Blood cannot inherit the Kingdom of God', *NTS* 2 (1955–6), pp. 151ff.). This body, made of 'dust' and animated by 'soul', **cannot inherit** an order which is spiritual and immortal. It is therefore as necessary for the living to be transformed at the parousia as it is for the dead to be raised in 'spiritual' bodies. Since a new subject—the transformation of the living—is introduced in this verse, it is more properly treated as introducing a new paragraph (as in *RV*) than as concluding the foregoing one (as in *RSV*).

51. If any one asks how this can be, Paul says that he has received the answer in the form of **a mystery**: some aspect of the divine purpose thus far concealed but now communicated by special revelation (see 2.7). In 1 Th. 4.13–17 the Thessalonian Christians were reassured 'by the word of the Lord' (presumably an utterance of Jesus) about the lot of those of their number who 'fell asleep' before the parousia: they would suffer no disadvantage, for at the parousia 'the dead in Christ' would rise first. Here the Corinthians have been told further that 'the dead in Christ' will rise with 'spiritual' bodies: now they are told by revelation what will happen to those still alive at the parousia.

We shall not all sleep, but we shall all be changed: although **not all** believers will die before the parousia, all of them, living as well as dead, will have to **be changed** to conform to the conditions of the resurrection age. The textual tradition shows great variety in the number and position of the negatives in this sentence: P^{46} reads 'We shall not all sleep, nor shall we all be changed' (which might imply that only the dead will be changed); Aleph AC 33 etc. read 'We shall all sleep, but we shall not all be changed' (all mankind will die, but only the dead in Christ will be changed); the Western text, represented by D* and several Old Latin authorities, reads 'We shall all rise, but we shall not all be changed' (only those who are acquitted in the post-resurrection judgment will receive spiritual bodies or, as Tertullian interprets this reading in *De resurrectione carnis* 42, only those still alive will need to be changed). The text of B and the bulk of later manuscripts, versions and citations (translated in *RSV*) best agrees with the context; the variations may be 'due to rival theories of the resurrection or to failure to understand Paul's language' (A. T. Robertson, *Introduction to the Textual Criticism of the NT* (1928), p. 159), or they may 'represent independent approaches to the same doctrine and adjustments to the changing Christian life' (K. W. Clark, 'Textual Criticism and Doctrine', in

Studia Paulina in honorem J. de Zwaan, ed. J. N. Sevenster and W. C. van Unnik (1950), p. 64).

52. in a moment, in the twinkling of an eye: moment is Gk *atomos*, an indivisible fragment of time; for *rhipē*, **twinkling** (lit. 'casting'), P^{46}, with 1739 and the Western codices D G, has *rhopē*, 'inclination'. The split-second speed of the transformation, and its coincidence with **the last trumpet** which heralds the parousia, exclude rival views such as that of 2 Bar. 50.1-51.10, where the bodies of the dead, raised without change of form in order to receive equitable judgment, are thereafter transformed in accordance with the verdict—those of the justified being vested with angelic glory, while those of the condemned waste away in torment.

The **last trumpet** plays a recurring part in apocalyptic: the 'great trumpet' which will be blown for the return of the exiles in Isa. 27.13 (cf. Mt. 24.31) is probably an eschatological counterpart of the 'loud trumpet' which announced the year of jubilee (Lev. 25.9); the Feast of Trumpets (the civil New Year's Day), which introduced the penitential season culminating in the Day of Atonement (Lev. 23.24; cf. Ezek. 45.20), also served as an important precedent (cf. Mishnah, *Rôš ha-Sānāh* 1.2, where 'all who come into the world' are judged by God on this New Year's Day). In 1 Th. 4.16f. 'the trumpet of God' is sounded at the Lord's descent from heaven, when the dead in Christ are raised and living believers are 'caught up together with them in the clouds to meet the Lord in the air'. The designation of this **trumpet** as the **last** one may simply refer to its ushering in the end of the present world-order; cf. also Rev. 11.15ff., where the last of the seven trumpets announces the consummation of the kingdom of God and 'the time for the dead to be judged', for the servants of God to be rewarded and for the earth's destroyers to be destroyed. So here, when **the trumpet** sounds, **the dead will be raised imperishable, and we** (the living) **shall be changed**: as in 1 Th. 4.15, 17, Paul includes himself among the survivors (but see 1 C. 6.14); a new perspective is evident in 2 C. 4.13-5.10.

53. It is doubtful if **perishable** and **imperishable** (Gk *phthartos, aphtharsia*) can be so sharply distinguished from **mortal** and **immortality** (Gk *thnētos, athanasia*) that the former refers exclusively to the dead and the latter exclusively to the living (so J. Jeremias; see note on verse 50); the correlated terms are too nearly synonymous to be kept strictly apart in this way. But at any rate Paul does mean that the dead will rise in bodies which are not liable to corruption, while the bodies of the living will exchange mortality for **immortality.**

54. This event will mark the fulfilment of two *OT* scriptures. **'Death is swallowed up in victory':** the words of Isa. 25.8, 'he will swallow up death for ever' (Hebrew *lā-neṣaḥ*), are reproduced here not in the deviant LXX version ('death has grown strong and swallowed up') but in a form similar to that of the versions of Aquila and Theodotion, where Hebrew *lā-neṣaḥ* is translated *eis nikos* (lit. 'to victory', a rendering adopted also by LXX in several other passages, though not here, through confusion of this Hebrew idiom with another sense of the root *nṣḥ*). For another use of the verb 'swallow up' (Gk *katapinō*) in a similar context see 2 C. 5.4.

55. **'O death, where is thy victory? O death, where is thy sting?':** this quotation from Hos. 13.14 has a common term with the former not only in the important word **death** but also (as reproduced here) in the word *nikos*, **victory**—a word which appears in no known Greek version of the passage (LXX has *dikē*, 'judgment'), but which is probably selected by Paul to provide an extra link with Isa. 25.8. In the original context of Hosea, Death and Sheol, personified, are invited to come and be the executors of Yahweh's judgment against Ephraim: 'O death, where are your plagues? O Sheol, where is your destruction?' Paul, for his part, treats the double question as a defiant challenge to death to do its worst. LXX renders 'destruction' (Hebrew *qeṭeb*) by *kentron*, **sting.** Aleph and the Byzantine authorities, with TR, follow the LXX rendering of Sheol as 'Hades' (cf. *AV*), but this is contrary to Paul's usage ('Hades' occurs nowhere in the Pauline corpus); he prefers to use **death** twice over. The 'last enemy' will be destroyed then (cf. verse 25), and so certain is his destruction that the believer in Christ can defy him in the prophet's words here and now.

56. Paul adds an interpretative gloss: **The sting of death is sin.** 'Death employed Sin to stab for itself an opening into human nature' (C. A. A. Scott, *Christianity according to St. Paul* (1927), p. 51). The reign of death rests on **the power of sin,** but when sin is overcome, death loses its terror (Rom. 5.12, 20) Christ, who 'died to sin, once for all' (Rom. 6.10), thereby set his people free from sin, and thus drew the sting of death. Death is

still an enemy, but a disabled one, since Christ triumphed over
it; when his people die, they are no longer the prisoners of death,
but sleep in the certainty of awaking in resurrection.

the power of sin is the law: because sin, as Paul describes the
human situation in Rom. 7.7ff., gains a foothold by means of the
law, and then fans out to occupy all the territory of Mansoul.

57. But over sin and death alike God **gives** his people **the
victory** (the note of the two quotations in verses 54f. is continued),
and this victory is their participation in Christ's victory, secured
to them by the Spirit: 'the law of the Spirit of life in Christ Jesus
has set me free from the law of sin and death' (Rom. 8.2).

Concluding Exhortation **15.58**

58. With the resurrection hope thus reconfirmed, let them
adhere steadfastly to the gospel as it was delivered to them, not
shifted from this foundation by any plausible argument in keeping
with the prevalent climate of opinion around them, and let them
confidently redouble their efforts to serve the Lord. If the resurrection hope were a phantom, these efforts would indeed be futile;
but since that hope was securely established, they knew **that in
the Lord** their **labour** was **not in vain** (cf. 9.26f.; 15.10; Gal.
2.2; Phil. 2.16 for Paul's concern that his own labour should not
be in vain).

THE QUESTION OF THE COLLECTION FOR JERUSALEM **16.1-4**

16.1. Now concerning the contribution for the saints: the
form of words in which this new subject is introduced suggests that
the Corinthians' letter included a question about it. Evidently
they had heard about it, and were eager to know how they could
share in it (cf. 2 C. 8.1of.; 9.2). The **saints** are the members of the
Jerusalem church (cf. 2 C. 8.4; 9.1, 12); they are the foundation-
members of the new people of God, and if Gentile Christians are
also 'saints' (cf. verse 15; 1.2) it is because they have been incorporated as 'fellow citizens with the (original) saints' (Eph.
2.19).

The **contribution** or 'collection' (Gk *logeia*) for Jerusalem
was an enterprise to which Paul attached high importance. During
the visit of Paul and Barnabas to Jerusalem at which they reached
the agreement with the leaders there about their respective spheres
of ministry (see on 1.12; 2 C. 10.13-16), those leaders urged them

to remember 'the poor' of the Jerusalem church (Gal. 2.10). Thi
perhaps amounted to a request that Paul and Barnabas shoulc
continue the ministry begun when they carried famine-relief fund
from the church in Syrian Antioch to Jerusalem (Ac. 11.30). Pau
described himself as 'eager' to do this very thing (Gal. 2.10) anc
during his Aegean ministry he organized a contribution to be
taken to Jerusalem from the Gentile churches of his own planting
This, as he saw it, was (a) an acknowledgment by the Gentil
churches of the spiritual debt they owed to the mother-church i
Jerusalem, (b) a practical token to the Jerusalem church of th
genuineness of the Gentile Christians' faith, (c) a means of bindin
Jewish and Gentile Christians more closely together (see hi
account of the matter in Rom. 15.25–28). It is possible that wha
was from his viewpoint a voluntary gift was in the eyes of th
Jerusalem leaders a tribute due, comparable to the annual hal
shekel which Jews throughout the world contributed to th
maintenance of the temple and its ministry (cf. K. Holl, Gesam
melte Aufsätze II (1928), pp. 44ff.; and for the whole subject
K. F. Nickle, *The Collection* (1966)).

This is the first reference to the collection in Paul's survivin
writings: the directions to **the churches of Galatia** may hav
been given orally or in writing, but not in the extant letter to th
Galatians. (The **churches of Galatia** here are probably thos
of Gal. 1.2; they were situated in the Roman province of Galati
though there is no agreement on the question whether they wei
in the ethnic region of Galatia in the north-central part of th
province or, as is more probable, in the cities of Pisidian Antioc
Iconium, Lystra and Derbe in the south of the province.)

2. The direction to the church of Corinth, as to the Galatia
churches, is that Sunday by Sunday each member should se
aside a proportion of his weekly income, so that when Pa
arrives the money will be ready. It is doubtful whether there
any liturgical significance in this mention of **the first day e
every week**, except that the week was plainly introduced to th
Gentile churches from the earliest days. Nor were the individu
sums to be taken to church and handed over to the communi
treasurer: each member is to **put something aside** *par' heaut
*'at home', **and store it up** there.

3. The money was to be taken to Jerusalem by approve
delegates of each contributing church. The Greek is more ar

biguous than *RSV*, and Paul himself may have intended to supply the delegates with letters of accreditation (cf. *NEB*: 'I will give letters of introduction to persons approved by you'). It is probably some of these delegates who are listed in Ac. 20.4.

4. If it seems advisable that I should go also: he does not say 'if the Lord wills', as in 4.19; he may mean that circumstances at Jerusalem and elsewhere will indicate whether it is **advisable** (Gk *axion*, 'fit') for him to accompany the delegates. By the beginning of A.D. 57 he had decided to go in person (Rom. 15.25ff.), and a few months later he carried out his decision (Ac. 20.16, 22; 21.17; 24.17).

CONCLUDING REMARKS 16.5-24

FURTHER PLANS, PERSONALIA AND EXHORTATIONS 16.5-14

5. I will visit you after passing through Macedonia: cf. Ac. 19.21. A change of plan is indicated in 2 C. 1.15f., involving a visit to Corinth before going to Macedonia as well as after; but that plan too was changed.

6-7. I will stay with you or even spend the winter: he did spend the winter before setting out for Jerusalem in Corinth (cf. Ac. 20.2f.; Rom. 16.1, 23); that, however, was probably not the next winter after writing 1 Corinthians, but the next after that. **wherever I go:** a further indication that his plans were rather flexible at this time.

just in passing: in view of his current plans, a visit to Corinth on his way to Macedonia would be but a brief one.

if the Lord permits: as in 4.19, this refers to something he fully intends to do, subject only to divine guidance or overruling (cf. Jas 4.15).

8. I will stay at Ephesus until Pentecost: Pentecost (the Feast of Weeks) was the festival of wheat-harvest, seven weeks after the presentation of the firstfruits (see on 15.4, 20; cf. Lev. 23.15ff.). Paul was therefore presumably writing in the spring (cf. 5.7; 15.20). We cannot conclude that the Christian Pentecost was celebrated in the churches at this early date; but for the regulation (or at least reckoning) of Paul's journeys by the Jewish sacred year cf. Ac. 18.21 (Western text); 20.6, 16; 27.9.

9. a wide door for effective work: lit. 'a great and effective door' (where **door** is a metaphor for 'opportunity'; cf. 2 C. 2.12; Col. 4.3).

many adversaries: cf. Ac. 19.23ff.; 20.19.

10–11. When Timothy comes: lit. 'if Timothy comes', but his coming is not in serious doubt. Cf. 4.17; and for Paul's commendation of him cf. Phil. 2.19ff.

put him at his ease . . . let no one despise him: this suggests that Timothy's personality was diffident rather than forceful, and that those who judged superficially would not be greatly impressed by him, especially as he was probably quite young (cf. 1 Tim. 4.12).

with the brethren: who they are is not clear; one of them was probably Erastus (Ac. 19.22).

12. Apollos: see on 1.12; 3.4–6; 4.6. It is evident from this reference that Paul's relations with Apollos were perfectly friendly.

with the other brethren: probably with Timothy and his travelling companions.

it was not at all his will: **his** has no equivalent in the Greek text, and the meaning is probably 'it was not at all God's will for him' (so *RSV* footnote; for this absolute use of *thelēma*, 'will', cf. 1 Mac. 3.60; Mt. 18.14; Rom. 2.18).

He will come when he has opportunity: whether Apollos ever did visit Corinth again we have no means of knowing.

13–14. stand firm in your faith: i.e. (probably) your trust in God.

be courageous: Gk *andrizesthe*, 'play the man'. The vigilance, steadfastness, courage and strength which are inculcated here are commonplaces in *NT* paraenesis (cf. Eph. 6.10ff.); as in 13.13, **love** is enjoined above all (cf. Col. 3.14).

RECOGNITION OF LEADERS 16.15–18

15–16. One of the roots of the trouble at Corinth was a tendency to anarchy, a failure to give due recognition to those who were qualified to be 'administrators' in the church (12.28). (A recurrence of similar trouble called forth the letter of Clement to the Corinthians a generation later.) To remedy this state of affairs Paul directs his readers' attention to **the household of Stephanas** (i.e. Stephanas and his household), his **first converts in** the province of **Achaia** (lit. 'the firstfruits of Achaia'; cf. 1.16, where

he says he baptized them himself); they had shown themselves
worthy of recognition as pastors and administrators because they
had **devoted themselves to the service of the saints** (here
plainly the Christians of Corinth). To such persons as these and
to others doing similar service in the church they ought **to be
subject.** Function, not status, was the important thing in the
church's ministry: those who did the work were to receive the
appropriate recognition and respect.

17–18. Perhaps it is this reference to 'the household of
Stephanas' that reminds Paul to say a word in appreciation of
Stephanas and his two companions who had recently come to
Ephesus from Corinth, probably carrying the letter to Paul from
the Corinthian church and bringing further news orally. **Fortunatus and Achaicus** evidently shared the ministry of **Stephanas**;
at Ephesus they **refreshed** Paul's **spirit** as they were accustomed
to refresh their fellow-Christians at home. Again Paul calls for
recognition to be given **to such men.**

FINAL GREETINGS AND BENEDICTION 16.19–24

19. The churches of Asia: those founded in Ephesus and
other Asian cities during Paul's present ministry there (cf. Ac.
19.10).

Aquila and Prisca are usually mentioned in the reverse order.
They were the couple who moved to Corinth when Claudius's
edict expelled Jews from Rome in A.D. 49 (Ac. 18.2); when Paul
came to Corinth they had recently arrived there and they were
henceforth among his closest friends. They were well known in
the Corinthian church, but when Paul left Corinth they left with
him and settled in Ephesus (Ac. 18.18ff.). It was probably at
Ephesus that they risked their lives for Paul (Rom. 16.4). Their
house evidently served as a meeting-place for part of the Ephesian
church (cf. Rom. 16.5). See pp. 19, 32.

20. All the brethren: in particular, Paul's fellow-missionaries
who were with him at the time.

a holy kiss: cf. 2 C. 13.12; Rom. 16.16; 1 Th. 5.26. Perhaps this
had already become part of the church's regular liturgy (cf.
I Pet. 5.14), as it was later (cf. Justin, *First Apology* lxv.2).

21. The final greetings in Paul's own hand authenticated the
letter as his; cf. Gal. 6.11; Col. 4.18; 2 Th. 3.17. He habitually
dictated his letters to amanuenses (cf. Rom. 16.22).

F

22. If any one has no love for the Lord, let him be accursed (Gk *anathema*): apart from Tit. 3.15, this is the only occurrence of the verb *phileō* in the Pauline corpus (otherwise Paul regularly uses *agapaō* as the verb to love). The sentence may be a quotation—possibly from a liturgical interchange (it might be the counterpart to some such words as 'If any one loves the Lord, let him draw near' or '. . . let him be blessed'). This possibility is rendered the more plausible by the invocation **Our Lord, come!** immediately following, which may have been the congregation's response in confirmation of the ban. We may indeed have here 'the remains of the earliest Christian liturgical sequence we possess' (J. A. T. Robinson, *Twelve NT Studies* (1962), p. 157; cf. also C. F. D. Moule, 'A Reconsideration of the Context of *Maranatha*', *NTS* 6 (1959–60), pp. 307ff.).

Our Lord, come! This represents Aramaic *māranā-ṭā*, which Paul uses without translating it into Greek, presumably because the Aramaic form was current as an invocation in the Greek-speaking churches (cf. the use of Hebrew 'amen', 'hallelujah', 'hosanna', etc.). It would be possible to divide Paul's *maranatha* as *māran 'aṭā*, 'our Lord has come', but in the light of the ample evidence for the invocation 'Come, O Lord' or 'Come, Lord Jesus' in early Christianity (cf. Rev. 22.20), the imperative construction is much more probable. The form *maranatha* appears as part of the eucharistic liturgy in *Didache* x.6 (significantly enough coming, probably as a response, immediately after the words, 'If any one is holy, let him come; if any one is not, let him repent'); and it was presumably in a eucharistic setting that it was current among Greek-speaking Christians (for the linking of the Eucharist with the hope of the parousia, cf. 11.26). Their use of this Aramaic form points to the Palestinian origin of the ascription to Jesus of 'Lord' as the title of supremacy; it is a testimony to the place given to the exalted and expected Christ in the worship of the most primitive church.

23–24. With the prayer for grace and the assurance of the apostle's **love** the letter is concluded.

INTRODUCTION
to
2 Corinthians

INTRODUCTION TO 2 CORINTHIANS

1. BACKGROUND AND OCCASION OF 2 CORINTHIANS

When 1 Corinthians was despatched, Paul hoped to pay a visit to Corinth before too long—not indeed so soon as he may have intended when he wrote 1 C. 4.18–21, for he planned to remain at Ephesus for a few more weeks at least—until Pentecost, and then to pass through Macedonia in the course of the summer and autumn and so come to Corinth, where he might possibly spend the winter—probably the winter of A.D. 55–56 (1 C. 16.5–9).

Not long afterwards he modified this plan, and decided to visit Corinth twice—once on his way to Macedonia, and again on his return from Macedonia. After the second of these two visits to Corinth he planned to set sail for Palestine (2 C. 1.15f.), because by that time (he hoped) the collection of the gift for Jerusalem in the Gentile churches both east and west of the Aegean would be complete (cf. 1. C 16.1–4).

A number of things made it impossible for him to carry out these plans as he had arranged. One was the deadly peril which befell him 'in Asia' (2 C. 1.8–10); if we knew its character and details, much that is obscure to us with regard to Paul's movements around this time might be plainer. Another was news of further trouble in Corinth, which made it necessary for Paul to pay an urgent visit to the church there. From allusions here and there in 2 Corinthians it may be inferred that 1 Corinthians was not as effective as Paul could have wished in checking those tendencies in the church which he deplored, and Timothy was not strong enough to enforce the apostle's directions. It may indeed have been Timothy who brought back such a report that Paul decided that nothing would serve but a direct confrontation with the church. This visit—the 'second visit' of 2 C. 13.2—was a painful one for Paul and his converts alike (2 C. 2.1). The opposition to Paul came to a head, and one member of the church in particular took the lead in defying his authority. Paul was deeply humiliated (cf. 2 C. 12.21) and withdrew—perhaps fulfilling his plan to 'pass through Macedonia'.

He then sent the Corinthians a stinging letter—one which he

assures them he wrote 'out of much affliction and anguish of heart and with many tears' (2 C. 2.3f.). This letter (which may be called 'Corinthians C') was sent by the hand of Titus, and when Titus had set off with it Paul began to be sorry he had sent it. In it he assured the Corinthians of his love for them, but demanded that they give evidence of the love they professed for him by acknowledging his apostolic authority, and in particular by subjecting to church discipline the man who had taken the lead in defying his authority. He assured Titus, as he gave him the letter to take to Corinth, that the Corinthians' hearts were in the right place and that they would show themselves as they really were by gladly rendering him the obedience which the letter demanded. He had now to wait and see if this confident assurance proved to be well grounded or not.

Back in proconsular Asia he was assailed by severe depression if not also by extreme external danger. If such danger did beset him at this time (cf. 2 C.1.8–10), it subsided, and he made his way to the Troad, hoping to greet Titus on his return from Corinth. In spite of opportunities for evangelism there he could not settle down to take advantage of them. He waited probably until navigation across the Aegean had ceased for the winter, and since he now knew that Titus would not be sailing straight across to Troas from Corinth but would be taking the land-route through Macedonia, he himself set out for Macedonia, and there too was a prey to inward anxiety as well as unspecified external troubles (2 C. 7.5).

But then Titus met him, and brought good news from Corinth. The 'tearful letter' had been completely effective: the Corinthian Christians were stung to such a pitch of indignation in their zeal to vindicate themselves in Paul's eyes and assure him of their love and loyalty that they were in danger of going to the opposite extreme in making a scapegoat of the offender against whom Paul had demanded disciplinary measures. There were still some complaints that Paul's changes of travel plans were disconcerting; in particular, why did he leave Macedonia without visiting them as he had promised to do? But the general mood was one of reconciliation: Titus was delighted with their attitude and communicated his delight in his report to Paul. Paul immediately sent a further letter (our 2 Corinthians), which we may call 'Corinthians D', in which he responded to Titus's news with an outpouring of open-hearted affection. He explains that his one reason for not visiting them again was to avoid giving them further pain; he urges them to forgive the offender because his demand for discipline against him was due to no personal resentment but to his resolve to test the church's love and obedience. Now that they had satisfied him on this score, they should show the offender full friendship and fellowship, and prevent his dejection from overwhelming him.

The sense of euphoria which Titus's news had engendered in Paul encouraged him to wear his heart on his sleeve and enlarge on the glories and trials of the apostolic ministry. During the period of strained relations following the despatch of 1 Corinthians, it had not been expedient to follow up the instructions about the Jerusalem fund given in 1 C. 16.1–4, but now he can raise the subject again, and use the example of the Macedonian churches' liberality to encourage the Corinthians to give generously (2 C. 8–9).

2. THE PROBLEM OF 2 C. 10–13

Nothing in 2 C. 1–9 prepares the reader for the rude shock administered by the opening words and sustained argument of 2 C. 10–13, in which Paul warmly defends his apostolic authority and denounces with savage irony visitors who came to Corinth and endeavoured to displace his authority in the church there by their own or by that of the leaders whose names they invoked. To explain the abrupt change of tone by such a suggestion as that Paul had a bad night between dictating chapter 9 and chapter 10 is incredibly frivolous. While chapters 1–9 are not free from criticism and self-defence, there is nothing in them comparable to the invective of (say) 11.13–15, and the mood which they reflect is quite different from that of chapters 10–13. This calls for a serious explanation.

One explanation which has won widespread support is that in 2 C. 10–13 there has been preserved part of the 'tearful letter' or 'Corinthians C'. This view, propounded by A. Hausrath in *Der Vier-Capitel Brief des Paulus an die Corinthier* (1870), was widely adopted in the English-speaking world through the influence of J. H. Kennedy, *The Second and Third Letters of St. Paul to the*

Corinthians (1900). There is no intrinsic improbability in this hypothesis, if internal evidence warrants it: we can understand that if 'Corinthians C' had lost its beginning and 'Corinthians D' had lost its ending, the two might have been put together by an editor who did not notice that the former part of the resultant composite document was written after the latter part.

The identification of 2 C. 10–13 with part of 'Corinthians C' has been supported by a number of arguments tending to show that the contents of 2 C. 10–13 correspond to features of 'Corinthians C' as it is referred to in 2 C. 1–7. The following sets of parallels demand our attention:

2 C. 10–13	2 C. 1–7
11.11: Because I do not love you? God knows I do!	2.4: I wrote . . . to let you know the abundant love that I have for you.
12.15: If I love you the more, am I to be loved the less?	
10.6: being ready to punish every disobedience, when your obedience is complete.	2.9: I wrote, that I might test you and know whether you are obedient in everything.
13.10: I write this while I am away from you, in order that when I come I may not have to be severe.	1.23: it was to spare you that I refrained from coming to Corinth.
	2.3: I wrote as I did, so that when I came I might not be pained by those who should have made me rejoice.
10.8ff.: even if I boast a little too much of our authority . . .	3.1: Are we beginning to commend ourselves again?
10.1: I . . . am . . . bold to you (*tharrō eis hymas*).	7.16: I have perfect confidence in you (*tharrō en hymin*).

On the other hand, there are a few considerations which remind us that such parallels do not point inescapably to the identity of 2 C. 10–13 with part of 'Corinthians C':

(a) 2 C. 10–13 may conceivably have been written 'with many

tears', but it does not read like that: it is written more in anger than in sorrow.

(b) The main targets of Paul's attack in 2 C. 10–13 are not the Corinthian Christians but the interlopers who masquerade as apostles of Christ; his main criticism of the Corinthians is for their readiness to accept these people at their own valuation, and consequently to depreciate their one true apostle, whose concern is for their lasting good.

(c) The main point of 'Corinthians C', the demand for discipline against 'you know who' (Gk *ho toioutos*), is totally absent from 2 C. 10–13; it is not even hinted at. It may be maintained that this came in a part of 'Corinthians C' which is now totally lost, but this plea shares the weakness of most arguments from silence.

(d) Impressive as the parallels are, it would not be difficult to find parallels almost as impressive between references to 'Corinthians C' in 2 C. 1–7 and passages in 1 Corinthians. For example, 2 C. 1.23 could echo 1 C. 4.18f.; 2 C. 2.3 could echo 1 C. 4.21; 2 C. 2.9 could echo 1 C. 4.14; 2 C. 3.1 could hark back to 1 C. 9.1ff.; 'and indeed, any three lines promising a visit for the punishment of offenders but expressing at the same time the hope that such punishment might prove unnecessary would do as well' as any of these passages in 1 Corinthians or 2 C. 1–7 (C. H. Buck, 'The Collection for the Saints', *HTR* 43 (1950), p. 6).

(e) The language of 2 C. 10.10f., 'his letters are weighty (Gk *barys*, which might well mean 'severe') and strong . . .', would be most applicable as a back-reference to 'Corinthians C'—although indeed it would not be inapplicable to 'Corinthians B', nor yet, so far as can be judged, to 'Corinthians A'.

(f) The reference in 2 C. 12.18 to Titus and 'the brother' who accompanied him to Corinth is the conclusive argument against any view which dates 2 C. 10–13 before 2 C. 1–9. (Even if chapters 8 and 9 are held to have been originally separate from chapters 1–7, their content indicates a date later than 'Corinthians C'.) There is no evidence for a visit by Titus to Corinth earlier than that of 2 C. 7.6ff., which had such a happy issue; indeed, the passage implies that this was his first contact with the Corinthians, whom until then he had known only from Paul's glowing report of them (which his own experience now corroborated). The reference to his part in organizing the collection at Corinth

(2 C. 8.6ff.) does not suggest that he had had anything to do with this business there previously. Neither Titus nor any other representative of Paul is mentioned, or even envisaged, in this connection in 1 C. 16.1–4. The words 'as he had already made a beginning' (2 C. 8.6) do not mean that he had made a beginning with this business, but rather that as he had made such a good beginning in his relations with them recently by helping to restore their feeling of confidence towards Paul, so he should now continue the good work by helping them with the collection— 'this grace also' (*RV*, more literally than *RSV*).

The verbs of sending in 2 C. 8.17, 18, 22; 9.3 may be epistolary aorists, but those of 12.18a certainly refer to a mission that has already taken place, as is clear from the force of the aorists of 12.18b. It is most difficult to understand 2 C. 12.18 of any other mission than that of 8.6ff. (for the mention of one 'brother' only as Titus's companion in 12.18 see note *ad loc*.); this being so, 2 C. 10–13 cannot be dated before 2 C. 1–9, and cannot be regarded as part of 'Corinthians C'.

But if 2 C. 10–13 belongs chronologically after 2 C. 1–9, we have still to account for the abrupt transition from chapter 9 to chapter 10. Only two possibilities seem worth considering: either (i) chapters 10–13 are part of the same letter as chapters 1–9, but written after some fresh news had come from Corinth, indicating that the condition of the church was by no means so happy as it had appeared to be when Titus brought his good news from Corinth to Paul in Macedonia, or (ii) chapters 10–13 belong to a later letter, which must be called 'Corinthians E'.

The former possibility recalls that envisaged at the end of 1 C. 4, but the two situations are not comparable. There is no abrupt transition from 1 C. 4 to 1 C. 5; the hypothesis of fresh news coming in between the dictating of the two chapters is based on indications at the end of chapter 4 that the letter is drawing to a close. Here, in addition to the abrupt transition, we have to allow time not only for fresh news to have come from Corinth but also for Titus and his companion(s) to have arrived there, since in 2 C. 12.18 the Corinthians are expected to be in a position to say how they conducted themselves during their visit. It is more probable that 2 C. 1–9 was sent to Corinth soon after it was completed (taken perhaps by Titus if the relevant aorists in 2 C. 8.6ff. are epistolary). After an interval Paul heard of the arrival in

Corinth of the interlopers whom he attacks in 2 C. 10–13, and of their success in captivating many members of the church. This was probably not the first time that Corinth had received such visitors (in addition to the implications of the presence of a 'Peter party' in the church in 1 C. 1.12, we have to think of the 'some' of 2 C. 3.1 who brought letters of recommendation), but nowhere else in the Corinthian correspondence is it suggested that their influence on the church was on the scale described in 2 C. 10–13. These four chapters are best regarded as the major part of a fifth letter—'Corinthians E'.

If 2 C. 10–13 be identified with 'Corinthians C', then Paul's Corinthian correspondence has a happy ending. It is far otherwise if these four chapters are the last portion of this correspondence that has survived—but life, including church life, tends to be like that. (On the sequel to 2 Corinthians see pp. 255f.)

3. STRUCTURE AND DATE OF 2 CORINTHIANS

On the structure of 2 Corinthians we have come to one tentative conclusion—that chapters 10–13 form the sequel to chapters 1–9, whether they were completed in time to be sent along with chapters 1–9 as part of the same letter or were despatched later as a separate communication (cf. J. Munck, *Paul and the Salvation of Mankind*, E.T. (1959), pp. 168ff.). On the whole, the second of these alternatives seems the more probable (cf. C. H. Buck, 'The Collection for the Saints', *HTR* 43 (1950), pp. 1ff., especially 9ff.). If chapters 10–13 represent a separate communication, it appears to lack the initial salutation; this may have been omitted by an editor who put our 2 Corinthians together. Otherwise the integrity of 2 C. 10–13 is not in question; R. H. Strachan, indeed, made 2 C. 13.11–14 the conclusion of 2 C. 1–9, but that was on the supposition that 2 C. 10–13 represent 'Corinthians C' (Commentary, pp. 145f.).

The integrity of 2 C. 1–9 is not undisputed. Several students of the letter have regarded 2 C. 6.14–7.1 as an intrusive paragraph, interrupting the apostle's plea in 2 C. 6.1–13 and 7.2–4, and have variously treated it as a fragment of 'Corinthians A', or of some other Pauline letter, or of a non-Pauline document. But the very difficulty of accounting for its intrusion into what seems, at first sight, an alien context could be used in favour of recognizing it as a Pauline digression (see discussion on pp. 213f. below). That he has digressed before 2 C. 7.2 is suggested by his repetition there of the appeal of 2 C. 6.13, as though he were resuming a train of thought momentarily broken off ('Open your hearts to us' catches up 'widen your hearts also').

A much more substantial digression, running from 2.14 to 7.4 and dealing with the apostolic ministry, interrupts Paul's account of the turmoil of mind which he suffered as he travelled from the Troad to Macedonia, hoping to meet Titus on his way back from Corinth, and the joyful relief which he experienced when at last Titus reached him with his good news. This digression has been treated as part of a separate letter to the Corinthians—e.g. by G. Bornkamm, *Die Vorgeschichte des sogenannten Zweiten Korintherbriefes* (1961), appearing in an abridged English version, 'The History of the Origin of the So-called Second Letter to the Corinthians', *NTS* 8 (1961–2), pp. 258ff., reprinted in *The Authorship and Integrity of the NT* (SPCK Theological Collections 4 (1965)), pp. 73ff. Bornkamm rightly sees that this 'digression' is earlier than 2 C. 10–13, since in it the interlopers of 2 C. 10–13 have begun to arrive but the church has not yet been carried away by them. But since he identifies 2 C. 10–13 with the 'tearful letter', which was self-evidently earlier than 2 C. 1.3–2.13 and 7.5–16, he is compelled to distinguish three letters, in this chronological order: (*a*) 2 C. 2.14–7.4, on the apostolic ministry; (*b*) 2 C. 10–13, the 'tearful letter'; (*c*) 2 C. 1.3–2.13; 7.5–16, the letter of relief and reconciliation. That 2 C. 2.14–7.4 constitutes a real digression rather than a separate composition is shown by the transition from its closing words to the opening words of Paul's resumption of his personal narrative (7.5ff.); 7.4 anticipates 7.16 and the 'For even . . .' of 7.5 would be out of place if 7.5 originally followed on directly from 2.13.

Bornkamm further regards the two 'collection' chapters, 2 C. 8 and 9, as two separate units, the former preparing the way for the mission of Titus and his companions and the latter presupposing that they have already reached Corinth. There is no need to separate chapter 8 from what precedes it: the atmosphere of relief and reconciliation which breathes in chapter 7 afforded a ready opportunity for Paul to take up a subject which was very much on his mind at the time, but of which it would not have been politic to remind the Corinthians during the recent period of tension. While the transition from chapter 8 to chapter 9 may seem a little awkward, the references to the sending of 'the brethren' to Corinth in 9.3–5 are written from the same perspective as those in 8.6, 16–23; the aorist of 9.3 is as likely to be epistolary (*RSV* 'I am sending') as those in 8.17ff. J. Héring sees that chapter 9 was sent about the same time as chapters 1–8, but in that case there is no need to regard it as a separate note, as he does (Commentary, p. 65); such a separate note would be superfluous.

Both in chapter 8 and in chapter 9 Paul speaks of the energy with which the Corinthians threw themselves into the business of the collection a year before (8.10; 9.2)—an expression (Gk *perysi*) which might denote anything from 9 to 15 months. We should probably not dissociate this reference from 1 C. 16.1–4, in which Paul responded to the initiative which the Corinthians took in asking about their part in the collection. If 1 Corinthians was sent between Passover and Pentecost of A.D. 55 (see p. 25), 2 C. 1–9 will have been sent early in A.D. 56, and 2 C. 10–13 a few weeks later. (Mention should be made of the argument of L. P. Pherigo ('Paul and the Corinthian Church', *JBL* 68 (1949), pp. 341ff.) that Paul wrote 2 C. 10–13 after his release from the Roman imprisonment of Ac. 28.30f.; but there is nothing in 2 C. 10–13 which presupposes such a setting, and one so late.)

4. PAUL'S OPPONENTS IN CORINTH

The identity and character of the visitors to Corinth who set themselves, not without some success, to undermine Paul's authority in the church, have been debated with animation, especially in recent years. Against the traditional view that they were judaizing emissaries from Jerusalem there has been a tendency to view them as Gnostics of ecstatic temperament and libertine ethics; a pioneeer in this representation was W. Lütgert (*Freiheitspredigt und Schwarmgeister in Korinth: ein Beitrag zur Charakteristik der Christuspartei* (1908)). He denied that they were Judaizers on the ground that they do not appear to have advocated circumcision, as their counterparts who troubled the Galatian churches certainly did. It is difficult to dispute his argument in this regard, but they may have been emissaries from Jerusalem without being Judaizers.

This was pointed out by E. Käsemann ('Die Legitimität des Apostels', *ZNW* 41 (1942), pp. 33–71), who added that they could have been (self-styled) 'men of the Spirit' (*pneumatici*) without being Gnostics. In Käsemann's judgment, they invoked the authority of the Jerusalem apostles (the 'superlative apostles' of 2 C. 11.5; 12.11), with doubtful justification; and part of Paul's embarrassment in refuting their claims arises from his desire to unmask them without seeming to attack the apostles themselves. If, like 'some' in 2 C. 3.1, these visitors carried 'letters of recommendation' from the Jerusalem church, Paul was also concerned to expose the hollowness of their pretensions without questioning the authority of the community with whose recommendation they journeyed. (From what other source, apart from Paul himself, could letters of recommendation be issued which would carry such weight among the Gentile churches?)

Käsemann's arguments called forth a reply from R. Bultmann (*Exegetische Probleme des zweiten Korintherbriefes* (1947), pp. 20ff.), but his main contention remains unshaken—that the issue between Paul and these opponents is not *gnōsis*, not spiritual gifts, but his apostolic *exousia*, his liberty and authority. The opponents asserted that no teaching could be validated unless it was authorized by Jerusalem: if Paul acted in independence of Jerusalem, he lacked the commission of Christ which they possessed (see note on 2 C. 10.7), for he cut himself loose from the source of spiritual authority and 'walked according to the flesh' (2 C. 10.2, *RV*). If the church of Corinth wished to enjoy the blessings of the Spirit, it must recognize the authority of Jerusalem.

In Paul's eyes, these arguments did not affect his personal status so much as the truth of the gospel and the nature of the church. If his ministry bore the stamp of divine approval, if the Corinthian church was the seal of his apostleship 'in the Lord' (1 C. 9.2), then the opposition of these intruders was opposition not merely to him but to the Lord who commissioned him, to the Spirit who empowered him and to the gospel which he proclaimed: it followed that theirs was 'another Jesus . . ., a different spirit . . ., a different gospel' (2 C. 11.4). Such men were no true apostles of Christ but false apostles; while claiming to be servants of Christ they were in reality servants of Satan (2 C. 11.13–15, 23); instead of pioneering a mission-field of their own, they preferred to be parasites on 'other men's labours' (2 C. 10.15).

In trying to establish their authority over against Paul's, they claimed to be 'Hebrews', 'Israelites', 'descendants of Abraham' (2 C. 11.22), and to have had special experience of 'visions and revelations of the Lord' (2 C. 12.1). Paul does not dispute these claims, but affirms that he himself can produce stronger credentials than theirs. In addition, though he is ashamed to have to say so (for his Corinthian converts should spontaneously have undertaken his defence), he has endured far more hardships in the discharge of his ministry than they have done. If they assert their authority by lording it over the Corinthians and living at their expense, he exercises his liberty by tending them with paternal care and spending and being spent for them.

The intruders are best recognized as Palestinian Jews—not Judaizers in the Galatian sense, but men who conceived it as their mission to impose the authority of the mother church over the Christian world. Paul saw in their activity a breach of the agreement which he and Barnabas had reached some ten years before with the Jerusalem leaders, by which the latter would concentrate on the apostolate to the Jews and he and Barnabas on the Gentile mission (Gal. 2.6ff.); if he does not say so openly, this is probably because he wishes to avoid the very appearance of criticizing the Jerusalem apostles. 'Paul, who learnt at Corinth what it is to be weak in Christ, shows there perhaps more clearly than elsewhere his full stature of Christian intelligence, firmness, and magnanimity' (C. K. Barrett, 'Christianity at Corinth', *BJRL* 46 (1963–4), p. 297.

(This subject is treated also by T. W. Manson, *Studies in the Gospels and Epistles* (1962), pp. 210ff.; J. Munck, *Paul and the Salvation of Mankind*, E.T. (1959), pp. 168ff.; H. J. Schoeps, *Paul*, E.T. (1961), pp. 74ff.; G. Friedrich, 'Die Gegner des Paulus im 2. Korintherbrief', in *Abraham unser Vater: Festschrift für O. Michel*, ed. O. Betz *et al.* (1963), pp. 181ff.; W. Schmithals, *Die Gnosis in Korinth* (1965²), pp. 106ff.; D. Georgi, *Die Gegner des Paulus im 2. Korintherbrief* (1964).)

ANALYSIS OF 2 CORINTHIANS

FIRST SECTION   **1.1–2.13** REMOVAL OF MISUNDERSTANDING.
                (a) **1.1–2** Salutation.
                (b) **1.3–7** Thanksgiving for divine comfort.

THE SECOND LETTER OF PAUL TO THE
CORINTHIANS

THE SECOND LETTER OF PAUL TO THE
CORINTHIANS

SALUTATION 1.1–2

1.1–2. For the salutation see notes on 1 C. 1.1–3. In place of
Sosthenes **Timothy** is here associated with Paul in the greeting,
as regularly when Timothy was in Paul's company at the time
of writing (cf. Phil. 1.1; Col. 1.1; 1 Th. 1.1; 2 Th. 1.1; Phm. 1, and
see note on 1 C. 4.17). Whether Timothy, because of Paul's great
confidence in him (cf. 1 C. 16.10), was given a larger part in the
composition of such letters than (say) Sosthenes or Silvanus, is an
interesting question on which no certainty is attainable.
all the saints who are in the whole of Achaia: e.g. members
of the church of Cenchreae (cf. Rom. 16.1).

THANKSGIVING FOR DIVINE COMFORT 1.3–7

**3. Blessed be the God and Father of our Lord Jesus
Christ:** these words (cf. Eph. 1.3; 1 Pet. 1.3) introduce a christianized form of a synagogue *berākāh*, an ascription of praise to God.
The description of God as **the Father of mercies and God of
all comfort** (cf. Rom. 15.5), which goes back to such *OT* texts
as Ps. 103.13, 17; Isa. 51.12; 66.13, can be paralleled in the synagogue liturgy (cf. the prayer *'Ahabah Rabbah*, where he is called
'the merciful and compassionate Father'). This designation, which
is specially appropriate to Paul's present situation, sets the tone
for 2 C. 1–9.

4–7. Having recently experienced **the comfort** of **God**, Paul
finds himself better able than before to communicate to others the
comfort he himself has received. As the **affliction** he endures for
the gospel's sake is accepted by him as a sharing **in Christ's
sufferings** (cf. Phil. 3.10), and accepted the more gladly for the
comfort and salvation of fellow-Christians (cf. Col. 1.24), so
the comfort he receives **through Christ** is readily extended to his
fellow-Christians. Christ, who suffered personally on the cross,
continues to suffer in his people on earth so long as the present
aeon lasts (cf. Ac. 9.4f.); Paul's desire is to absorb as much as
possible of this suffering in himself so that his converts may have
less of it to endure. The recent strained relations between Paul and
the Corinthian church called for a generous measure of comfort

and conciliation if unreserved friendship and mutual confidence were to be restored, and this initial emphasis on comfort (Gk *paraklēsis*, which includes the ideas of help and encouragement) is maintained throughout 2 C. 1–9.

PAUL'S DELIVERANCE FROM DEADLY PERIL 1.8–11

8–11. The **affliction** which Paul had recently **experienced in Asia** has been variously understood. It may have been an illness which nearly proved fatal (so M. Goguel, E. B. Allo, C. H. Dodd); the language in which he describes it, however, suggests rather some deadly danger from without (so G. S. Duncan, H. Clavier) from which there seemed to be no hope of escape. Paul himself considered death to be the certain outcome—**we felt that we had received the sentence of death**—so much so that, when at last he was **delivered ... from so deadly a peril** (lit. 'from so great a death'), he greeted his deliverance as a miracle wrought by **God who raises the dead** (here again we may detect an echo of a synagogue benediction). If it was some external danger, the task of identifying it calls for speculation beyond the exegete's province. It would be a later experience than the 'fighting with beasts at Ephesus' mentioned in 1 C. 15.32: it is most natural to place it between the completion of 1 Corinthians and the writing of 2 C. 1–9. The hostility of some of the 'many adversaries' of 1 C. 16.9 had perhaps proved exceptionally effective. But, against all reasonable hope, Paul had escaped the danger in a manner which he could only interpret as the action of God in response to his own prayers and the prayers of his friends. The experience had the effect of encouraging him to **rely** more than ever **on God**: the God who had saved him from such unprecedented danger was well able to **deliver** him **again**. Here was incentive enough both for renewed **hope** in God and also for redoubled **prayer** for Paul on the part of his friends, with the result that thanksgiving to God would increase because of the further **blessing granted in answer to many prayers.**

Whatever the nature of Paul's **affliction ... in Asia** may have been, it left a permanent mark on his mind, even if we do not go so far as to treat it as 'a sort of second conversion', a psychological watershed by reference to which his epistles may be dated to the period preceding it or the period following it (cf. C. H. Dodd, 'The Mind of Paul', *New Testament Studies* (1953), pp. 67ff.). In 2

Corinthians the effect of this experience is specially evident in 4.7–5.10.

EXPLANATION OF HIS RECENT CONDUCT 1.12–2.4

A plea for understanding 1.12–14

12. Paul's recent conduct, particularly his disconcerting change of travelling plans, had been felt to be strange and inconsistent by many of his Corinthian friends. Hence he assures them that his own **conscience** bears clear witness to the **holiness and godly sincerity** of his behaviour towards men in general and especially towards themselves. Even in changing his plans he has been true to a higher consistency, being guided **not by earthly wisdom but by the grace of God.**

13–14. He hopes that as they read they will **understand** his motives **fully**, as already they understand them **in part**—thanks, no doubt, to the reconciling visit lately paid them by Titus (7.6ff.). He boasts of them to others here and now (cf. 7.14; 9.2), and looks forward to **the day of the Lord Jesus** (cf. 1 C. 5.5) when he can point to them with pride, as to his converts elsewhere (cf. 1 Th. 2.19f.; Phil. 2.16; 4.1), as evidence of his apostolic service; and he hopes that on that day they will have as much cause to be proud of him (cf. 5.12) as he of them.

Answer to the charge of vacillation 1.15–24

15–16. I wanted to come to you first: this in itself marks a change of plan as compared with 1 C. 16.5–7; there he says he will visit them after, not before, his projected journey in Macedonia; here he speaks of his intention to visit them both before and after his Macedonian journey, so that they **might have a double pleasure** (Gk *charan*, 'joy', for which there is a strongly attested variant reading *charin*, 'grace', 'favour').

have you send me on my way to Judea: with the collection for Jerusalem. In 1 C. 16.4 he was not sure if he would go to Jerusalem in person; now he has decided to accompany the delegates of the churches on their journey there (cf. Rom. 15.25). This indicates that the plan of a double visit to Corinth was subsequent to that of a single visit announced in 1 C. 16.5–7 (and accordingly that it was conveyed to them between the writing of 1 C. and of 2 C. 1–9). On Paul's visits to Corinth see pp. 164ff., 250.

17. was I vacillating . . .? The question, introduced by the negative *mēti*, expects the answer 'No', but Paul is aware that some Corinthians were giving it the answer 'Yes'.

like a worldly man: lit. 'according to flesh' (Gk *kata sarka*; cf. 5.16; 10.3), where 'flesh', as habitually in Paul, denotes unregenerate humanity.

ready to say Yes and No at once: or to say Yes one day and No the next (lit. 'that with me there should be Yes, yes, and No, no'). The thought here is quite different from that of Mt. 5.37 or Jas 5.12.

18. As surely as God is faithful: lit. 'God is faithful', as in 1 C. 1.9; but here God's faithfulness is invoked to confirm Paul's assurance that he was not guilty of vacillation. In all his dealings with the Corinthian church, whether in preaching the gospel or in discussing travel-plans, he was conscious of his responsibility as the apostle of Christ: this forbade him to say **Yes and No** in one breath, as though nothing mattered but the whim of the moment.

19-20. There was no such **Yes and No** about **the Son of God** whom he and his companions proclaimed: in him **all the promises of God find their** answering **Yes** (cf. Rom. 1.2)—a fulfilment which his people acknowledged in their worship with the confirmatory **Amen**, uttered **through** Christ, or in Christ's name, **to the glory of God** (for God's glory is manifested when his self-revelation in Christ finds a spontaneous response in his people's worship). Not only does this passage attest the primitive use of the Hebrew **Amen** ('sure', 'steadfast') in the Hellenistic churches; it has an inner coherence in Paul's use of a variety of words which embody the same Hebrew root. While this could not have been appreciated by his Greek readers, it was probably present to Paul's mind—not that he necessarily thought in terms of a triliteral Semitic root, as we do, but recognized the assonance in the various forms. **God is faithful** (*neʾĕmān*) . . . in Christ **it is always Yes** (*ʾāmēn*; for Gk *nai* and Hebrew *ʾāmēn* used as synonyms see Rev. 1.7) . . . **all the promises of God find their Yes** (*ʾāmēn*) **in him** (in Rev. 3.14 he is called 'the Amen') . . . **we utter the Amen through him** (for Hebrew *ʾāmēn* as a response to Gk *nai* cf. Rev. 22.20) . . . **it is God who establishes us** (preachers and converts together), i.e. makes us steadfast (Gk *bebaiōn*, perhaps recalling the same Hebrew root), **in Christ** (Gk *eis christon*, lit.

'into Christ'). The gospel preached in Corinth, in the mouth of three witnesses (cf. 13.1)—Paul, Silvanus (Silas) and Timothy (cf. Ac. 18.5)—announced that God's promises to mankind had been fulfilled in Jesus. The Corinthian church acknowledged this gospel as the basis of its existence: every time the members greeted the recital of the saving act of God by their responsive **Amen** they bore witness that they had been caught up into this saving act. If this certainty characterizes issues of such paramount importance, it is foolish to suppose that in less important matters Paul should vacillate between **Yes and No**. If he changed his plans, he had good reason for doing so. Far from adopting 'worldly' standards, he regulated his whole life, in great and small things alike, in terms of his apostolic calling (cf. 1 C. 9.19–27), as one who had learned to 'walk by the Spirit'. (This exegesis of verses 15ff. is greatly indebted to W. C. van Unnik, 'Reisepläne und Amen-Sagen . . .', in *Studia Paulina in honorem J. de Zwaan* (1953), pp. 215ff.)

21. us with you: the apostle's standing is bound up with that of his converts (cf. verse 14; 1 C. 3.5–4.16; 9.2).

has commissioned us: lit. 'has anointed us', i.e. with the Spirit; **us** is probably inclusive here, embracing 'us with you'.

22. he has put his seal upon us and given us his Spirit in our hearts as a guarantee: this unction of the Spirit bestowed on believers is spoken of both as a seal (Gk *sphragis*) by which God reserves them for himself against the day of final and total redemption (cf. Eph. 1.13; 4.30) and as a **guarantee** or pledge (Gk *arrhabōn*, a word of Semitic origin; cf. Gen. 38.17f.) which they have as an assurance of the inheritance of glory awaiting them in the resurrection age (cf. 5.5; Eph. 1.14). The figure of sealing is used of Jesus' special endowment with the Spirit (at his baptism) in Jn 6.27 (synonymous with the 'anointing' of Ac. 10.38). (For the significance of this figure cf. G. W. H. Lampe, *The Seal of the Spirit* (1951).) The present interval between Christ's resurrection and theirs is the age of the Spirit, who not only makes effective in them what Christ has done for them and communicates to them the power of their living and exalted Lord, but also enables them, as those who are incorporated in his risen life, to live in the present enjoyment of the glory yet to be revealed (cf. Rom. 8.9–27, and especially verse 23 where the Spirit is the 'first fruits'—Gk *aparchē* —or initial instalment of all that will be theirs when the new creation is consummated). See E. Dinkler, 'Die Taufterminologie in 2 Kor. i.21f.', in *Neotestamentica et Patristica* (*Suppl. to NovT* 6, 1962), pp. 173ff.

23. I call God to witness: a characteristic Paulinism (cf. Rom. 1.9; Phil. 1.8; 1 Th. 2.5, 10).

It was to spare you that I refrained from coming to Corinth: his change of plan was due to no instability of purpose; it arose from his apostolic and pastoral concern, a concern the more intense because he and they were 'anointed' and 'sealed' with the same Spirit, and *the Spirit* must not be grieved (cf. Eph. 4.30). To carry out his plan of visiting them in the existing circumstances would have caused them grief and shame; **to spare** them such humiliation he stayed away until happier relations were restored between him and them.

24. Not that we lord it over your faith: their **faith** (cf. Hebrew *'ĕmūnāh*, also related to the root *'āmēn*) was a matter of their direct response to God's grace in Christ; it was by faith that they had their standing before him (cf. Rom. 5.2; 11.20; 1 C. 15.1). Even an apostle had no right of intervention or dictation here; his congenial responsibility was rather **to work with** them **for** their **joy,** and therefore he chose to postpone visiting them again until the occasion would be one of mutual rejoicing.

A painful visit and a tearful letter **2.1–4**

2.1. not to pay you another painful visit: these words (lit. 'not to come to you again in sorrow') are best understood as implying that Paul had already paid them one **visit** which proved to be **painful**—'the second visit' of 13.2. It is less natural to take them to mean simply that he decided not to pay them **another . . . visit** which in the circumstances would (unlike any previous visit) be a **painful** one (cf. R. Batey, 'Paul's Interaction with the Corinthians', *JBL* 84 (1965), pp. 139f.). The earlier **painful visit** which is to be inferred was probably later than the despatch of 1 Corinthians, since no such painful visit is implied in that letter, and appears to have been marked by the culmination of the anti-Pauline trend at Corinth. Cf. pp. 164, 250.

2. Since Paul's joy was bound up with theirs (cf. 1.24), it would be paradoxical to cause unnecessary **pain** to the only people capable of making him **glad.**

3. I wrote as I did: instead of paying them another painful visit he **wrote** them a letter, hoping that its effect would be such

that when he did pay them another visit it would be a happy one
for him and them. For the realization of this hope, see 7.8ff.

4. This letter, written **out of much affliction and anguish of
heart and with many tears**, has traditionally been identified
with 1 Corinthians, but for a century now the identification has
been seriously questioned, though it continues to find able defen-
ders. While in some sections of 1 C. Paul does take his friends at
Corinth sharply to task, it does not give the impression of having
been composed in the state of spiritual distress described here,
and it ends calmly and factually enough. Elsewhere in his correspondence Paul speaks of weeping as he writes (cf. Phil. 3.18), but
there is not a hint of this in 1 C., nor any reference to his **affliction
and anguish of heart**. Again, while 1 C. includes the great
exhortation to love in chapter 13, it does not in any exceptional
way emphasize Paul's love for the Corinthian church, although
this is naturally assumed throughout (cf. 1 C. 4.21; 16.24; but
contrast the strong asseverations of 2 C. 11.11; 12.15). Even if 1
C. as we have it were held to include parts of more than one letter
(cf. p. 25), it would be difficult to identify any one of its component
parts with the letter described here. It is more satisfactory to
regard this tearful letter as having been written after 1 C., even if
we have to assume that (like the 'previous letter' of 1 C. 5.9) it is
entirely lost—unless part of it survives in 2 C. 10–13 (see pp. 166ff
for this view).

A CALL TO FORGIVENESS **2.5–11**

5–8. If anyone has caused pain: reference is now made to an
individual whose behaviour had **caused pain** not only to Paul
himself but also **in some measure** to the whole church. For this
he had been disciplined by the church—**the majority** might
imply that there was a minority which held out either for a more
severe or less severe **punishment**, but should more probably be
interpreted of the general body of members (Gk *hoi pleiones*, RV
'the many', with which may be compared the Qumran designation
of the general assembly of the community; cf. also 4.15). Paul now
tells them that the offender has been punished enough, and that
the time has come for them **to forgive and comfort him**, and
reaffirm their **love for him**, lest he should **be overwhelmed by
excessive sorrow**. This offender has traditionally been identified
with the man whose expulsion is ordered in 1 C. 5.5, and who

like the offender here (verses 6f.), is there called 'such a one'. Tertullian knew of this identification as current in his day (*c.* A.D. 218), and refuted it fiercely (*De pudicitia* 13–15). His rigorist principles were outraged by the suggestion that a temporary spell of disciplinary treatment, followed by unreserved restoration to church fellowship, could be envisaged as an adequate penalty for incest; even so, some of his arguments against the identification are sufficiently objective to retain their validity. 'Deliverance to Satan for the destruction of the flesh' (1 C. 5.5) suggests something more drastic and permanent than temporary suspension from certain privileges of church membership which seems to be envisaged here. Paul might well be accused of 'lightness' or lack of seriousness (Gk *elaphria*, translated 'vacillating' in 1.17) if, after the solemn sentence of 1 C. 5.3–5, 13, he now recommended such a lenient course for the offender. It is better to regard the offender here as someone who had been foremost in the opposition to Paul— **not to me** (verse 5) means 'not only to me' or 'not primarily to me'.

9. If this was the offender's fault, Paul demanded sanctions against him in order to **test** the church's obedience to his apostolic authority (cf. the later allusion to the affair in 7.12; see also 10.6). Once this obedience had been shown, his purpose was achieved. There was now the danger that the church, in its revulsion and indignation (cf. 7.11), might proceed too far in its disciplinary measures against the offender. Whatever his offence, the man was now thoroughly penitent, and any continuance of the discipline might cause spiritual harm both to him and to the community at large.

10. I also forgive: this language suggests some injury done to Paul himself, which called for his personal forgiveness, in a way for which the situation of 1 C. 5 makes no provision (see note on 7.12). Paul, however, dismisses the personal aspect of the injury as hardly worth mentioning; his forgiveness is granted as a matter of course: **What I have forgiven, if I have forgiven anything, has been for your sake.** The man's behaviour was more of an embarrassment to the Corinthian church than it was to Paul: they felt that they were all somehow involved in the breach of hospitality and courtesy to their apostle and 'father in Christ' which such behaviour occasioned, and so they found it more difficult to **forgive** him than Paul did.

in the presence of Christ: perhaps in the light of the forgiveness which they had all received through Christ (cf. Col. 3.13; Eph. 4.32).

11. to keep Satan from gaining the advantage over us: any undue prolongation of the discipline would have led to division and tension in the community which **Satan**, the author of strife, could exploit to its undoing. Satan is not here, as in 1 C. 5.5, the executor of divine judgment, but the sower of discord among brethren.

we are not ignorant of his designs: Gk *noēmata*, a word which in *NT* is found only in Paul's writings, and (except in Phil. 4.7, where it is rendered 'minds') always with some adverse implication (cf. 3.14; 4.4; 10.5; 11.3). Cf. Eph. 6.11, 'the wiles (Gk *methodiai*) of the devil'.

PAUL'S UNREST AFTER SENDING THE TEARFUL LETTER 2.12-13

It is not difficult to reconstruct the general course of events surrounding Paul's arrival in Troas (see p. 165). Shortly before his departure for Troas he had sent Titus to Corinth with the tearful letter (cf. 7.5-16). His mind was so agitated by his concern for his Corinthian friends and his anxiety about their response to his letter that he could not settle down to missionary activity in Troas, despite the wide open opportunities for such activity that presented themselves there. But the transition from verses 11 to 12 is abrupt: perhaps he implies that his experience in Troas provided him with a notable instance of Satan's 'designs', in exploiting his unhappiness over Corinth to hinder the advance of the gospel in Troas.

12. When I came to Troas: Alexandria Troas, a seaport a little way south on the Asian side of the Aegean entrance to the Dardanelles (cf. Ac. 16.8, 11), founded by Antigonus and Lysimachus about 300 B.C. and more recently reconstituted as a Roman colony by Augustus. Even if Paul was inhibited in his evangelization of the place at this time, Ac. 20.6ff. indicates the presence of a church there not long afterwards. T. W. Manson suggests that the definite article here (Gk *eis tēn Trōada*) points to the district (the Troad) rather than to the seaport of Troas alone (*Studies in the Gospels and Epistles* (1962), p. 216; so, earlier, W. Kelly, Commentary, *ad loc.*). (But in Ac. 20.6 the same phrase, with the article, refers unambiguously to the seaport.)

a door was opened: cf. 1 C. 16.9 for the same figure.

13. my mind could not rest: when he resumes and continues his narrative in 7.5 he does not say **my mind**—lit. 'my spirit' (Gk *pneuma*)—but 'our (i.e. my) flesh' (Gk *sarx*), RSV 'our bodies'. In both places the language denotes the absence of inner tranquillity, but the variation in wording shows that lines between Paul's psychological terms should not be too sharply drawn.

I did not find my brother Titus there: on his way back to Paul with news of the Corinthian situation.

I took leave of them and went on into Macedonia: perhaps he waited at Troas until he was sure that navigation had ceased for the winter and there was now no chance of Titus's arriving by sea from Greece. For his own part, he could not risk setting sail from Troas to Piraeus or Cenchreae in case Titus came some other way (cf. W. L. Knox, *St. Paul and the Church of the Gentiles* (1939), p. 144).

Paul's narrative breaks off here and is taken up at 7.5. This need not imply that 2.14–7.4 is an interpolation editorially inserted from another Pauline letter (7.5, with its transitional *kai gar*, 'for even', follows on immediately from 7.4, not from 2.13); 2.14–7.4 is a lengthy digression on Paul's part, caused by the contrast between the agitation of mind which he has just described and his present sense of relief and rejoicing.

THE APOSTOLIC MINISTRY 2.14–7.1

THE TRIUMPHAL PROGRESS OF THE GOSPEL 2.14–17

14. The present joy which has expelled his recent anxiety finds expression in a paean of thanksgiving **to God, who in Christ always leads us in triumph:** the apostles are joyful participants in their commander's triumphal procession, not (like the disarmed principalities and powers of Col. 2.15) the unwilling captives driven before his car.

the fragrance of the knowledge of him: there may be an allusion to the perfumes sprinkled along the triumphal way. Here **the fragrance** (Gk *osmē*) is **the knowledge of** God spread abroad by the apostles in the gospel: Christ himself is the embodiment of that **knowledge.** The figurative language used in various rabbinical documents of the Torah is here used of Christ: he, not the Torah, is 'the embodiment of knowledge and truth' (Rom.

2.20; cf. Col. 2.3) and the life-giving remedy against sin and death
(see T. W. Manson, '2 Cor. 2.14–17; Suggestions towards an
exegesis', in *Studia Paulina in honorem J. de Zwaan*, ed. J. N
Sevenster and W. C. van Unnik (1953), pp. 155ff., where extended
medicinal and pharmacological meanings of *osmē* are brought into
play).

15–16. If Christ, proclaimed in the gospel, is 'the fragrance of
the knowledge' of God, the apostles, as heralds of the gospel
share his fragrance and are thus **the aroma** (Gk *euōdia*) **of Christ
to God.** The perfumes which strewed the path of a triumphal
procession increased the joy of the participants but for those
captives who were to be executed at the end of the procession they
were **a fragrance from death to death** (for this characteristic
ally Pauline formation cf. 3.18; Rom. 1.17). So the knowledge of
God proclaimed in the gospel is a message **from life to life**
(telling of life and leading to life; cf. Rom. 6.22f.) for those who
respond to it in faith and are thus on the way to salvation (cf. 1 C
1.18), but a message **from death to death** (deadly in nature and
effect; cf. *NEB*: 'a deadly fume that kills') for those who impeni
tently refuse to believe it and are thus on the way to perdition
(**those who are perishing**, as in 4.3; 1 C. 1.18). Similar language
is used of the Torah in *Deut. Rabba* i.6, *TB Šabbaṭ* 88*b*, *Yômâ* 72.
and elsewhere, where it is said to be an elixir of life for Israel, or
for those who treat it worthily, but a deadly poison for the nation
of the world, or for those who treat it unworthily (where 'elixir' and
'poison' are renderings of the one Hebrew or Aramaic substantive
sam, which, like Gk *osmē*, may variously mean 'perfume', 'spice'
'drug', etc., as the context requires). It is not in their own right
that the apostles have this 'aromatic' quality, but as those who
spread abroad the 'fragrance' of Christ (or, in language used
elsewhere in the epistle, proclaim the gospel, or show forth the
light of God's glory, or convey the message of reconciliation). It
stands to reason that none could be **sufficient for these things**
(cf. 3.5f.) apart from a special endowment of spiritual grace.

17. We are not . . . peddlers of God's word: the gospel had
been entrusted to Paul and his fellow-apostles as a sacred steward
ship; they were not to treat it as **peddlers** or hucksters (Gk
kapēleuontes), who were commonly suspected of adulterating the
goods they handled with a view to increasing their own profit
The phrase used here has thus practically the same sense as 'to

tamper with God's word' (4.2). It is part of the apostles' commission **as men of sincerity** to ensure that 'the divinely ordained remedy for sin is offered pure and unadulterated to those for whom it is intended' (T. W. Manson in *Studia Paulina*, p. 161), to deliver the gospel as they themselves received it from God, speaking as in his presence and as the representatives of Christ (cf. 5.20). As in Gal. 1.11ff., Paul concentrates here on his receiving the gospel and his commission to preach it directly from God (see note on 1 C. 15.3).

THE MINISTRY OF THE NEW COVENANT 3.1-18

Paul's credentials 3.1-3

3.1. Are we beginning to commend ourselves again?: as in 1 C. 2-4 (cf. also Paul's sustained and impassioned apologia in 2 C. 10-12, with special reference to 12.19).
letters of recommendation: Gk *systatikai epistolai*, 'letters establishing' the bearer's identity and credentials, such as were probably carried by emissaries from the Jerusalem church to the Christian communities in Corinth and elsewhere, as they were carried by delegates from the Jewish authorities in Judaea to synagogues in the 'Dispersion' (cf. Ac. 9.2; 22.5; also Ac. 18.27; Rom. 16.1).

2. Paul's ministry is certificate enough of his apostolic authority, especially in a church like that of Corinth, which owed its existence to his ministry. Such a church was for him a living **letter of recommendation, written** (he says) **on your hearts:** *RSV* is probably right in preferring **your** (*hymōn*, the reading of Aleph 33 and a few other manuscripts) to 'our' (so *AV, RV, NEB*, rendering *hēmōn*), the majority reading. The change which the gospel had effected in their **hearts** was manifested in their lives, so as **to be known and read by all men.**

3. The metaphor is developed further: the Corinthian church is a letter of which Christ is the author; Paul is either the messenger by whom it was **delivered** (Gk *diakonētheisa*, 'ministered' or 'administered') or perhaps the amanuensis who took it down; it was **written not with ink but with the Spirit of the living God.** This contrast between **ink** and **Spirit** reminds Paul of the contrast between the old covenant and the new, but in view of the material on which the Decalogue, the old covenant code, was engraved, he thinks not of parchment or papyrus (which would have been suitable for **ink**) but of **tablets of stone** as contrasted with **tablets of human hearts** (lit. 'tablets, hearts of flesh') on which the terms of the new covenant are inscribed. This language echoes Jer. 31.33, where under the new covenant Yahweh will write his law on his people's hearts, and Ezek. 11.19; 36.26, where he promises to give them 'a heart of flesh' in place of their 'stony heart'.

Letter and Spirit 3.4–6

4. Such is the confidence that we have: confidence in the validity of his apostolic commission, confirmed by the inception and growth of the church of Corinth.

5–6. our sufficiency is from God: the repetition of **sufficient** (Gk *hikanos*), **sufficiency** (*hikanotēs*) and **qualified**, i.e. 'made sufficient' (*hikanōsen*), may reflect the occasional use of *hikanos* in LXX as one of the renderings of *šadday* ('Almighty'). (Cf. Col. 1.12; and see C. H. Dodd, *The Bible and the Greeks* (1935), pp. 15f.) The apostolic commission carries divine enabling with it, making Paul and his colleagues effective **ministers of a new covenant.** The gospel **covenant** is **new** (cf. 1 C. 11.25) by contrast with the covenant established between Yahweh and Israel at the foot of Sinai (Exod. 24.3–8); that was based on **a written code**, 'the book of the covenant' (Exod. 24.7), but this is fulfilled **in the Spirit** (cf. Rom. 8.3f., where the 'just requirement of the law' which the old order was powerless to translate into action, is 'fulfilled in us, who walk not according to the flesh but according to the Spirit').

the written code (lit. 'the letter', Gk *gramma*) **kills:** it pronounces the death-sentence on the law-breaker, and since it does not impart the power to keep the law, everyone under the old covenant is liable to that sentence (cf. Dt. 30.17f.; Gal. 3.10, quoting Dt. 27.26; Rom. 7.5, 9–11). This attitude differs radically from the rabbinical statement that 'while Israel stood below engraving idols to provoke their Creator to anger . . ., God sat on high engraving tablets which would give them life' (*Exod. Rabba* xli.1 on Exod. 31.18).

the Spirit gives life: the Spirit of God is the very principle of life in the old creation (cf. Ps. 104.30) and in the new (Ezek. 37.5f., 9f., 14), and those who 'serve not under the old written code but in the new life of the Spirit' (Rom. 7.6) are set 'free from the law of sin and death' (Rom. 8.2; cf. Rom. 8.10f.; 1 C. 15.45b). It is by the Spirit that the new covenant, established by the sacrifice of Christ (1 C. 11.25), becomes effective in the lives of his people.

The fading glory of the old covenant and the surpassing glory of the new
3.7–18

7–8. Paul now presents a commentary or *midrash* on Exod. 34.29–35, in order to establish that the proclamation of the gospel (to which he was called) is attended by even greater glory than the giving of the law. When Moses came down from Sinai with the tablets of the law, his face shone because he had been talking with God face to face, so much so **that the Israelites could not look** (Gk *atenisai*, 'look steadfastly', *RV*) **at** his **face because of its brightness** (cf. Philo, *Life of Moses* ii.70). (*RSV* in this section uses 'splendour', 'brightness' and 'glory' to render the one Gk word *doxa*.) Yet the law which Moses brought was **the dispensation** (*diakonia*, ministry) **of death**, and it was a **fading** glory which radiated from his face; it might reasonably be concluded, then, that the ministry of life, **the dispensation of the Spirit**, with which the apostles were entrusted, would **be attended with greater splendour**, with unfading glory. The **fading** of the glory on Moses' face is inferred from Exod. 34.33f., which is interpreted here as meaning that his face was 're-charged' with glory every time he went into the presence of Yahweh in the 'tent of meeting'. Paul follows LXX, which says that Moses' face was 'glorified' (*dedoxasmenon*, translated 'had splendour' in verse 10 below); the Hebrew text says that it emitted rays or beams, using the verb *qāran*, from the same root as *qeren* ('horn'), whence, through the Latin Vulgate, which says that his face was *cornuta* (lit. 'horned'), Moses was traditionally pictured as sprouting horns from his brow (as in Michelangelo's statue).

9. The law is **the dispensation of condemnation**, because it condemns the law-breaker; the gospel is **the dispensation of righteousness**, because it proclaims 'the righteousness (justifying action) of God through faith in Jesus Christ for all who believe' (Rom. 3.22; cf. 1 C. 1.30; 2 C. 5.21).

10–11. The glory that attended the giving of the law under the old covenant, splendid as it was, is so outshone by the glory which invests the gospel that it pales into insignificance and loses its

splendour; but the surpassing **splendour** of the new covenant is **permanent** and can never be outshone.

12. such a hope: the hope springing from assurance of the unfading glory of the gospel which Paul and his fellow-apostles were commissioned to proclaim.

we are very bold: lit. 'we use great boldness (frankness)'. Gk *parrhēsia* (cf. 7.4), originally 'freedom of speech', came to include within its range of meaning not only 'boldness' and 'frankness' but also 'freedom of access' (cf. Heb. 10.19), such as Moses exercised when he entered Yahweh's presence 'with unveiled face' (see note on verse 18). On *parrhēsia* in *NT* see W. C. van Unnik, 'The Christian's Freedom of Speech', *BJRL* 44 (1961–2), pp. 466ff.

13. The statement of Exod. 34.33 that Moses **put a veil** (mask) **over his face** (the imperfect tense indicates that this was his habitual practice) is taken to mean, not that he thus made it possible for the Israelites to look at him without being dazzled, but that he wished to prevent them from seeing that the brightness on his face was fading.

14-15. The Israelites' inability to see the glory shining from Moses' face, fading though that glory was, is treated as a parable of their descendants' present inability to realize the transitory character of the Mosaic order and to recognize the unfading glory of the gospel dispensation.

their minds were hardened (rendered insensitive): both then, in the wilderness (cf. Dt. 32.5, 15–18; Pss. 78.7f., 17–20, 32ff.; 106.13ff. for the sense, if not the wording), and **to this day** (an echo of Dt. 29.4, used in Rom. 11.8 as a *testimonium* of Israel's 'hardening'). The same verb *pōroō* ('harden') and its derivate *pōrōsis* ('hardening') are used in Rom. 11.7, 25, of the temporary 'hardening' which 'has come upon part of Israel', impeding their acceptance of the gospel.

when they read the old covenant: that the Mosaic covenant is **old** is implied by Jeremiah's announcement of a 'new' one (cf. Heb. 8.13). This might be regarded as by far the earliest instance of the use of Gk *palaia diathēkē* in the sense of 'Old Testament' (i.e. the Hebrew scriptures), but probably the reference is more particularly to the Torah; cf. the parallel clause in verse 15, **whenever Moses is read.** When the Torah is read in synagogue, they cannot see that the order of which it speaks is a temporary one, which has now been superseded by Christ. The **veil** which covered

Moses' face—**that same veil**—is in this application transferred
to the **minds** of the Jews; because of it they cannot apprehend the
truth. This is another theme which has influenced Christian art, as
in the sculptured portrayal of the blindfolded synagogue alongside
the clearly-seeing church in Strasbourg and Rochester Cathedrals.

16. when a man turns to the Lord the veil is removed: a
general principle extracted from Exod. 34.34, 'whenever Moses
went in before the LORD to speak with him, he took the veil off',
and parallel to 'only through Christ is it taken away' (verse 14).

17. Now the Lord is the Spirit: this should probably be
understood as Paul's exegesis of Exod. 34.34; **the Lord** in that
text means **the Spirit.** Paul elsewhere distinguishes between **the
Lord** (i.e. Christ) and **the Spirit** (cf. 1 C. 12.4f.; 2 C. 13.14), but
dynamically they are one, since it is by the Spirit that the life of
the risen Lord is imparted to believers and maintained within
them (cf. Rom. 8.9–11; see also note on 1 C. 15.45b).
where the Spirit of the Lord is, there is freedom: Gk *eleutheria*,
used here with little distinction from *parrhēsia* (verse 12). Cf. Rom.
8.15, 'you did not receive the spirit of slavery to fall back into fear',
which implies that the Spirit of sonship, which they did receive, is
the Spirit of freedom (cf. also Rom. 8.2).

18. we all: all Christians, not apostles only.
with unveiled face: by contrast with Israel, but Paul may also
have in mind the Semitic idiom in which 'to uncover the face
(head)' means 'to behave boldly (frankly)'. If so, then **with
unveiled face** has practically the same meaning as 'with boldness'
(Gk *parrhēsia*) and may help to explain Paul's use of the latter
expression in verse 12. See W. C. van Unnik, *Die semitische
Achtergrond van ΠΑΡΡΗΣΙΑ in het Nieuwe Testament* (1962); 'With
Unveiled Face', *NovT* 6 (1963), pp. 153ff.
beholding: Gk *katoptrizomenoi*, 'beholding as in a mirror' (Gk
katoptron, synonymous with *esoptron* in 1 C. 13.12; see note *ad loc.*)
or possibly 'reflecting as a mirror does'; the verb in the middle
voice regularly bears the former sense but the following context
indicates that the latter sense (attested for the active voice) is also
present here. As Moses reflected the divine glory to which he was
exposed, so Christians, **beholding** the surpassing glory which
shines in the gospel, which is nothing less than **the glory of the
Lord** himself, reflect that glory, **being changed into his likeness:**
lit. '(into) the same image' (*eikōn*; cf. 4.4). The verb *metamorphoō*

G

(in the passive, as here) is used in Rom. 12.2 of the transformation wrought by the gospel in the lives of believers by the renewal of their minds; in Mk 9.2 (Mt. 17.2) it is used of the transfiguration of Jesus.

from one degree of glory to another: lit. 'from glory to glory', a Pauline turn of phrase (cf. 2.16). J. Héring suggests that 'from glory' indicates the source of the transformation (**the glory of the Lord**) and 'to glory' its result ('to be manifested only at the time of the resurrection').

This transformation is being wrought within at present by **the Lord who is the Spirit**: lit. 'from (the) Lord (the) Spirit', a reference to the first sentence in verse 17 (although apart from this context Gk *apo kyriou pneumatos* might be rendered 'from the Spirit of the Lord'). It is a curiosity of exegesis that finds in verses 17f. a gnostic gloss (see also note on 5.16) which originally ran: 'Now the Lord is the Spirit, and where the Spirit of the Lord (i.e. the Spirit who is the Lord) is, there is freedom, as from the Lord who is the Spirit' (W. Schmithals, *Die Gnosis in Korinth* (1965²), pp. 299ff.).

THE HARDSHIP AND GLORY OF APOSTOLIC SERVICE 4.1–5.10

Paul's Source of Encouragement 4.1

4.1. having this ministry: the ministry of the new covenant (3.6).

by the mercy of God: lit. 'as we have received mercy' (cf. 1 Tim. 1.13, 16); the clause may be construed either with the preceding words (so *RSV*) or with those immediately following.

we do not lose heart: the plural **we** throughout this chapter, unlike 'we all' in 3.18, means 'we apostles' (cf. 1 C. 4.9), and more especially denotes Paul himself. So glorious is the commission he has received that it outweighs in his estimation all the distressing experiences which he has to undergo in discharging it; they might well make any one **lose heart**, but the dignity of his ministry and the assurance that its success and his own ultimate triumph depend on God's power, not on his, fill him with hope that eclipses everything that might otherwise drive him to despair. The train of thought begun in verse 1 is taken up again in verse 16; meanwhile he turns aside to say more about his ministry and what is involved in fulfilling it.

The Divine Treasure and the Earthen Vessels **4.2-15**

2. There is no 'veil' in the new covenant, as there was in the old: everything is open and above board where the gospel is concerned, and everything must be open and above board where its preachers are concerned. Paul denies that he stoops to use methods unworthy of his message—such methods as some religious propagandists of his day did not scruple to employ; cf. 1.12, and the similar disclaimer in 1 Th. 2.3-7, 10.

we refuse to . . . tamper with God's word: see note on 2.17; here the verb is *doloō*, 'handle deceitfully' (*AV, RV*). He does not falsify or water down the message with which he has been entrusted. **by the open statement of the truth:** no veil of concealment obscures the gospel (cf. 3.14f.) as he proclaims it: he endeavours to deliver it faithfully as he had received it and so to **commend** himself (cf. 3.1) **to every man's conscience in the sight of God,** over and above his care to maintain the testimony of his own conscience (1.12).

3-4. even if our gospel is veiled: in spite of his claim to state the truth openly, some of Paul's critics maintained that his message was obscure in that it lacked the perspicuity of true revelation, and that he himself lacked the openness of a true messenger of God. Among certain people, he concedes, the message is indeed a **veiled** one, in the sense that 'a veil lies over their minds' (3.15) and prevents them from appreciating its truth; but they are **those who are perishing** or 'on their way to perdition' (cf. 2.15; 1 C. 1.18); they are **the unbelievers,** whose **minds** (Gk *noēmata*; see note on 2.11) have been **blinded** by **the god of this world** or 'age' (Gk *aiōn*). This is a reference to Satan, called 'the ruler (*archōn*) of this world (*kosmos*)' in Jn 12.31; 14.30; 16.11 (cf. 1 Jn 5.19b). Because 'this age' is dominated by him, it is 'the present evil age' (Gal. 1.4; cf. 'the epoch of Belial' in the Qumran texts), but believers already enjoy through the Spirit the life of the world to come and **the god of this world** has no power to blind their minds.

Those **minds** which he has **blinded** are thus prevented **from seeing the light of the gospel of the glory of Christ:** Gk *augazō*, when transitive (as here), means 'see'; the Byzantine text makes it intransitive by adding *autois* ('to them'), hence *AV* 'shine unto them'. The genitival phrase **of the glory** is not merely

equivalent to the adjective 'glorious' qualifying **gospel** (as in
AV); **the glory of Christ** (cf. 'the glory of the Lord', 3.18) is
unfolded in **the gospel. Christ**, in turn, **is the likeness** (Gk
eikōn, 'image') **of God** (cf. Col. 1.15): 'perhaps the concept
"image of God" provided Paul with a thought-form with which
he elucidated the eternal relation of the Father to the Son'
(A. Schlatter, *Theologie des Neuen Testaments* ii (1910), p. 299). There
is, moreover, a link with Gen. 1.26f.; if man was created 'in the
image of God', then Christ, being himself **the image of God**, is
the archetype of man, and those who (in the words of 3.18),
'beholding the glory of the Lord, are being changed into his likeness (image)', are being conformed anew to that archetype and
experiencing the Creator's purpose in bringing man into being
(cf. Col. 3.10). That the creation narrative was in Paul's mind is
further evident from verse 6. Cf. J. Jervell, *Imago Dei* (1960),
pp. 173ff.

5. For what we preach is . . . Jesus Christ as Lord: the
conjunction **for** indicates that the sentence introduced by it
explains or reasserts the implication of the phrase 'the gospel of
the glory of Christ'; it is he, proclaimed **as Lord**, who is the
subject-matter of the message, and **not ourselves.** The herald does
not draw attention to himself or devise his own proclamation; so
the apostles are their hearers' **servants for Jesus' sake:** for the
word *doulos* used in this way cf. 1 C. 9.19.

6. The gospel light mentioned in verse 4 is as much the creation
of God as was the **light** which he called into existence in the
beginning. **'Let light shine out of darkness'** is a paraphrase
of Gen. 1.3, 'Let there be light', incorporating the contextual
reference to 'darkness' (Gen. 1.2, 4f.). The same Creator **has
shone in** the **hearts** of believers to illuminate them with **the
knowledge of** his **glory . . . in the face of Christ**: a presentation, perhaps, of Christ as Divine Wisdom (cf. Wis. 7.25f., where
Wisdom is 'a pure emanation of the glory of the Almighty;
. . . a reflection of eternal light, a spotless mirror of the working
of God, and an image of his goodness'), but more certainly a
reminiscence of Paul's conversion experience, when 'the glory of
that light' from heaven which outshone the sun (Ac. 22.11, *RV*;
26.13) blinded his eyes to everything else. Nor can we overlook
the contrast between the fading glory on Moses' face (3.7ff.) and
the permanent and unveiled glory **in the face of Christ**.

7. we have this treasure: the 'light of the knowledge of the glory of God' displayed in the gospel.

in earthen vessels (Gk *en ostrakinois skeuesin*): the apostles themselves. They were expendable, but the **treasure** was of indestructible worth. It has been suggested that Paul thinks of Gideon's torches concealed in jars, whch were broken when the moment came to show the light (Jg. 7.19f.); this is possible, but doubtful. The pottery lamps which could be bought for a copper or two in the Corinthian market-place provided a sufficient analogy: it did not matter how cheap or fragile they were so long as they showed the light. The worthlessness of the **vessels** is evidence that **the transcendent power** which attends the preaching of the gospel, the change which it effects in human lives, is God's and not the apostles'.

8–11. No one troubles to handle a cheap piece of earthenware with specially tender care. The worthlessness and fragility of the vessels, the weakness and insignificance of the apostles, is emphasized in verses 8 and 9 in language reminiscent of 1 C. 4.9–13, but here a contrast is drawn between the apostles' sufferings (cf. 1.8–10) and their preservation, the wretchedness of their lot viewed by wordly standards and their triumph by the mercy of God, culminating in the contrast between their **always carrying in the body the death** (Gk *nekrōsis*, 'putting to death') **of Jesus** and the purpose and consequence of their doing so: **that the life of Jesus may also be manifested in our bodies.** The use of *nekrōsis* ('dying') instead of *thanatos* ('death') indicates that what is in view here is not identification with the death of Christ in baptism but that daily exposure to danger and death for his sake which constitutes their sharing in his sufferings (cf. 1.5f.; 1 C. 15.31; Phil. 3.10; see R. C. Tannehill, *Dying and Rising with Christ* (1967), pp. 85ff.). This might be regarded as Paul's counterpart to Jesus' words about taking up one's cross and following him. But while the mortality of the fragile body was an experience constantly present, the life-giving Spirit within was the guarantee of sharing in Jesus' resurrection life and enabled them to manifest the power of his risen life in their **mortal flesh** here and now (cf. 5.5; Rom. 8.10f.). Verse 11 elucidates verse 10 by repeating its thought in slightly different language. The two verses together convey with exceptional power and poignancy Paul's conception of his apostolic existence (cf. also 12.9f.).

12. These experiences are the lot of Christians in general, but Paul accepts more than his fair share of affliction for Christ's sake so that, while **death is at work** in him, **life** may be their portion (see note on 1.4–7).

13–14. Applying to himself the language of Ps. 116.10 (115.1, LXX; MT bears a different meaning: 'I kept my faith, even when I said . . .'), Paul affirms that he speaks with the **spirit of faith** when he contemplates the certainty of resurrection. As in 1 C. 6.14 (see note *ad loc.*), God's raising of Christ from the dead is to him the proof that he too will be raised **with Jesus** (cf. 1 Th. 4.14, 'through Jesus, . . . with him') and brought, together with his converts, **into the presence** of Christ (cf. 11.2) or of God (cf. 1 C. 8.8)—i.e. at the parousia.

15. it is all for your sake: a repetition of the note of verse 12. The remainder of the sentence raises questions of grammar and construction. (Cf. B. Noack, 'A Note on II Cor. iv. 15', *Studia Theologica* 17 (1963), pp. 129ff.) One literal rendering would be: 'in order that grace, having abounded (cf. Rom. 5.20), may because of the thanksgiving of the many (*dia tōn pleionōn tēn eucharistian*) overflow to the glory of God'. That is to say, **more and more people**, hearing of the **grace** granted so abundantly to Paul in all his afflictions, will thank God for this and so it will redound **to the glory of God.** But *RSV* takes *perisseusē*, aorist subjunctive of *perisseuō* (translated 'may overflow' in the literal rendering offered above), as transitive (**may increase**) with **the thanksgiving** (*tēn eucharistian*) as its object; *dia* then governs the genitive *tōn pleionōn* in a prepositional phrase (lit. 'through the many'; cf. 2.6) which may be attached either (as in *RSV*) to the preceding clause (**as grace extends**) or to the following clause (**may increase thanksgiving**)—and a consideration of the expression of a very similar thought in 9.11f. suggests that the latter is more probable: thanksgiving to God for the grace shown to Paul increases 'through the many' as they (**more and more people**) get to hear of it. That man's gratitude is the proper response to God's grace is a biblical commonplace: 'in the New Testament, religion is grace, and ethics is gratitude' (R. N. Flew *Jesus and his Way* (1963), p. 13, quoting *Letters of Thomas Erskine* p. 16). Cf. also 1.11.

Momentary Affliction and Eternal Glory **4.16–18**

16. we do not lose heart: resuming the course of thought begun in verse 1. While the afflictions endured for the gospel's sake may cause Paul's **outer nature** (lit. 'outer man') to waste away, the life-giving Spirit who dwells within him renews his 'inner man' day by day. This 'inner man' (cf. Eph. 3.16) is the 'new creation' of 5.17 (cf. Col. 3.10), which will be consummated in the immortal nature to be put on at the resurrection (see notes on 5.1ff.). Therefore he does not allow his troubles and infirmities to 'get on top' of him. His spiritual resilience might amaze onlookers, but they could not see the inner resources which supplied him with constant sustenance and refreshment.

17. In the light of this, he can view his suffering in its true perspective and refer to it as **this slight momentary affliction** (lit. 'the present lightness of affliction'). This characterization of what he had to endure should be compared with the catalogue of his hardships in 11.23–27. It is in comparison with **the eternal weight of glory** that lies in store for him that all these hardships appear as **this slight momentary affliction.** His choice of the expression **the weight of glory** may be influenced by the fact that in Hebrew **weight** and **glory** come from the same root *kbd*. It is because the coming **glory** is so 'weighty' that the present **affliction** seems so **slight** (Gk *elaphron*, 'light'), just as the eternity of the coming **glory** makes the **affliction** seem **moment-ary.** It is not simply that the **glory** is the compensation for the **affliction**—true, 'the sufferings of this present time are not worth comparing with the glory that is to be revealed to us' (Rom. 8.18)—rather, the **glory** is the product of the **affliction,** produced in measure **beyond all comparison** (Gk *kath' hyperbolēn eis hyperbolēn,* itself a hyperbolic phrase, 'more and more exceedingly'). Cf. Rom. 8.17, 'provided we suffer with him in order that we may also be glorified with him'; but the relation between the suffering and the glory is stated more clearly here.

18. The contrast between the visible order, which is **transient,** and the invisible, which is **eternal,** is a familiar theme in Plato and his followers, but parallels which may be adduced from their writings to Paul's present affirmation are more formal than material. His hardships, and the 'outer man' that wastes away because of them, belong to the **transient** realm of **the things**

that are seen: but he turns his attention away from them to concentrate on the **eternal** realm of **the things that are unseen**, to which his 'inner man' belongs and where his hope of glory is secure (cf. Col. 1.27; 3.1–4).

The Christian's Sure Hope 5.1–10

This passage has given rise to a wealth of variant interpretation which cannot be discussed adequately in the space available here. It represents a further stage in Paul's thinking about the resurrection life as compared with his treatment in 1 C. 15. But now Paul makes no appeal to a 'word of the Lord' as in 1 Th. 4.15, nor does he claim to be imparting a 'mystery' or fresh revelation as in 1 C. 15.51f. In these earlier letters he had reckoned with the probability, or at least the possibility, that he would be among those who would still be alive on earth at the parousia and be 'changed' without dying (1 Th. 4.15, 17; 1 C. 15.51ff.; but see note on 1 C. 6.14); now his recent encounter with what seemed certain death (1.8ff.) and his constant exposure to the risk of death (4.10–12) have brought about a change in his perspective—a change which the passage of time would in any case have occasioned —and he thinks in terms of dying before the parousia. But if he does, what will be the mode of his existence between death and resurrection? Must he endure some kind of disembodied state in the interval? To some people of a different tradition (see note on 1 C. 15.12) disengagement from the shackle of the body was something infinitely desirable, but while Paul longed to be delivered from the present mortal body it was in order that he might exchange it for one that was immortal: to be without a body of any kind would be a form of spiritual nakedness from which his mind shrank. He had no special revelation to help him with this problem, but he tackles it in the light of what he already knows, both from revelation and from experience. The resurrection principle he sees to be already at work in the people of Christ, by grace of the indwelling Spirit; in some sense the spiritual body of the life to come is already being formed, as the inner man undergoes daily renewal, so that physical death will mean no hiatus of disembodiment but the immediate enjoyment of being 'at home with the Lord'.

In addition to the exposition of these verses in the standard commentaries, important studies of them appear in the following

places: H. A. A. Kennedy, *St. Paul's Conception of the Last Things*
(1904), pp. 262ff.; G. Vos, *The Pauline Eschatology* (1930), pp.
185ff.; A. Oepke in *TWNT* 1, 1933 (E.T. 1964), *s.v. γυμνός*;
W. L. Knox, *St. Paul and the Church of the Gentiles* (1939), pp.
128ff.; J. Lowe, 'An Examination of Attempts to detect Development in St. Paul's Theology', *JTS* 42 (1941), pp. 129ff.; W. D.
Davies, *Paul and Rabbinic Judaism* (1948), pp. 310ff.; R. Bultmann,
Theology of the NT 1, E.T. (1952), pp. 201f.; J. A. T. Robinson,
The Body (1952), pp. 75ff.; J. N. Sevenster, 'Some Remarks on the
γυμνός in II Cor. v. 3', in *Studia Paulina in honorem J. de Zwaan*,
ed. J. N. Sevenster and W. C. van Unnik (1953), pp. 202ff., and
'Einige Bemerkungen über den "Zwischenzustand" bei Paulus',
NTS 1 (1954–5), pp. 291ff.; E. Best, *One Body in Christ* (1955),
pp. 161, 219; A. Feuillet, 'La demeure céleste et la destinée des
chrétiens', *Recherches de Science religieuse* 44 (1956), pp. 161ff.,
360ff.; R. F. Hettlinger, '2 Corinthians 5.1–10', *SJT* 10 (1957),
pp. 174ff.; O. Cullmann, *Immortality of the Soul or Resurrection of the
Dead?* (1958), pp. 52ff.; E. E. Ellis, 'II Corinthians v. 1–10 in
Pauline Eschatology', *NTS* 6 (1959–60), pp. 211ff. (reprinted in
Paul and his Recent Interpreters (1961), pp. 35ff.); R. Berry, 'Death
and Life in Christ', *SJT* 14 (1961), pp. 60ff.; M. E. Thrall, *Greek
Particles in the NT* (1962), pp. 82ff.; D. E. H. Whiteley, *The
Theology of St. Paul* (1964), pp. 248ff.; C. F. D. Moule, 'The
Influence of Circumstances on the Use of Eschatological Terms',
JTS, n.s. 15 (1964), pp. 1ff. (esp. pp. 11f.), and 'St Paul and
Dualism: the Pauline Conception of Resurrection', *NTS* 12
(1965–6), pp. 106ff.; F. W. Danker, 'Consolation in 2 Cor. 5:
1–10', *Concordia Theological Monthly* 39 (1968), pp. 552ff.

5.1. we know: the confidence thus expressed is his own, but it
is a confidence which all believers can share.
the earthly tent we live in: lit. 'our earthly house of tent
(bivouac)'; the latter noun (Gk *skēnos*) is probably used to
emphasize the temporary character of this dwelling, by contrast
with the **house . . . eternal in the heavens.** The **earthly tent**
(cf. 'this earthy tent' in Wis. 9.15) is practically identical with the
'outer nature' of 4.16 or the 'physical body' of 1 C. 15.44. When
the time comes for it to be **destroyed** (or, if we carry on the
thought of a tent, 'taken down'), a more permanent **building**
awaits us. So sure is Paul of this that he says **we have** it; it is laid
up for us **in the heavens** because Christ, our life, is there (cf.

1 C. 15.20; Col. 3.1–4). It is **not made with hands** (Gk *acheiropoiētos*), an adjective used in *NT* to denote divine or heavenly workmanship (cf. Mk 14.58; Col. 2.11), as against 'hand-made' (*cheiropoiētos*), which denotes material structures or human workmanship (cf. Mk 14.58; Ac. 7.48; 17.24; Eph. 2.11; Heb. 9.11, 24); **a building from God** (originating with him) and **a house not made with hands** are thus synonymous expressions (for the 'spiritual body' of 1 C. 15.44). Some commentators see here the idea of integration into the body of Christ, but this is unsuitable to the context; moreover, the distinctively Pauline concept of the body of Christ (cf 1 C. 12.12–27) is not elsewhere related to the life to come, but to the present existence of the church 'militant here in earth'.

2. Here: lit. 'in this', which most versions take (rightly) to mean 'in this tent' (cf. verse 4); Gk *en toutō*, however, can bear the sense 'hereby', 'for this reason' (cf. Jn 16.30; 1 C. 4.4), and a possible (but less probable) meaning would be: 'It is for this reason that we groan, knowing that a heavenly abode awaits us and longing impatiently to receive it'.

we groan: under the hardships of the present life; the thought is amplified in verse 4, where the same Gk verb (*stenazomen*) is rendered in *RSV* 'we sigh' (cf. Rom. 8.23 for its use in a very similar context).

long to put on our heavenly dwelling: the Gk word is *oikētērion*, slightly different from *oikodomē* ('building') and *oikia* ('house') in verse 1, but synonymous with them; now, however, Paul oscillates between the figure of a building to dwell in and a garment **to put on.** The verb here is *ependysasthai*, which, if the force of the prefix *ep-* (*epi*) is stressed, would mean 'put on over' (so *NEB*; contrast the simpler *endysasthai* occurring twice in 1 C. 15.53). See note on verse 4.

3. so that: the Greek text has *ei ge kai* (Aleph C with the majority of MSS) or *eiper kai* (P[46] B D G and a few others), neither of which readings is properly rendered **so that.** The former is best translated 'on the assumption, of course, that . . .'; the latter (whose early attestation is impressive) 'if indeed' or 'since indeed'. Whichever be preferred, the clause is to be interpreted as a parenthesis, explaining why we 'long to put on our heavenly dwelling': it is 'on the assumption, of course, that (*or* since, indeed), having put it on, we shall **not be found naked**'.

by putting it on: Gk *endysamenoi* (aorist participle), catching up *ependysasthai* ('to put on') in verse 2, and therefore equivalent to it in sense. The prefix *epi*, which it lacks, can be understood from the antecedent verb, if it has special significance. For *endysamenoi* there is a mainly Western variant *ekdysamenoi* (attested by D* with Marcion, Tertullian, Chrysostom and the Old Latin, and implied by F G), 'having put off'. This would make the parenthesis mean 'on the assumption, of course, that, having put off (the present mortal body), we shall (nevertheless) not be found naked'; but there is no good reason to reject the better attested *endysamenoi*. The implication, in either case, is that we shrink from being **naked**—deprived of embodiment or 'housing' of any sort. The gnosticizing members of the Corinthian church might regard such 'nakedness' as desirable (cf. *Gospel of Thomas* 21; 37, where the stripping off of garments may be a figure for sloughing off the body); but for someone of Paul's outlook the body was an essential means of communication with the environment, and to lack a body of any kind would be to experience fearful isolation.

4. in this tent (Gk *skēnos*, as in verse 1): the phrase expands 'in this' (*RSV* 'here') of verse 2, and indeed verse 4 as a whole is an expansion of verse 2, recapitulating and amplifying its sense after the parenthesis of verse 3.

we sigh with anxiety: lit. 'we groan (*stenazomen*, as in verse 2), being weighed down' (cf. Wis. 9.15, 'a perishable body weighs down the soul'—a thought more Platonic than Pauline). The verb *bareō* ('weigh down') was used in the aorist passive in 1.8 (*RSV* 'we were . . . crushed'), and the reference here too may be to the burden of affliction which life in this mortal body involved. Under this burden the apostle might well **sigh** and long for the dismantling of the earthly tent, 'provided that' (the classical force of Gk *eph' hō*, represented simply by **that** in *RSV*) his desire was not for complete disembodiment but for investiture with the heavenly body once he was released from the mortal body and its burdens—**not that we would be unclothed** (*ekdysasthai*), **but that we would be further clothed** (*ependysasthai*). The adverb **further** conveys the force of *epi* in *ependysasthai*, 'put on over' (so *NEB* again); it almost suggests that the new body could be put on like an overcoat, above the clothes already being worn. So instantaneous is the changeover from the natural to the spiritual body—'in a moment, in the twinkling of an eye' (1 C. 15.52)—

that there will be no interval of conscious 'nakedness' between the one and the other.

so that what is mortal may be swallowed up by life: cf. 1 C. 15.53f. both for the verb 'swallow up' (*katapinō*) and for the idea of what is mortal putting on immortality. In 1 C. 15 this takes place at the parousia in those believers who are still alive then, while those who have died will rise in bodies which are not liable to corruption. But may it not be (Paul seems to imply here) that for those who do not live until the parousia the new body will be immediately available at death? He does not say that it will, presumably because he had received no clear revelation to this effect, but he approaches the brink of such a statement.

We cannot reconcile this fresh insight (if indeed it was in Paul's mind) with 1 C. 15.23, 51ff., by the supposition that he is thinking of a temporary integument for the intermediate state pending his investiture with the imperishable resurrection body; the 'dwelling' of which he speaks is 'eternal in the heavens' (verse 1), and it is doubtful if this dwelling can be envisaged even as an initial and 'temporary phase of the eternal body' (cf. D. E. H. Whiteley, *The Theology of St. Paul* (1964), p. 260). A more satisfactory reconciliation could be proposed, if the emphasis on instantaneous change (excluding any period of 'nakedness') were amplified by the suggestion that in the consciousness of the departed believer there is no interval between dissolution and investiture, however long the interval may be by the calendar of earth-bound human history. Paul does not make this suggestion, but it would be a legitimate extension of his thought.

5. He who has prepared us: lit. 'wrought us' (Gk *katergasamenos*).

this very thing: endowment with immortal bodies (cf. Phil. 3.21).

the Spirit as a guarantee: Gk *arrhabōn*, as in 1.22. The gift of **the Spirit** is an assurance both that this is God's purpose for his people and that the purpose will be fulfilled. Here and now this life-giving Spirit is progressively transforming them into the likeness of 'the glory of the Lord' and thus preparing them for the time when, invested with the 'spiritual body' (one which is totally animated by the Spirit), they will 'bear the image of the man of heaven' (1 C. 15.44–49; cf. Rom. 8.11).

6. So we are always of good courage: as opposed to 'losing

heart' (4.1, 16), because this hope of ours is fixed on 'the things
that are unseen' and is confirmed to us by the Spirit.

at home in the body: i.e. in this earthly body.

we are away from the Lord: not that there is no opportunity of
communion with him now (cf. 12.8f.); Paul is **away from the
Lord** now only in comparison with the 'face to face' vision to
which he looks forward 'then' (1 C. 13.12). Philo speaks of this
bodily life as a state of being away from home (Gk *apodēmia*; cf.
Paul's present use of *ekdēmeō*, 'to be away'), a 'sojourning as in a
foreign land' (*Who is the heir of divine things?* 82, 267), but by
contrast with liberation from the body, not with being 'at home
with the Lord' (verse 8).

7. for we walk by faith, not by sight: a parenthesis, making
it clear in what sense we are 'away from the Lord'—not absolutely,
but in the sense that at present our communion with him is maintained **by faith**, not experienced in unimpeded vision.

8. We are of good courage: resumed from verse 6 after the
parenthetic verse 7.

away from the body: i.e., again, from this earthly body.

at home with the Lord: clothed, presumably, with the heavenly
body, but Paul is no longer so much concerned with this as with
nearness to the Lord (the heavenly body is but the means by which
this nearness is made possible); cf. Phil. 1.21, 23, where 'to die is
gain' because for him 'to depart' means to 'be with Christ, for that
is far better'.

9. we make it our aim: 'we are ambitious' (Gk *philoti-
moumetha*).

to please him: now that we are **away** from him (in the sense of
verse 6) as we certainly shall be when we are **at home** with him
(in the sense of verse 8)—or perhaps, but less probably, whether
the day of judgment finds us still in mortal body on earth or
already **at home** with him in a state of glory.

**10. for we must all appear before the judgment seat of
Christ:** in 1 C. 4.1-5 Paul has stated that he is not concerned
about men's assessment of his faithfulness in discharging his
stewardship because 'it is the Lord who judges me'. He repeats the
same thought here, presenting this prospect as a motive for his
ambition to win the Lord's approval, and reminds his readers that
they, with him, **must all** be made manifest before Christ's tribunal
(Gk *bēma*); cf. Rom. 14.10, 'we shall all stand before the judgment

seat (*bēma*) of God'. The unity of the Father and the Son in judgment as in salvation is as axiomatic for Paul as it is for the Fourth Evangelist (Jn 5.22, 27; cf. also Ac. 17.31).

so that each one may receive as his due **good or evil:** praise (as in 1 C. 4.5) or blame; cf. Eph. 6.8; Col. 3.25.

in the body: lit. 'by means of (*dia*) the body'; this mortal body may belong to the transient order, but believers are accountable for its deeds; they are not morally indifferent (cf. Rom. 6.13, 19; 8.13; 1 C. 6.13ff.). Unbelievers too, of course, are liable to divine judgment (Rom. 2.5ff., 16), but it is with believers that Paul is concerned here.

THE MESSAGE OF RECONCILIATION 5.11–6.13

The Preachers' Motive 5.11–15

11. Paul returns to the subject of his apostolic ministry—a ministry which he discharges in **the fear of the Lord:** not in the slavish fear which is incompatible with the Spirit of freedom (3.17; Rom. 8.15) but **knowing** that he must one day render the Lord an account of his service. This *fear* is inseparable from the 'hope' which makes him and other ministers of the new covenant 'very bold' (3.12).

we persuade men: in the preaching of the gospel; the present tense (*peithomen*) means rather 'we try to persuade' (cf. *NEB*: 'we address our appeal to men').

what we are is known to God: lit. 'we have been made manifest to God'; the same verb (the passive of *phaneroō*) is rendered 'appear' in verse 10, and the implication is that Paul endeavours to be as transparently open to God now as he must be at the judgment seat.

to your conscience: as well as to his own (1.12). He hopes by his manner of life to commend himself 'to every man's conscience' (4.2), but his own Corinthian converts should be foremost in bearing witness to the purity of his conduct and motives.

12. not commending ourselves . . . again: cf. 3.1.

giving you cause to be proud of us: as Paul boasted of them to others, however much he might have to criticize them to their face (cf. 1.14; 7.4, 14; 8.24; 9.2f.).

who pride themselves on a man's position: lit. 'in appearance' or 'face' (Gk *en prosōpō*); the same people (or same kind of

people) are described in 11.18 as those who 'boast of wordly
things' (lit. 'according to the flesh', Gk *kata tēn sarka*; cf. verse 16
below). Corinth was visited by men who did their best to belittle
Paul's commission and impugn his motives in the eyes of his
converts (cf. 10.2ff.; 1 C. 9.1ff.); Paul gives his converts material
for a reply.

13. Some of Paul's critics disparaged him by saying he was
mad; be it so, he answers; that is **for God** to assess, not for men.
There might be a veiled reference here to his visions and ecstatic
experiences (cf. 12.1ff.); the verb rendered **we are beside ourselves** is cognate with *ekstasis* (whence 'ecstasy'). If so, these are
matters between himself and God, but in his dealings with the
Corinthians he eschewed ecstasy and acted rationally, in his
right mind (cf. 1. C 14.15-19, 'with the spirit . . . with the
mind').

14. the love of Christ: probably Christ's love for men.
controls us: or 'confines (Gk *synechei*) us' to this conclusion (cf.
NEB: 'leaves us no choice').
one has died for all; therefore all have died: this probably
means that **one has died** as the representative of **all** his people,
and **therefore all** of them are deemed to **have died** in the person
of their representative; 'the death of one was the death of all'
(C. Hodge). The second **all** has the article (Gk *hoi pantes*), indicating that the reference is to the **all** for whom **one has died.**
Christ is the 'last Adam', whose life-giving death has given birth
to the new creation as truly as the death-dealing disobedience of
the first Adam has doomed the old creation (cf. Rom. 5.12ff.;
1 C. 15.22). It is difficult to interpret the aorist 'all died' (*apethanon*)
to mean that all were under sentence of death, or actually 'dead
through the trespasses and sins' (Eph. 2.1), for which reason
Christ accepted death in their place—true though that is to Paul's
thought (cf. verse 21; 1 C. 15.3; Rom. 5.6, 8). The **all** of this
passage (cf. 1 Tim. 2.6) is synonymous with the second 'many' of
Rom. 5.15, 19 (cf. Mk 10.45; 14.24; Heb. 9.28).

15. those who live: i.e. those who, having died with Christ,
have risen with him. Christ's resurrection, like his death, was
representative (cf. Rom. 6.3ff.; Col. 2.13, 20; 3.1ff.). But **those
who live** in this newness of life with him belong to a new order of
existence: 'the death of Christ is something in which all his
followers have a share, and equally they share in his risen life,

which means that they can no longer live their old selfish life but must live for him who inaugurated the new life for them by dying and rising again' (T. W. Manson in *Studia Paulina in honorem J. de Zwaan* (1953), p. 156).

Ambassadors for Christ 5.16–21

16. Life in the old creation is lived 'according to the flesh' (Gk *kata sarka*). The adjective **human** in *RSV* **from a human point of view** might well have been replaced by 'worldly' (cf. *NEB*: 'With us therefore worldly standards have ceased to count in our estimate of any man'). Life in the new creation brings with it quite different standards and criteria. Paul has already shown (1 C. 1.18ff.) how an appreciation of Christ crucified involves a trans-valuation of values and in particular the turning upside down of secular canons of wisdom and power. No man presents the same appearance when viewed from the vantage-point of the new order ('according to the Spirit') as he does when seen 'according to the flesh'; and this is pre-eminently true of one's assessment of Christ. Before his conversion Paul had a clear picture of Christ in his mind; now he knows it was a wrong picture. This is equally true whether he means (as he probably does) that he had a wrong conception of the Messiah ('even if we have known a Messiah according to the flesh', e.g. a political Messiah) or that he had a wrong conception of Jesus of Nazareth (which he would readily have acknowledged, although this is the less likely sense here); in either case it was 'worldly standards' that had counted with him then, but as it is, 'even if once they counted in our understanding of Christ, they do so now no longer' (*NEB*). He is not contrasting his own post-Easter knowledge of Christ with the knowledge that the Twelve had of him before the cross, neither is he deprecating an interest in the Jesus of history as something improper, or at least spiritually irrelevant, for a Christian (cf. R. Bultmann, *Faith and Understanding*, E.T., i (1966), pp. 217, 241; H. J. Schoeps, *Paul*, E.T. (1961), pp. 57, 72, 79). Did he avoid asking or learning anything about the earthly life of Jesus when he talked with Peter and James at Jerusalem in the third year after his conversion (Gal. 1.18f.; see notes on 1 C. 15.5, 7)? Still more curious than these misinterpretations is the argument that verse 16 is a gnostic gloss (W. Schmithals, *Die Gnosis in Korinth* (1965²), pp. 286ff.; cf. note on 3.17).

17. a new creation: the man **in Christ** shares his Lord's risen life (cf. Gal. 2.20); he has experienced a new birth and anticipates by faith the 'new heaven and new earth' of which the prophet spoke (Isa. 65.17; 66.22); he has already crossed the bridge from **the old** age to **the new.** This co-existence of life 'by faith' in the eternal age with life 'by sight' in this transient age sets up the tensions described above (4.8–5.10). But it will not last indefinitely: when the order that is seen disappears for ever, 'the things that are unseen' will alone survive.

18. All this is from God: in all the action of the gospel the initiative is his; the new order, like the old, is his creative work.

who through Christ reconciled us to himself: in the context **us** may have primary reference to the apostles (the 'ambassadors for Christ' of verse 20), but of course it embraces all believers. God took the initiative when **through Christ** (what this means is stated in verse 21) he conveyed his proclamation of peace to the world; those who have responded to this proclamation with the obedience of faith have been effectively **reconciled** to him (cf. Rom. 5.10f.; Col. 1.22).

gave us the ministry of reconciliation: again, **us** means primarily, but not exclusively, the apostles; the 'ministry of the new covenant' includes the 'publishing of peace' (Isa. 52.7, quoted in Rom. 10.15; cf. Ac. 10.36; Eph. 6.15).

19. The proclamation of peace is that **God was in Christ reconciling the world to himself:** what is indicated unobtrusively by the absence of the comma after **Christ** (present in *AV*) is expressed clearly in the marginal rendering: 'in Christ God was reconciling . . .'. The form **was . . . reconciling** (Gk *ēn . . . katallassōn*) is a periphrastic imperfect: Paul is not here combining with his statement about reconciliation a statement about the incarnation. The periphrastic construction emphasizes the imperfect or continuous aspect of the verb; only with the response of faith can the aorist tense be used as in verse 18.

in Christ: hardly to be distinguished from 'through Christ' in verse 18, except in so far as it emphasizes how completely God and Christ are at one in this work of reconciliation.

not counting their trespasses against them: i.e. justifying them; cf. Rom. 4.6–8, where Ps. 32.2a, 'blessed is the man against whom the Lord will not reckon his sin' is quoted to show how 'God reckons righteousness apart from works'. 'Peace with God through our Lord Jesus Christ' is the portion of all who are 'justified by faith' (Rom. 5.1; cf. the juxtaposition of justification and reconciliation in Rom. 5.9f.). **entrusting to us the message** (Gk *logos*, 'word') **of reconciliation:** cf. the last clause of verse 18; the gospel is here spoken of as a treasure (cf. 4.7) deposited with the apostles. 'The work of God in Christ is reconciliation; but this process of reconciliation still goes on and the followers of Christ are made partakers in it. . . . Paul's exposition of the activity of Christ constantly carries the idea that it is a shared activity' (T. W. Manson in *Studia Paulina in honorem J. de Zwaan*, p. 156).

20. ambassadors: announcing their king's amnesty.

for Christ: Gk *hyper christou*, the same phrase as is rendered **on behalf of Christ** later in the verse. They are God's **ambassadors** but their proclamation (which is not so much theirs as his) involves an appeal to the name and work of **Christ.**

God making his appeal through us: the verb *parakaleō* has also the more authoritative note of exhortation, but the following **we beseech** (*deometha*) justifies the rendering **appeal** here. No object is expressed in the original with **we beseech**, although English style expects one; the supplied **you** should not be taken to mean Paul's Corinthian readers, who are presumed to have been reconciled (cf. verse 18), but those to whom he and his colleagues preach the gospel.

be reconciled: aorist tense; the hearers are urged to appropriate by faith the reconciliation procured by the death of Christ.

21. he made him to be sin (Gk *hamartian epoiēsen*): this remarkable expression (which amplifies 'through Christ . . . in Christ' in verses 18f.) can best be understood on the assumption that Paul had in mind the Hebrew idiom in which certain words for **sin** (*ḥaṭṭā't, 'āšām*) mean not only **sin** but 'sin-offering'; in this case we have a parallel here to Rom. 8.3, where God is said to have sent his Son 'as a sin offering' (*RSV* mg). A probable *OT* source is Isa. 53.10, where the Servant of Yahweh is made (or makes himself) an *'āšām* (*RSV* 'an offering for sin'; LXX has *peri hamartias*, the same expression as Paul uses in Rom. 8.3); cf. also Isa. 53.6. We have seen the same general sense in 1 C. 15.3. The sacrificial idiom implies that in the hour of death Christ offered his life to God as an atonement for the sins of men (a thought elaborated especially in Hebrews).

who knew no sin: an affirmation of the sinlessness of Christ inwardly in conscience (cf. 1 Jn 3.5) as well as outwardly in action (cf. 1 Pet. 2.22).

so that in him we might become the righteousness of God: a positive statement of justification in Christ (cf. verse 19), uniquely worded. In 1 C. 1.30 God is said to have made Christ 'our righteousness' (cf. Jer. 23.6; 33.16); if here **we** are made **the righteousness of God** in Christ (cf. Gal. 2.16f.; Phil. 3.19), it is probably by analogy with the preceding statement that Christ was 'made sin for us'. Paul has chosen this exceptional wording in order to emphasize the 'sweet exchange' whereby sinners are given a righteous status before God through the righteous one who absorbed their sin (and its judgment) in himself.

Apostolic Entreaty **6.1–13**

6.1. Working together with him: or, 'as fellow-workers (for him)'; **with him** has no explicit equivalent in the original. Cf. 1 C. 3.9, *RSV* ('we are fellow workmen for God'), with J. A. Bengel's note *ad loc.*: 'we are God's workmen and fellow-workmen one with another' (*Gnomon Novi Testamenti*). (Cf. also 1 Th. 3.2, *RV* mg.) **we entreat you:** in contrast to 5.20, the Corinthian Christians are the express object of this entreaty. (The Gk verb here is *parakaleō*, translated 'make appeal' in 5.20.) **not to accept the grace of God in vain:** as they would if they abandoned the faith and life of the gospel for pagan ways, or exchanged it for 'a different gospel' (cf. 11.4) which emphasized human achievement in place of divine grace (cf. Gal. 2.21), or even resisted Paul's appeal for personal reconciliation (cf. 6.13; 7.2). Cf. Ac. 20.24, 'the gospel of the grace of God' (in that speech which, of all ascribed to Paul in Ac., most closely resembles the Pauline epistles).

2. For he says: the words quoted from Isa. 49.8 are addressed by Yahweh to his Servant, commissioning him to release the captives and restore the exiles. Paul follows up the quotation with an interpretation of the type which the Qumran texts have taught us to call *pesher*, applying it, like so much else in the same context, to the gospel age: they must avail themselves of the grace of God **now**, while the opportunity lasts (cf. Heb. 3.12–15).

3. Paul returns to the subject of his apostolic **ministry**, in spite of his assurance in 5.12. His commission had been questioned, his motives had been disparaged, his conduct had been impugned;

that his opponents should do this was bad enough, but it was worse that some of his converts in Corinth should be disposed to pay heed to their insinuations. If he had no other reason for exercising scrupulous care, he states, it would be reason enough that unexemplary conduct on the part of the minister reflects adversely on the ministry (cf. 1 C. 10.32–11.1). 'The Christian Church . . . stands or falls by the integrity of its ministers' (E. G. Rupp).

4–5. His conduct and endurance of suffering not only attest the genuineness of his apostleship but provide an example to others. Nine forms of suffering are arranged in three sets of three: (*a*) general suffering (**afflictions, hardships, calamities**), (*b*) suffering endured at the hands of men (**beatings, imprisonments**, riotous onsets), (*c*) sufferings endured by way of self-discipline (**labours**, wakeful nights, fastings). The **hunger** is voluntary, not involuntary; cf. 11.27 where, in another catalogue of sufferings, involuntary and voluntary hunger are separately mentioned, the latter being expressed, as here, by Gk *nēsteiai*, 'fastings'.

6–7. Next he enumerates the qualities he endeavoured to cultivate and display in the course of his service, culminating in the armour **of righteousness** (or integrity) **for the right hand** (meaning perhaps for attack) **and for the left** (for defence); cf. 10.3f. and the fuller development of the figure in 1 Th. 5.8; Eph. 6.11–17. The mention of **the Holy Spirit** in a list of virtues is striking: it is by the Spirit that these virtues are fostered, and they are the evidence of his indwelling presence.

8–10. The vicissitudes of the apostolic life are summarized in pairs of antitheses, somewhat after the fashion of 1 C. 4.10–13; 2 C. 4.8f. The **dishonour** and **ill repute** with which they are visited by men are more than compensated for by the **honour** and **good repute** of which they are assured in God's sight. The two assessments—the worldly and the divine—are set side by side in some detail: by worldly standards they are **impostors, unknown, dying, punished** ('disciplined by suffering', *NEB*), **sorrowful, poor** and penniless; by the standards of the eternal order they are **true, well known**, living, preserved from death, **always rejoicing**, enriching **many** and **possessing everything**, including 'the world, life and death, the present and the future' (1 C. 3.22). The second and third divisions of verse 9 echo Ps. 118.17f.: 'I shall not die, but I shall live . . . The LORD has chastened me sorely, but he has not given me over to death'.

11. Our mouth is open: we speak freely (cf. 3.12; 4.2).
our heart is wide: the fact that P^{46} Aleph B have 'your heart',
which is manifestly unsuitable to the context, is a reminder that
antiquity of attestation is not always a pointer to the true reading.
This clause recalls the Gk text of Ps. 119 (LXX 118).32: 'thou
enlargest my understanding (lit. "heart")'. In this context it is
affection more than understanding that is implied.

12. There was no sense of restraint in Paul's feeling for the
Corinthians: if there was any restraint or reserve between them,
it was on their part, not on his.

13. In return: 'fair play', as children say in their games: if
there is no restraint in my affection for you, let there be none in
your affection for me.

A CALL TO SEPARATION **6.14-7.1**

The warm approach and appeal of verses 11-13 are continued in
7.2 ('Open your hearts to us'); the flow of thought is interrupted
by 6.14-7.1. It has therefore been widely supposed that these six
verses have found their way into this position from some other
source—that they are (for example) a fragment of the 'previous
letter' of 1 C. 5.9. This identification was first put forward, it
seems, by A. Hilgenfeld (*Hist.-krit. Einl. i.d. NT* (1875), p. 287);
see the discussion between R. Whitelaw, F. H. Chase and W.
Sanday in *Classical Review* 4 (1890), pp. 12, 150ff., 248f., 317f.,
359f. The 'previous letter', indeed, warned the Corinthian
Christians against fornication, whereas these six verses do not
mention this kind of conduct (if they warn against one practice
more than another, it is idolatry); nevertheless, the warning not
to be **mismated with unbelievers** could have been misunderstood along the lines of 1 C. 5.10.

It has further been maintained, however, that these six verses
have a number of un-Pauline features: for one thing, in their brief
compass they contain eight words not found elsewhere in *NT*—
those translated **mismated, partnership, accord, Belial,
agreement, move among** (*emperipateō*, from Lev. 26.12, LXX),
welcome (*eisdechomai*, from Ezek. 11.17; 20.34, 41, LXX), and
defilement (*molysmos*, found in LXX at 1 Esd. 8.83; Jer. 23.15; 2
Mac. 5.27). Over and above that, a number of scholars—first,
apparently, K. G. Kuhn (cf. *RB* 61 (1954), p. 203, n. 1)—have
pointed out affinities between these verses and Qumran literature,

such as the dualistic antitheses, including that between light and darkness, the reference to Belial, the idea of the community as a temple, the conflation of *OT* citations, and the general emphasis on separation, to the point where P. Benoit can call the passage 'a meteor fallen from the heaven of Qumran into Paul's epistle' ('Qumran and the *NT*' in *Paul and Qumran*, ed. J. Murphy-O'Connor (1968), p. 5), while others have regarded it as the christianized reworking of a Qumran paragraph by someone other than Paul (cf. J. A. Fitzmyer, 'Qumrân and the interpolated Paragraph in 2 Cor 6, 14–7, 1', *CBQ* 23 (1961), pp. 271ff.), perhaps by the editor of 2 Corinthians (cf. J. Gnilka, '2 Cor 6: 14–7: 1' in *Paul and Qumran*, pp. 48ff.).

But while the verses contain features characteristic of Qumran, these features are not peculiar to Qumran, and the theory of interpolation at this particular point involves a certain bibliographical improbability. Paul is quite capable of digressing, and it may be argued that while he is pleading for mutual open-heartedness he reflects that the reason for the restraint which he deprecates on his readers' part is their uneasy awareness that they have not made the complete break with idolatrous associations which he had earlier urged upon them (1 C. 10.14ff.); hence this exhortation.

14–16a. Do not be mismated (more literally, 'do not become diversely yoked', Gk *heterozygeō*) **with unbelievers:** an extension to human life of the principle underlying Dt. 22.10 (cf. the treatment of Dt. 25.4 in 1 C. 9.9). The five rhetorical questions which follow are introduced by the interrogative pronoun *tis* ('what?') preceding five successive synonyms: *metochē* (**partnership**), *koinōnia* (**fellowship**), *symphōnēsis* (**accord**, 'harmony'), *meris* ('portion') and *synkatathesis* (**agreement**); in the five antitheses, **righteousness . . . light . . . Christ . . . a believer . . . the temple of God** belong together on one side, as do **iniquity . . . darkness . . . Belial . . . an unbeliever . . . idols** on the other. Each question presupposes a negative answer, like the sequence of questions in Am. 3.3ff. For the antithesis between **light** and **darkness** cf. Rom. 13.12; Eph. 5.8–14; Col. 1.12f.; 1 Th. 5.2–8; Jn 1.5; 3.19–21; 8.12; 9.4f.; 12.35f.; 1 Jn 1.5–7; 2.8–11; it is as pervasive a feature of the *NT* as it is of Qumran literature.

Belial (Gk *Beliar*, by dissimilation): the personalization of evil, here equivalent to Antichrist. In *OT* Hebrew *beliyya'al* means 'worthlessness' or 'perdition'; cf. the familiar phrase 'son(s) of

Belial' (Dt. 13.13, etc.) and the parallelism of the word with
'death' and 'Sheol' in 2 Sam. 22.5f. // Ps. 18.4f. In Jubilees, the
Testaments of the Twelve Patriarchs, the *Ascension of Isaiah*, the
Sibylline Oracles and some of the Qumran texts **Belial** is the arch-
enemy of God or the demonic counterpart of the 'prince of light'
(1 QM 13.10ff.; cf. also Jub. 1.20; *Test. Levi* xix.1; CD iv.13;
Asc. Isa. i.8f.; ii.4; *Or. Sib.* iii.63, 73). In *Test. Levi* xviii.12 he is
to be bound by the 'new priest' of the age to come. In Samaritan
literature it is he who tempted Eve (M. Gaster, *The Samaritans*
(1925), p. 64). The last of the five questions may echo Hos. 14.8,
'what have I to do with idols?'

16b. The sequence of questions now gives place to an important
affirmation, followed by a supporting catena of *OT testimonia*. **we
are the temple of the living God:** cf. 1 C. 3.16f.; 6.19; here, as
there, the word is *naos*, 'sanctuary'. For a discussion of the temple-
figure in its present context see B. Gärtner, *The Temple and the
Community in Qumran and the NT* (1965), pp. 49ff.

I will live in them and move among them: this first *testimonium* is a conflation of Lev. 26.11f. with Exod. 25.8 and Ezek.
37.27a (cf. Rev. 21.3); this is involved in their being **the temple
of God.**

I will be their God, and they shall be my people: the ancient
language of covenant (Lev. 26.12; Jer. 32.38; Ezek. 11.20; 36.28;
37.27b; cf. Rev. 21.3), which carried the corollary that they must
be holy as he is (cf. Lev. 11.44, etc.; Mt. 5.48 // Lk. 6.36; 1 Pet.
1.15f.).

17. Since God dwells among them, they must withdraw from
everything that is incompatible with his holiness.
Come out ... and touch nothing unclean: from Isa. 52.11;
the quotation illustrates the transition from ceremonial to ethical
purity. Those who see in 6.14–7.1 part of the 'previous letter' of 1
C. 5.9 suggest that *exelthein* ('go out') in 1 C. 5.10 echoes **Come out**
(*exelthate*) here. **I will welcome you:** cf. Ezek. 11.17; 20.34, 41;
Zeph. 3.20.

18. I will be a father to you: cf. 2 Sam. 7.14; Jer. 31.9.
you shall be my sons and daughters: from Hos. 1.10 (quoted
also in Rom. 9.26), with **daughters** added to **sons** (cf. Isa. 43.6).
says the Lord Almighty (Gk *kyrios pantokratōr*): a clausula
particularly common in the LXX of Zechariah and Malachi,
where, as very frequently (though not invariably) throughout the

Gk *OT*, *kyrios pantokratōr* represents Hebrew *yhwh ṣᵉḇā'ōt* ('LORD of hosts'; contrast *kyrios sabaoth* in Rom. 9.29).

Similar catenae of *OT* quotations appear elsewhere in Paul's writings (cf. Rom. 3.10-18; 9.25f.; 15.9-12), although here the quotations are more than usually interwoven so as to produce a comprehensive combination of admonition and promise by God to his people.

7.1. these promises: those quoted in 6.16b, 17b, 18. **let us cleanse ourselves:** so as to be in practice what we are by divine calling (cf. 1 C. 6.11, 'you were washed, you were sanctified').

from every defilement of body and spirit: lit. 'of flesh (*sarx*) and spirit'. This is not Paul's distinctive use of 'flesh' (*sarx*), but he was quite capable of using the word in its ordinary sense, especially as in 1 C. 5.5, in correlation with **spirit** (cf. the correlation of Hebrew *bāśār* and *rûaḥ*, e.g. in Isa. 31.3; a Qumran example is provided in 1 QM 7.5, where the 'sons of light' who take part in the holy war must be 'perfect in spirit and flesh'). Cf. Col. 2.5, 'absent in body (*sarx*, 'flesh') . . . with you in spirit'—a passage similar to 1 C. 5.3 where, however, *sōma* ('body') is used, as also in 1 C. 7.34, 'holy in body (*sōma*) and spirit' (a phrase otherwise comparable to the present one). In 2 C. 12.7 also 'flesh' (*sarx*) has its ordinary physical sense; see note *ad loc*.

make holiness perfect: bring holiness to completion (cf. 3.18; 1 Th. 5.23).

in the fear of God: cf. 5.11.

RESTORATION OF MUTUAL CONFIDENCE 7.2-16

PAUL'S AFFECTION FOR THE CORINTHIANS 7.2-4

This short paragraph serves as transition from Paul's exposition of the apostolic ministry to the resumption of his personal narrative from which he digressed after 2.13.

2. Open your hearts to us: Gk *chōrēsate hēmās*, 'make room for us' (i.e. in your hearts), repeating the entreaty of 6.13.

we have wronged no one . . .: once again, after a digression (cf. 4.2; 6.3), Paul defends his behaviour against misrepresentations which he knew to be current and which, if heeded, might make his readers receive his affectionate overtures with coolness. Cf. also 1.12; 1 Th. 2.9f.; 2 Th. 3.7f.

we have taken advantage of no one: the verb is *pleonekteō* (as in 12.17), frequently translated 'covet' (cf. Ac. 20.33, where, however, the verb is *epithymeō*, 'desire'). Cf. 1 Sam. 12. 1-5.

3. I do not say this to condemn you: he does not want them to suppose that he imagines they harbour such unworthy thoughts of him (cf. 1 C. 4.14).

I said before: cf. 6.11.

to die together and to live together: cf. Horace, *tecum uiuere amem, tecum obeam libens*, 'with thee I'd love to live, with thee I'd gladly die' (*Odes* iii.9.24)—but the setting is different. Perhaps Paul puts death first because it is a more probable prospect than life.

4. I have great confidence in you: lit. 'great is my boldness (*parrhēsia*) towards you' (cf. 3.12; 4.2), a repetition in different words of the first clause of 6.11.

I have great pride (*kauchēsis*) **in you:** see notes on 1.14; 5.12.

I am filled with comfort: this catches up the note struck at the beginning of the letter (cf. 1.3ff.); one way in which he received the comfort of God was by the renewal of friendly relations with his Corinthian friends.

With all our affliction: cf. 1.4ff.; 4.8, 17; 6.4.

I am overjoyed: a very emphatic form of words, 'I superabound (Gk *hyperperisseuō*, as in Rom. 5.20) with joy'.

THE JOYFUL SEQUEL TO THE TEARFUL LETTER **7.5-16**

5. For even when we came into Macedonia: while this carries on Paul's narrative directly from the point to which he had brought it in 2.13, the conjunction **for** links this sentence to that immediately preceding: Paul tells them why he is 'overjoyed'; it is because of the good news brought by Titus.

our bodies: lit. 'our (i.e. my) flesh (Gk *sarx*)'; it is difficult to press a distinction between 'flesh' here and 'spirit' in 2.13 (see note *ad loc.*), as though, for example, this reference might be to a recurrence of his 'thorn in the flesh' (see note on 12.7). He may use 'flesh' here to emphasize the weakness of human nature which is so much influenced by external circumstances and inward moods.

rest: Gk *anesis*, 'relaxation', 'relief' (so also in 2.13; cf. 8.13).

fighting without: a reference, perhaps, to 'many adversaries' in Macedonia as earlier in Ephesus (1 C. 16.9).

fear within: especially lest Titus's mission of reconciliation in Corinth should prove to have been fruitless.

6. God, who comforts the downcast: a designation in the same vein as those of 1.3, 4a. The adjective is *tapeinos*, translated 'humble' in 10.1

the coming of Titus: i.e. his arrival (Gk *parousia*).

7. your longing: to see Paul and assure him of their affection.

your mourning: for the temporary estrangement.

your zeal: to put the matter right and discipline the offending party.

8–10. even if I made you sorry: in 2.4 he has told them that his **letter** was not intended to cause them pain (the same verb *lypeō* is used both here and there); the pain was but a means to an end, which has now been attained. Therefore, although at the time he **did regret** having sent the letter, he does not **regret** it now, because of the happy outcome. The **grief** (Gk *lypē*) it caused them was temporary; it was moreover a **godly grief** (a grief 'according to God'), which differs from **worldly grief** in that it produces **repentance** (a change of heart which **leads to salvation** and will never be rued), not **death**. Cf. *Test. Gad* v.7, 'true repentance according to God . . . guides the mind to salvation'.

you suffered no loss through us: they were the gainers because of the salutary effect of his painful letter.

a repentance that . . . brings no regret: lit. 'repentance not to be repented of' (Gk *metanoia . . . ametamelētos*), an oxymoron.

11. That the **grief** produced in the Corinthians was **godly** has been evidenced by their prompt reaction to Paul's letter, their energetic determination to right whatever wrong had been done.

what punishment: lit. 'revenge', 'avenging' (Gk *ekdikēsis*), a reference to the 'punishment' (*epitimia*) of 2.6.

you have proved yourselves guiltless: by taking action which both **cleared** themselves and satisfied Paul's purpose expressed in 2.9, 'that I might . . . know whether you are obedient in everything'.

12–13a. it was not . . . but: i.e. 'not so much . . . as'.

the one who did the wrong: the man who is referred to in 2.5 as having 'caused pain' not only to Paul personally but 'in some measure' to them all.

the one who suffered the wrong: probably Paul himself (see notes on 2.8, 10). The identification of the wrongdoer with the offender of 1 C. 5.1ff. would almost inevitably imply that the injured party here was the 'father' of that passage, whose wife his son had taken; but if the father was still alive, the offence was much more heinous than the notes *ad loc.* have assumed it to be, and the acceptance of whatever discipline 'the majority' had imposed (2.6) as satisfying the severe terms of 1 C. 5.5 is even more improbable than has been suggested in the note on 2.5–8.

in order that your zeal for us might be revealed to you: not only that Paul himself might assure them of his love and test their obedience (2.4, 9) but that they themselves might be shocked into realizing, **in the sight of God**, how strong was the bond of affection and loyalty binding them to him. This goal had been achieved: **therefore we are comforted** (perfect tense).

13b–14. Paul's personal **comfort** and joy were enhanced by the delight which the success of his mission had brought to Titus. Paul had boasted to him (hoping against hope, perhaps) that his Corinthian friends were loyal and sound at heart, and the event had **proved** his **boasting** to be **true**. The experience brought spiritual refreshment to Titus, and Paul felt greatly relieved that he had not been **put to shame**, as he would have been had his boasting proved hollow.

as everything we said to you was true: cf. 1.17f.

15. The Corinthians had secured a new and firm friend in Titus, on whose mind a deep and abiding impression had been made by their reception of him and their ready **obedience** to the apostle's directions. This led to further contacts between them and Titus (cf. 8.6, 16f.).

fear and trembling: cf. 1 C. 2.3; Eph. 6.5; Phil. 2.12 for this Pauline phrase. Here it is an ampler description of the 'alarm' (*phobos*, 'fear') of verse 11.

16. I rejoice: catching up verse 4b (cf. verses 7, 13b).

I have perfect confidence (Gk *tharreō*) **in you:** catching up the thought of verse 4a, but in a form presenting a striking antithesis to 10.1b, 'I am bold (confident) *against* you', where the same verb *tharreō* is used.

THE COLLECTION FOR JERUSALEM 8.1–9.15

In this section Paul returns, after the lapse of a year (more or less), to the subject of the collection for Jerusalem, previously mentioned in 1 C. 16.1–4. On that earlier occasion he gave directions for the gathering and transmission of the money, but in the intervening period of tension between him and part at least of the Corinthian church their interest in the matter would have waned, and he would have judged it inexpedient to remind them of it. But now, with the restoration of happier relations, the subject could be raised again, and Paul raises it, with all the delicacy and tact at his command. He wanted the Corinthians' contribution to be generous, but at the same time he wanted it to be completely voluntary. The whole purpose of the exercise, as Paul conceived it, would be vitiated if at any stage he appeared to be requiring their participation in the scheme by apostolic authority or by anything that savoured of pressure.

A NEW MISSION FOR TITUS 8.1–24

8.1. the grace of God: the response made by **the churches of Macedonia** (e.g. Philippi, Thessalonica and Beroea) to God's grace conveyed in Christ (cf. verse 9), and itself a reflection of the divine grace (for the reciprocal sense of Gk *charis*, see note on 4.15). The Corinthians' contribution to this cause has been called their 'grace' (*charis*, *RSV* 'gift') in 1 C. 16.3.

2. in a severe test of affliction: the natural inference is that the Macedonian Christians (among whom Paul found himself at the time of writing) were just then passing through a specially trying time of tribulation, although we have but little clue to its nature or circumstances. Paul himself may have been involved in it (cf. the reference to 'affliction' in 7.4 and to the recent 'fighting without' in 7.5). Nevertheless, their tribulation and the **extreme poverty** which accompanied it, and was perhaps a consequence of it, did nothing to diminish **their abundance of joy**; the **poverty** and the **joy** together **overflowed in a wealth of liberality** (Gk *haplotēs*, as in 9.11, 13; cf. Rom. 12.8; so also Jos. *Ant.* vii.332; *Test. Issachar* iii.8).

3–5. Paul has begun to use the language of paradox to emphasize the Macedonians' astonishing generosity and he continues to use it: **they gave** not merely **according to their means** but **beyond their means** (lit. 'beyond their power', not merely *kata dynamin* but *para dynamin*), and they did so **of their own free will**. In their difficult circumstances Paul might well have hesitated to mention the collection to them, but they took the initiative by **begging . . . earnestly for the favour of taking part:** lit.

'for favour (grace) and participation (fellowship)'. The Gk words, *charis* and *koinōnia*, are set in a relation of hendiadys one with the other (cf. Rom. 1.5, 'grace and apostleship'). Perhaps we should render *koinōnia* 'fellowship' rather than merely 'participation'; their desire to take part in this **relief** (*diakonia*, 'ministry', as in 9.1; Rom. 15.31) **of the saints** (cf. 1 C. 16.1) was a sign of divine grace in their lives and a gesture of Christian fellowship both with others who were contributing and with the prospective recipients. Their eagerness in this matter, to a point beyond what Paul could reasonably have **expected**, could be explained only by the unreserved fulness of their devotion to Christ: if **first they gave themselves to the Lord**, then their property as well as their lives belonged to him (cf. 5.15); they were giving him but his own. Since Paul was the Lord's representative and the collection for Jerusalem was part of the Lord's service, then their putting themselves at Paul's disposal for this purpose was a partial repayment of the debt of love they owed to Christ.

by the will of God: i.e. their giving themselves to the apostle was as much **the will of God** as their giving themselves to the Lord.

6. Paul has emphasized the extraordinary liberality of the Macedonian churches not only for the information of his Corinthian friends but as an example for them to follow. They are relatively more affluent than the Macedonians, and the report of the Macedonians' spontaneous and sacrificial contribution will (he implies) make the Corinthians all the more eager to play their part and not to be outdone by their fellow-Christians in the north. **Accordingly** he is sending Titus (see, further, on 12.18) to help them with the final stages of their donation. Titus **had already made a beginning** among them on his recent mission of reconciliation: that was one manifestation of the grace of God in their midst, and now he is being sent back to **complete** among them 'this grace also' (*RV*)—this further manifestation of God's grace in their generous giving to the collection for Jerusalem. Far from suggesting that the recent strained relations had caused any slackening off in their weekly instalments (cf. 1 C. 16.2), Paul writes as though he assumes that these have been kept up, and that nothing remains to be done but a final, specially liberal, addition to complete what has already been set aside for this purpose.

7. The Corinthians had shown themselves richly endowed with all other spiritual gifts (cf. 1 C. 1.7), not least in their **love** for Paul, as their recent conduct had shown (cf. 7.6–11); let them show themselves richly endowed with the **gracious work** (*charis*, 'grace') of liberality also.

8. not as a command: the same phrase as in 1 C. 7.6. He disowns any idea of putting pressure on them; their giving will be acceptable only as it is the spontaneous expression of a **love** that **is genuine**—as genuine as that of the Macedonians whose eager **earnestness** in this matter was proof enough of *their* love and whose example is calculated to stir up the Corinthians to friendly emulation.

9. But a greater example than that of the Macedonians comes readily to a Christian mind: **the grace** shown by **our Lord Jesus Christ** is the supreme incentive for his people.

though he was rich: before his incarnation (cf. Phil. 2.6, 'though he was in the form of God').

for your sake he became poor: in incarnation (cf. Phil. 2.7f., 'emptied himself, taking the form of a servant . . . humbled himself and became obedient unto death').

so that by his poverty you might become rich: with all the endowments of grace and salvation (cf. 12.9; Rom. 5.1ff.; Eph.1.3; Phil. 4.11–13, 18f.). The adducing of Christ's *kenōsis* as an example to his followers to give generously is a daring but characteristic argument; cf. Eph. 5.2 and especially the quotation in Phil. 2.6–11 of a hymn on the humiliation and exaltation of Christ which, whatever its original setting and purpose may have been (cf. R. P. Martin, *Carmen Christi* (1967)), is used there as an incentive to Christians to live together in concord and mutual consideration.

10–11. I give my advice: cf. 1 C. 7.25 where the same expression (*gnōmēn didōmi*) is rendered 'I give my opinion' (*RSV*).

it is best for you now to complete: this hardly does justice to the force of Paul's imperative: 'For this is expedient for you. You were foremost . . . in desiring it . . . Now then complete the doing of it.'

a year ago: a reference either to the question in their letter to Paul which was answered in the instructions of 1 C. 16.1–4, or to their receipt of these instructions. For the time-indication (cf. 9.2) see p. 172.

you began: perhaps even before the Macedonians, who are not mentioned in 1 C. 16. 1–4.

not only to do but to desire: they might have undertaken **to do** it out of obedience to Paul, but he reminds them that the **desire** was expressed on their own initiative; he is only encouraging them to press forward to the prompt completion of an enterprise for which they had long since manifested such eager enthusiasm.

out of what you have: cf. 1 C. 16.2, 'as he may prosper'.

12. if the readiness is there: the principle laid down here is that which is inculcated by the incident of the widow's mite (Mk 12.41–44). Cf. Rom. 12.8.

13. that others should be eased and you burdened: this criticism of the collection may well have been voiced at Corinth during the recent unpleasantness: 'he is laying a burden on us in order to ease others'.

14. so that their abundance may supply your want: the prospects of the Jerusalem Christians' ever being in a position to repay the Corinthians' gift in kind were slim indeed—unless Paul means (as in Rom. 15.27) that the gifts which the Jerusalem church bestowed were spiritual, while it received material gifts in return.

that there may be equality: that the affluent should supply the deficiencies of the needy was as desirable between churches as it was between members in any one local church.

15. The quotation from Exod. 16.18 relates to the daily gathering of the manna: while the Israelites 'gathered, some more, some less', yet each was found to have 'gathered according to what he could eat', so there was neither excess nor insufficiency, but equality of provision 'to each according to his need'.

16–17. Paul has spoken of his 'urging' Titus to go back to Corinth to complete the administration of the fund which the church had accumulated, but Titus in fact needed no urging: he had conceived such affection for the Corinthians on his previous visit (7.13–15) that he was ready to go to them **of his own accord**, and perhaps had indeed set out. (It is possible, on the other hand, to interpret the aorist *exēlthen* as epistolary, and translate with *RSV* **he is going to you**; in that case Titus might be the bearer of the present letter. *RSV* 'we are sending' in verses 18 and 22 similarly renders an aorist form, treating it as epistolary. Cf. 9.3.)

18–19. Titus was Paul's own representative, but in order that no unworthy suspicions might be ventilated he was accompanied by an unnamed **brother** whom the contributing **churches** themselves (presumably those of Macedonia) had **appointed** to join Paul and his colleagues as they travelled from church to church collecting the gifts for Jerusalem. Traditionally this brother 'whose praise is in the gospel' (*AV*) has been identified with Luke (cf. Origen in Eusebius *HE* vi.xxv.6 and the Anglican collect for St. Luke's Day). In so far as this tradition is based on the identification of **the gospel** in this verse with the Gospel according to Luke it manifestly depends on an anachronistic misunderstanding of Paul's words, which are well paraphrased by *RSV*: **who is famous among all the churches for his preaching of the gospel.** We have no knowledge that Luke was famed in this respect. In view of his special association with Philippi—hinted at, among other things, by the fact that the first 'we' section of Acts ends and the second begins in that city (Ac. 16.17; 20.5f.)—it is conceivable that he was deputed by the Philippian church to be its representative among the delegates from other churches who accompanied Paul to Jerusalem (the author of the 'we' sections was one of the company enumerated in Ac. 20.4). Even so, the identification is doubtful; whoever this **brother** was, he was evidently so well known to the Corinthians that there was no need to name him. The view that **the brother** should be understood as 'his (i.e. Titus's) brother' (cf. A. Souter, 'A Suggested Relationship between Titus and Luke', *ExT* 18 (1906–7), p. 285; 'The Relationship between Titus and Luke', *ibid.*, pp. 335f.) has little to commend it; the precise point of this man's going with Titus was that he should be an independent guarantor of the probity of the administration of the money, and this end would have been defeated if critics had been given an opportunity to draw unfavourable attention to a blood-relationship between the two.

20–21. Paul was very much alive to the readiness with which his critics would seize upon any circumstance in this business which could be made to look suspicious: it was not enough that honesty should be practised (**in the Lord's sight**); it must be visibly practised (**in the sight of men**).Cf. Prov. 3.4, LXX.

22. If it is difficult to identify the 'brother' of verse 18, it is impossible to identify this additional **brother** who accompanied Titus and the other on this occasion. He was one whom Paul had frequently trusted with responsible commissions and who, in view of **his great confidence** in the Corinthians, may be assumed (like the anonymous messenger already mentioned) to have been well enough known to them not to require to be named.

23. Paul supplies the three messengers with credentials: **Titus,** as they have reason to know, is his **partner and fellow worker** in serving them; the two **brethren** who are with him are **messengers of the churches** and, because of their life and ministry, they are a credit to the name of Christ which they bear. It appears, then, that the second anonymous 'brother', as well as the first, was in some sense delegated by **the churches.** The designation **messengers** (Gk *apostoloi*) **of the churches** suggests a comparison with the Jewish *šᵉlûḥîm* or *šᵉlîḥîm*, who carried money and messages from or to central authorities (cf. K. H. Rengstorf *s.v.* ἀπόστολος, in *TWNT* i (1933; E.T. 1964), pp. 413ff.). Cf. Phil. 2.25, where Epaphroditus is the 'messenger' (*apostolos*) of the Philippian church to Paul.

24. As Paul had earlier 'boasted' to Titus about the Corinthians' loyalty to him personally (7.14), so now he had boasted to him and his two companions about their prompt and generous contribution to the Jerusalem fund: he expresses his confidence that on this occasion, as on the former, they will not let him down, but **give proof, before the** other contributing **churches,** of the genuineness of their Christian **love** (cf. verse 8; 9.13).

GENEROUS SOWING, GENEROUS REAPING **9.1–15**

9. 1–2. The connection of this paragraph with the preceding one has been felt to be somewhat awkward: the opening words— 'Now concerning the ministry to the saints . . .'—read as if the subject were being introduced afresh. The connection is less awkward in the Greek text than in *RSV*: verse 1 does not begin with *peri de*—as 1 C. 16.1 does, introducing a new topic—but with the resumptive *peri men gar*, and *gar* ('for') implies that some reference at least has been made to the subject in the preceding context. The substance of Paul's boasting about the Corinthians, mentioned briefly in 8.24, is amplified in 9.2–4, and the allusion to 'the brethren' in 9.3, 5, would be scarcely intelligible apart from 8.6, 16ff. Any awkwardness in the transition from 8.24 to 9.1 could easily be accounted for if there was a short break in dictating at this point. This is more probable than that 2 C. 9 is a separate note sent about the same time as 2 C. 1–8 (so J. Héring, p. 65) or shortly after 2 C. 8 (so G. Bornkamm in K. Aland *et al.*, *The Authorship and Integrity of the NT* (1965), p. 77). See W. G. Kümmel, *INT*, E.T. (1966), pp. 213f.

it is superfluous: because of their **readiness** (Gk *prothymia*, 'eagerness', as in 8.11f., 19), nevertheless he continues **to write** about it. He has not only boasted to Titus and his companions about the Corinthians' generosity but to the Macedonian Christians. **Achaia** (cf. 1.1) **has been ready since last year:** in 8.10 the Corinthians are said to have 'begun' a year before, but Paul regularly goes farther in praise of his converts to others than in addressing them directly.

your zeal has stirred up most of them: so the Corinthians' example was used as an incentive to the Macedonians, just as the Macedonians' example was used to the Corinthians (8.1–5).

3-4. I am sending the brethren: the three of 8.6, 16–23; the verb is aorist (*epempsa*), treated by *RSV* as epistolary (cf. 8.17, 18, 22). Another reason for the sending of the three commissioners to help the Corinthians with the completion of their offering is now mentioned: it is to make sure that Paul's **boasting** about them to the Macedonians will not be falsified by the event. It would certainly be embarrassing for Paul, not to mention the Corinthians themselves, if they were found **not ready** when he arrived with the delegates of the Macedonian churches, after his boasting so confidently about them.

5. to urge: the Gk verb is *parakaleō*, as in 8.6.
this gift: lit. 'blessing', Gk *eulogia*, translated **willing gift** in the next clause. Here *eulogia*, used in the sense of thanksgiving in 1 C. 10.16, takes on the correlative sense of 'act of grace', 'something which evokes thanksgiving' (cf. the twofold force of *charis* in 8.1, 6f., 9); or, as in Gen. 33.11; 1 Sam. 25.27, it may denote the material gift which accompanies and expresses a 'blessing' in the sense of a greeting or salutation. The opposite of such blessing is **exaction:** lit. 'covetousness' (*pleonexia*), something which is greedily extorted against the donor's will.

6. bountifully: lit. 'with blessings', 'with thanksgivings' (Gk *ep' eulogiais*), a similar usage of *eulogia* to that in verse 5. For the use of the word in an agricultural context, cf. Heb. 6.7, where the fruitful land 'receives a blessing (*eulogia*) from God'. Contributing to the Jerusalem fund is a form of sowing which will be followed by a rich harvest of blessing to the contributors. For the principle cf. also Prov. 11.25, LXX: 'every liberal soul receives a blessing' (*eulogoumenē*).

7. as he has made up his mind: lit. 'as he has chosen (preferred) in his heart'—a further principle to that of 1 C. 16.2 ('as he may prosper'); Paul is simply encouraging each one to give what he has already decided to give.

reluctantly: lit. 'out of pain' (Gk *ek lypēs*).

under compulsion: which might be felt if the collection was not ready when Paul arrived.

God loves a cheerful giver: from Prov. 22.8a, LXX ('God blesses a man who is cheerful and a giver'); cf. 1 Chr. 29.17 ('offering freely and joyously to thee') and *Leviticus Rabba* xxxiv.8, on Lev. 25.25 ('he who gives alms, let him do so with a cheerful heart').

8. They will not be the losers: 'the God of all grace' (as he is called in 1 Pet. 5.10) will multiply his grace in their lives as they show grace to others, and thus they will have **in abundance** more of his **blessing** to enjoy themselves and to share with others.

9. The quotation is from the description of 'the man who fears the Lord' (Ps. 112.9).

he scatters abroad: the sowing metaphor continued.

righteousness (*dikaiosynē*, rendering Hebrew *ṣᵉḏāqāh*) embraces all acts of piety, including (and particularly so here) almsgiving; cf. Dan. 4.27; Mt. 6.1.

endures for ever: in its effect and reward (see note on verse 11).

10. seed for the sower and bread for food: from Isa. 55.10.

your resources: lit. 'your seed for sowing'.

the harvest of your righteousness (from Hos. 10.12, LXX): the product of the charitable actions you have 'sown' (cf. verses 6, 9).

11. for great generosity: Gk *haplotēs*, 'singleness (of heart)', 'sincerity' (as in 8.2, where *RSV* renders 'liberality'; cf. verse 13). The effect of their enrichment will be opportunity for even more lavish giving, and hence for further **thanksgiving to God** on the part of those to whom their gifts are transmitted **through us** (i.e. through Paul and his associates).

12. this service: Gk *leitourgia*, which may convey a nuance of sacred service (Paul uses it in a sacrificial context in Phil. 2.17); the corresponding verb is used of this same offering in Rom. 15.27

(cf. also Phil. 2.30 for *leitourgia* used of the Philippians' service to Paul discharged by Epaphroditus).

overflows in many thanksgivings to God: the thought and wording are reminiscent of 4.15. How their gift has this effect is explained in verse 13.

13. the test of this service: the proof of their love (cf. 8.8, 24) which their offering (Gk *diakonia*, as in verse 1) will supply.

you will glorify God: taking the participle *doxazontes* ('glorifying') to have the same reference as the participle *ploutizomenoi* ('being enriched') at the beginning of verse 11. But since the participle does not stand in strict grammatical concord with anything in the immediate vicinity, it may as well apply to the grateful recipients in Jerusalem as to the generous donors in Corinth; that is to say, the Jerusalem Christians will welcome the gift as the visible evidence of the Gentiles' **obedience in acknowledging the gospel**, and will **glorify God** for his grace shown to them and through them.

the generosity of your contribution: 'the liberality (Gk *haplotēs*, as in verse 11) of the fellowship' (*koinōnia* as in 8.4, 'taking part').

14. they long for you: the receipt of the gift will create in the recipients a sense of intense affection towards the givers (for this sense of *epipotheō*, cf. the noun *epipothēsis* ('longing') in 7.7, 11) and will stimulate them to prayer on their behalf. Paul naturally says nothing here of his misgivings about the acceptance of the gift at which he hints in Rom. 15.31; possibly these misgivings arose from news which reached him later than the despatch of this letter, but even so he would not have mentioned them to the contributing churches.

the surpassing grace of God in you: as in the churches of Macedonia (8.1; cf. 8.6f.). The participle **surpassing** (*hyperballousa*) has been used in 3.10 of the 'surpassing glory' of the new covenant; here it implies that their generosity will be the spontaneous overflowing of the **grace** which God has poured into their lives (cf. the similar force of the participle *perisseuousa*, 'overflowing', in verse 12).

15. An ascription of **thanks** (*charis*) to the source of all grace for the supreme example of giving—God's **inexpressible gift** of his Son (cf. Rom. 8.32)—concludes Paul's plea for a generous contribution to the 'offering for the saints'.

VINDICATION OF PAUL'S APOSTOLIC AUTHORITY
10.1–13.14

The abrupt change of tone with which this section begins and
continues is discussed in the Introduction to 2 Corinthians
(pp. 166ff.).

PAUL'S ASSAULT ON CITADELS OF REBELLION 10.1–12

10. 1–2. I, Paul, myself: the two pronouns *autos* and *egō* emphasize that Paul's personal character and commission are at
issue (cf. Gal. 5.2; 1 Th. 2.18; also 2 C. 12.16); the very Paul who
is disparaged and misrepresented by his opponents is the one who
speaks with the apostolic authority vested in him by Christ. In
Christ's name, therefore, he makes his appeal, but the qualities
of Christ which he invokes are his **meekness** (*praÿtēs*, 'con-
siderateness', 'unassumingness') **and gentleness** (*epieikeia*, 'yield-
ingness', here perhaps, as in Wis. 2.19, the patient endurance of
abuse). This provides incidental confirmation of the Gospel portrayal of Jesus, although these two qualities are not specially
prominent in Paul's following rejoinder to his critics. Paul is decried because (for all the 'boldness' of his letters) he presents a
humble (*tapeinos*) demeanour **when face to face with** his cor-
respondents (cf. 1 C. 2.3). But, he implies in answer, Jesus
humbled himself in this way—cf. Mt. 11.29, where he is described
as 'gentle (*praÿs*) and lowly (*tapeinos*)'—instead of asserting his
divine authority; the servant must be content to follow his master's
example. Cf. R. Leivestad, 'The Meekness and Gentleness of
Christ', *NTS* 12 (1965–6), pp. 156ff.

bold to you when I am away: see note on 7.16 for two different nuances of the verb *tharreō*. It is for the Corinthians themselves
to decide whether or not he will have to show the same **boldness**
when he is **present** as they find in his letters written from a
distance.

such confidence as I count on showing: lit. 'the confidence
(*pepoithēsis*, as in 1.15; 3.4; 8.22) with which I reckon (*logizomai*)
to be daring (*tolmēsai*)'. **suspect:** 'reckon' (*logizomai*).

in worldly fashion: lit. 'according to (the) flesh' (*kata sarka*, as
in 1.17; 5.16), in the manner of one who is not indwelt and controlled by the Spirit of God.

3–4. we live in the world: Gk *en sarki*, 'in flesh', i.e. in mortal body, but this does not mean conducting our warfare *kata sarka* (cf. Eph. 6.12). Paul's critics probably represented him as conducting himself on a mundane level (cf. 1.17), whereas they themselves claimed to be 'spiritual' (see note on 1 C. 3.1). The **strongholds** we have to subdue, says Paul, belong to the spiritual order, and therefore must be stormed with spiritual, not worldly, tactics and **weapons** (siege engines), endowed with **divine**, not human, **power**.

5. These 'strongholds' are the **arguments** and designs which present an **obstacle to the knowledge of God** unfolded in the gospel, whether they are calculated to pervert the true gospel of divine grace and replace it by another form of teaching which brings the souls of men into bondage, or to destroy Paul's apostolic status in the eyes of his converts and thus hinder the further discharge of his commission. The tone of this attack on human wisdom or sophistry which limits the gospel by the measure of its own standards is similar to that in 1 C. 1.19ff.; 3.18ff., although he may not have the same persons in view. The fortresses and high towers which vaunt themselves against the divine revelation may reflect a spiritual interpretation of the tower of Babel, described by Philo as 'the stronghold (Gk *ochyrōma*, as here) built through persuasiveness of speech . . . to divert and deflect the mind from honouring God' (*Conf. Ling.* 129); cf. Prov. 21.22: 'A wise man scales the city of the mighty and brings down the stronghold (LXX *ochyrōma*) in which they trust'.

take every thought captive: the prisoners of war in this campaign are the thoughts or devices (Gk *noēmata*, as in 2.11; 3.14; 4.4) which rebel against the knowledge of God; they must be brought **to obey Christ**, the true wisdom.

6. If apostolic entreaty is ineffective, Paul is **ready** to exercise apostolic authority (see note on 2.9 and cf. 1 C. 5.3–5). To disobey this authority is to disobey Christ, in whose name it is exercised: **every** such **disobedience** must be punished when the time comes to make their **obedience** effective and **complete** (cf. J. Héring, *ad loc.*).

7. Look: Gk *blepete*, which can be taken as imperative (so *RSV*) or as indicative—in which case it might be interrogative ('Do you look on things according to appearance?'). But *kata prosōpon* should probably be taken here as in verse 2, not in the sense of *en prosōpō* in 5.12 (*RSV* 'on a man's position'): 'Look facts in the

face' (*NEB*). Paul's critics may disparage him, but if only the
Corinthians reflect on what they know of him (cf. 12.12), they
must conclude that his credentials are as valid as any that his
critics can claim.

If any one is confident that he is Christ's: the phraseology
recalls the affirmation 'I belong to Christ' (1 C. 1.12) and the
present context has therefore been used to throw light on the
meaning of that affirmation, notably by F. C. Baur, 'Die Christuspartei in der korinthischen Gemeinde', *Tübinger Zeitschrift für
Theologie* 5 (1831), Heft 4, pp. 61–206 (reprinted in *Ausgewählte
Werke*, ed. K. Scholder, 1 (1963), pp. 1–76). But there need be no
close relationship between the two passages: for one thing, the
situation in 1 C. 1.12 is a domestic one within the membership
of the Corinthian church, whereas the context suggests that the
reference here is to visitors from elsewhere, whose identity is more
fully revealed in what follows. They probably claimed Christ's
authority in a special degree, possibly as having seen him during
his ministry, but they could not claim it more absolutely than
Paul, whose gospel came to him 'through a revelation of Jesus
Christ' (Gal. 1.12).

8. If, in reply to his critics, Paul asserted more emphatically
than before this **authority, which the Lord gave** him, he was
no doubt charged with protesting overmuch. Others might claim
such authority without question, but Paul must not transgress the
limits of modesty and good taste. But where the situation demands
this course, Paul will assert his authority beyond his normal
practice, confident that the undeniable facts will vindicate his
assertion: **I shall not be put to shame.** And why should his own
converts object to his doing so? The **authority** which he received
has their permanent well-being in view: it was to 'build them up'.
He might talk of demolishing the hostile citadels of minds in revolt, but that was a very different thing from demolishing or
destroying (Gk *kathairesis*) his converts. (The wording is repeated
in 13.10.)

9–11. The charge that Paul was 'bold' when he was away had
reference to the note of authority in his letters. From his allusions
to the 'previous letter' (1 C. 5.9) and the 'severe letter' (2 C. 2.3ff.;
7.8ff.) it is evident that this note was struck in them; we hear it
repeatedly also in 1 Corinthians (e.g. 4.18–21) and 2 Corinthians
(e.g. 2.14–17), and especially in 2 C. 10–13. **'His letters are**

weighty and strong,' it was said, 'but that is by way of compensation for his ineffective presence and speech.' Paul was not eloquent, as Apollos was (Ac. 18.24), but he treated his lack of eloquence as an asset in his ministry (1 C. 1.17; 2.1, 4f.); it was a feature of the earthen vessel, so that the 'transcendent power' of the gospel he proclaimed owed nothing to any natural or cultivated rhetoric of his own (2 C. 4.7). He does not write now to 'frighten' them, any more than he wrote previously to cause them grief (2 C. 2.9; 7.12); he writes to secure their obedience. But if that obedience is not forthcoming, his speech and action on his next visit to Corinth will be fully as drastic as the weightiest of his letters could be (cf. 13.2–4, 10).

12. Other preachers came to Corinth and laid down the law dogmatically in the church. Paul will not **class or compare** (*enkrinai ē synkrinai*) himself with them, as though his ministry could be evaluated against theirs. They are interlopers; he is Christ's apostle to the Gentiles. Yet, strangely enough, some of the Corinthian Christians are readier to submit to the dictates of these interlopers, who come with no commendation but their own, than to their own apostle and father in God. These preachers indulge in such futile comparisons, measuring themselves against one another, and showing thereby their lack of **understanding**. (The Western text, attested by D* G and Ambrosiaster, omits **they are without understanding**; see note on verse 13.) Paul has already told the Corinthians that in the service of Christ it is Christ's commendation and assessment that matters: he himself will abide no man's judgment, for 'it is the Lord who judges me' (1 C. 4.3f.).

SPHERES OF SERVICE **10.13–18**

13. But we: Gk *hēmeis de*, omitted by the Western authorities D* G and Ambrosiaster (together with the preceding *ou syniasin*); the meaning then is: 'we do not compare ourselves with others, as they do, but measuring ourselves by ourselves and comparing ourselves with ourselves will not boast beyond measure (i.e. beyond the measure that has been laid down for us)'. This makes sense, but to measure oneself by oneself is a vain exercise; it is better to accept the non-Western text followed in *RSV*, which might be more literally rendered: 'But we will not boast beyond measure (*eis ta ametra*), but according to the measure (*metron*) of the sphere (*kanōn*) which God apportioned to us (as a) measure (*metron*)'. The normal meaning of *kanōn* is 'rule', and we might think of it as the measuring rod or line with which God, so to speak, has measured out Paul's sphere of apostolic ministry; but here by metonymy it means rather that sphere itself, a sphere which includes Corinth (**to reach even to you**). Cf. 1 Clement 41.1, where each church-member is exhorted 'not to transgress the appointed sphere (*kanōn*) of his ministry (*leitourgia*)'. Within that sphere Paul will 'boast' (he will exercise apostolic authority); to interfere in someone else's sphere of service would be to **boast beyond limit**; cf. Rom. 15.17ff., where he uses similar language and also describes such interference as 'building on another man's foundation' (see note on 1 C. 3.10). This is precisely what was being done by those interlopers who had invaded Paul's mission field and were trying to win the Corinthian Christians away from their allegiance to him.

14. we are not overextending ourselves: as Paul would be doing if he encroached on another mission field than his own, and as these visitors to Corinth were doing.

we were the first to come (Gk *ephthasamen*) **all the way to you**: Paul interpreted his commission to be apostle to the Gentiles as a commission to pioneer evangelism and made it his policy to pass over those areas, even in the Gentile world, 'where Christ has already been named' (Rom. 15.20). To each city which he evangelized, then, he was **the first to come ... with the gospel of Christ**, and his apostolic prerogative, sealed there by the existence of the local church (cf. 1 C. 9.2), should not be usurped or ignored by others.

15-16. beyond limit: Gk *eis ta ametra*, as in verse 13, again playing on the mutual 'measuring' of verse 12. Not only does Corinth fall within Paul's field of service, but he hopes that, as the **faith** of his converts there **increases**, the Corinthian church may in turn become a base for the extension of that **field** (*kanōn*) to the **lands beyond** Achaia: he thinks perhaps of other parts of the Balkan peninsula (cf. Illyricum, Rom. 15.19) and even the western Mediterranean (more particularly Spain, Rom. 15.24, 28), Gentile territories thus far unevangelized which therefore fell within his apostolic province. He would thus have no need to **boast ... in other men's labours** (*en allotriois kopois*) or **of work already done in another's field** (*en allotriō kanoni*). Some men

I

no doubt found it easier to take up a ready-made work than to plough virgin soil. If the men who did this in Paul's mission field were based on Jerusalem, then Paul might well complain that the apostolic agreement of Gal. 2.6–10, by which the Jerusalem 'pillars' were to go to the Jews and he and Barnabas to the Gentiles, had been infringed.

17. The quotation from Jer. 9.24 has already appeared in 1 C. 1.31, as a corrective to boasting of personal achievement or prestige. Here it is intended as a corrective to boasting in the exploitation of a situation which is someone else's responsibility. For an apostle to **boast** of what Christ had wrought through him in his allotted field of service (cf. Rom. 15.18) would be to **boast of** (or 'in') **the Lord**.

18. This verse echoes 3.1–3 and 1 C. 4.3–5; cf. also Rom. 2.29 for the importance of receiving one's praise 'not from men but from God'.

FALSE APOSTLES 11.1–15

11.1. Paul now invites them to put up with **a little foolishness** from him. The visitors who have tried to undermine his position at Corinth have had no compunction about parading their credentials. That Paul should speak of imitating them, and that to his own converts, would be unthinkable, if their readiness to listen to the visitors' disparagement of him had not forced him to do so (cf. 12.11). He is embarrassed by the necessity thus thrust upon him: he has just told them that self-commendation is no commendation, and now he proposes to embark on this foolish exercise himself.

2. Yet he stands in a unique relation to the Corinthian church: as her apostle and founder he has played the part of the one who has **betrothed** her **to Christ**, to whom he hopes to **present** her at the parousia as **a pure bride**, lit. 'a pure virgin' (cf. Eph. 5.25–27). He may have been acquainted with the Jewish conception of Moses as the *paranymphios* who presented Israel as a bride to Yahweh, although this is not attested in literature until later (e.g. *Mᵉkiltâ* on Exod. 19.17; *Exod. Rabba* xlvi.1 on Exod. 34.1); cf. also John the Baptist's similar depiction of his own rôle in Jn 3.29. Hence Paul guards the church of Corinth with affectionate **jealousy**—not self-regarding but **divine**—lest anything should rob her of her chastity between betrothal and the day of presentation.

3. The *OT* narrative of **Eve** occurs to his mind: Eve was 'beguiled' by **the serpent** into disobedience to God (Gen. 3.13; cf. 1 Tim. 2.13-15), and the Corinthians, he fears, may similarly be seduced from their loyalty to Christ. A haggadic version of the fall story which interpreted the serpent's seduction of Eve in a sexual sense is first attested in 4 Mac. 18.8, where the mother of the seven martyrs says (after a reference to the formation of Eve): 'nor did the false beguiling serpent sully the purity of my maidenhood'. This version may well have been known to Paul (see note on verse 14), although his language here is perfectly intelligible on the basis of Gen. 3. His verb **deceived** (*exēpatēsen*) echoes Eve's *ēpatēsen* (Gen. 3.13, LXX; cf. 1 Tim. 2.14a); he uses the compound *exapataō* (cf. Rom. 7.11; 1 Tim. 2.14b).

cunning: Gk *panourgia* ('rascality'; cf. 4.2; 12.16; 1 C. 3.19), perhaps a reference to the serpent's 'subtlety' (Gen. 3.1, although the LXX rendering is quite different).

a sincere and pure devotion: lit. 'the simplicity and the purity towards Christ' (P⁴⁶ Aleph B G etc.); the two nouns of quality are transposed in D, while 'and the purity' is absent from 1739 and the majority of Byzantine witnesses.

4. The seduction of which Paul is afraid would be effected if the Corinthians accepted **another Jesus** (*allon Iēsoun*) **than the one** Paul and his colleagues **preached**. He does not specify the difference between this 'other Jesus' and **the one we preached**; but since the Jesus whom Paul preached was the Messiah and exalted Lord who had now entered upon his reign (cf. 1 C. 15.25) and liberated his people from legal obligation, any attempt to impose such obligation on Christians, even if made in the name of Jesus, implied **another Jesus** than the one in whom Paul's hearers had originally believed, a Jesus who was not the true Messiah. The attempt need not be, as it was in the Galatian situation, to require that Gentile converts should be circumcised; from Paul's point of view even the food restrictions of the Jerusalem decree (Ac. 15.20, 29), if imposed as a matter of legal obligation, would compromise the freedom of the gospel. In view of the characterization of the visitors to Corinth as 'Hebrews' (verse 22), it is unlikely that the 'other Jesus' whom they are accused of proclaiming was conceived on Gnostic lines.

a different spirit: since the apostolic ministry is 'the dispensation of the Spirit' (3.8) and was discharged 'in demonstration of the

Spirit and power' (1 C. 2.4), the spirit by which this 'other Jesus' was proclaimed must be a **different spirit** (*pneuma heteron*) from the Spirit whom the Corinthian Christians **received** when they believed (1.22; 5.5; cf. 1 C. 12.13). Those who proclaimed the 'other Jesus' might claim to be spiritual men (see note on 10.3), but it was not by the Spirit of God that they were energized. It is doubtful whether there is any direct relation between what Paul says here and his declaration in 1 C. 12.3, where a criterion is laid down for judging prophetic utterances; if, however, the visitors claimed the prophetic gift, that criterion was applicable to them. **a different gospel** (*euangelion heteron*): cf. Gal. 1.6f., 'a different (*heteron*) gospel' which is not 'another (*allo*) gospel', since there is only one gospel—the message of salvation provided by divine grace to be accepted by faith, apart from legal works. A message, whether judaizing or gnosticizing, which presents the saving work of Christ as something to be appropriated in any degree by human attainment and merit, is in Paul's eyes a **different gospel**, proclaiming **another Jesus** in the power of **a different Spirit**. Paul nowhere charges the Jerusalem apostles with preaching such a message; in 1 C. 15.11 he indicates that they shared his own basic *kērygma*. The demarcation of spheres of apostolic activity in Gal. 2.7–9 implies that Paul and Barnabas were to preach the same essential gospel to Gentiles as James, Peter and John were to preach to Jews; and Paul's indignation at Peter's withdrawal from table-fellowship with Gentiles at Antioch (Gal. 2.11ff.)—a withdrawal which he describes as 'play-acting'—was the greater because he knew Peter to be at heart in fundamental agreement with himself with regard to the gospel of grace and the equality of Gentile and Jewish believers in Christ.

you submit to it readily enough: Pauline irony. 'You put up readily enough with someone who comes with a different message from that which brought you salvation: why not put up with the apostle who came with the message which did bring you salvation?' (A variant reading, *aneichesthe* for *anechesthe*, makes the construction hypothetical; cf. *AV* 'ye might well bear with him'.)

5. The **superlative apostles** (Gk *hyperlian apostoloi*) to whom, according to Paul's opponents, he himself was so **inferior** (cf. 12.11), can scarcely be other than the Jerusalem apostles, including James (as in Gal. 1.19). Such language, by whomsoever used, could not well be applied to men of lower apostolic status than theirs. By this time, perhaps, none of the Twelve was actually resident in Jerusalem, but Jerusalem would still be regarded as their home base. Their designation as **superlative apostles** might conceivably go back to the intruders in Corinth, who by this phrase invoked the authority of men whose commission and status were so incomparably superior, by their account, to anything that Paul could justly claim; but there is a strong flavour of irony about the expression, and it is more likely that it is Paul's way of summing up his opponents' portrayal of the Jerusalem leaders. We may compare his reference in Gal. 2.9 to 'James and Cephas and John, who were reputed to be pillars'; it may indeed be these three who are primarily in view here. Paul has no thought of depreciating their apostolic status; he is at pains to emphasize that his is **not in the least inferior** to theirs. He had received his commission from the risen Christ (1 C. 9.1; 15.8; Gal. 1.12), and, by his own account, so had they (1 C. 15.5-7). Even if he permits himself a measure of irony, it is rather at the expense of his opponents' portrayal of the Jerusalem apostles than at the expense of the apostles themselves; in fact, whatever he may have thought or felt about the failure to observe the delimitation of mission fields agreed upon at Jerusalem, he is studiously careful to avoid any overt criticism of the Jerusalem apostles, while he is unsparing in his denunciation of the intruders who invoked their authority (cf. verses 13-15). The point of the conjunction 'for' with which this sentence opens (untranslated in *RSV*) is: 'Please bear with me, for after all I reckon I am as much an apostle as those in whose name my critics claim to speak and act'.

6. Even if I am unskilled in speaking: cf. 10.10; Paul does not dispute this estimate of his eloquence. The word rendered **unskilled** is *idiōtēs* (cf. 1 C. 10.16, 23f.).

knowledge: Gk *gnōsis*; that he is not 'unskilled' or a mere amateur in this should by this time have become abundantly **plain** to them, as to all his subsequent readers (cf. 1 C. 2.6-13, 16b, for the content and source of his *gnōsis*). His opponents may have laid claim to a higher *gnōsis* than his, but he disallows their claim: such knowledge as they had belonged to the sphere of secular wisdom (cf. 1 C. 1.20f.) and, like that mentioned in 1 C. 8.1, tended to 'inflate' rather than to build up.

7-8. His refusal to accept material support from the Corinthian church (cf. 1 C. 9.15-18) still rankled. It was natural that they should resent this refusal when he consented to accept such **support** (Gk *opsōnion*, lit. 'wages', as in 1 C. 9.7, where *RSV* renders 'expense') from **other churches**, but had he accepted it from Corinth in the present situation, this would have been misrepresented by his critics, and worse still, some of the Corinthian Christians would have listened readily enough to their misrepresentations. Paul would rather die (1 C. 9.15) than have his converts think that he was sponging on them. If his critics asserted their authority by doing what he refused to do, sooner or later the Corinthians might make appropriate comparisons and draw the necessary conclusions.

9–11. When he first came to Corinth he supported himself by tent-making (Ac. 18.3) until his colleagues arrived **from Macedonia** (Ac. 18.5), bringing gifts from the Christians in that province—more particularly from those in Philippi (Phil. 4.15). Thus he **did not burden any one** in Corinth: the verb *katanarkaō*, used in this clause and 12.13f. (and nowhere else in the Greek Bible), means literally to 'benumb'; it is derived from *narkē*, the torpedo or electric ray which benumbs any one who touches it. The use of the verb in the sense of burdening is said by Jerome (*Epistle* cxxi.x.4) to be a Cilician idiom. (We might compare our colloquialism 'to sting someone for so much' in the sense of overcharging.) When later in this verse and in 12.16 Paul speaks of **burdening** his converts in the sense of living at their expense he uses more obvious words from the stem *bar-* (here *abarēs*, 'unburdensome'); cf. 1 Th. 2.7, 9; 2 Th. 3.8. Criticisms of his refusal will not move him to abandon this settled policy **in the regions of Achaia**; he is determined to maintain **this boast** of his (cf. 1 C. 9.15)—not because he does not **love** them, but because he does. The intensity of his feeling is indicated by his solemn asseverations: **As the truth of Christ is in me** and **God knows I do!**

12. A more immediate reason for his maintenance of this policy than anything previously mentioned now becomes apparent: he will give no opportunity to his intrusive critics to claim that in this respect he is no better than they are; he will not descend to their level. If they boast of the support they receive, he is glad that he can boast of his denying himself such support—although he has a better title to it than they have (1 C. 9.3–12).

13. Not so much for this conduct as for their perversion of the

true gospel **such men** are excoriated in the most scathing terms
as 'sham-apostles, crooked in all their practices, masquerading
as apostles of Christ' (*NEB*).

deceitful workmen: reminiscent of the 'workers of iniquity'
against whom the psalmists voice repeated complaints (Ps. 5.5,
etc.). **disguising themselves:** Gk *metaschēmatizō*; see note on 1
C. 4.6. The **false apostles** (*pseudapostoloi*) are not the 'superlative
apostles' of verse 5, but the interlopers who came in their name.
They may indeed have regarded Peter and even James in their
hearts as compromisers, although it was expedient to claim the
backing of their authority. Unlike the trouble-makers in the
churches of Galatia, they did not try to impose circumcision on
Paul's Gentile converts, but they did try to bring them into subjection to themselves. Perhaps they found a response on the part
of those who, at a slightly earlier stage in the Corinthian church's
life, said 'I belong to Cephas' (1 C. 1.12); this group might, for
example, have been ready to accept the provisions of the apostolic
decree as legally binding, whereas, so far as the food-regulations
were concerned, Paul took a more liberal line (see notes on 1 C.
8.1; 10.25-27). But it was not a difference of interpretation regarding the best way of maintaining a *modus vivendi* between Jewish
and Gentile Christians that called forth Paul's denunciation of
these people; it was their making such matters an essential condition of the gospel. With his language here may be compared the
'anathema' of Gal. 1.8f.

14-15. In the pseudepigraphic *Life of Adam and Eve* (one of the
witnesses to the haggadah referred to in the note on verse 3),
Satan appears to Eve 'wearing the form and brightness of an
angel' (ix.1). 'If he can disguise himself as a messenger of God,'
says Paul, '**it is not strange** that **his servants** should disguise
themselves as messengers of Christ; nevertheless, their behaviour
shows them to be not **servants of righteousness** but workers
of iniquity, and "all the workers of iniquity shall be scattered"'
(Ps. 92.9, *RV*).

PAUL BOASTS 'AS A FOOL' 11.16-29

16-19. After this digression on his opponents, Paul resumes his
'foolishness'; he is not really being **foolish**, because he is not in
earnest when he 'boasts' as these opponents do, but if his readers
do think this kind of talk is foolishness on his part, he asks them

to put up with him **as a fool**. He is not speaking now as their apostle, **with the Lord's authority**; but if others **boast of worldly things** (*kata tēn sarka*, 'according to the flesh'; cf. 5.12, *en prosōpō*), why should not he take a little time off and do the same? *Dulce est desipere in loco!* Of course **wise** men like the Corinthian Christians (cf. 1 C. 4.10, where the same adjective *phronimos* is used, although the irony here is more savage) must be accustomed to **bear with fools**; indeed they do so **gladly**, since the foolishness of others throws their own wisdom into relief! Well, let them bear with Paul when he assumes the rôle of a fool.

20–21a. The Corinthians bear with the boastful intruders who visit their church and dictate to them, treat them as **slaves**, live at their expense, put on superior **airs** among them and generally insult and humiliate them. Paul acknowledges, ironically treating it as something to be ashamed of, that he never went so far as that among them; the 'meekness and gentleness of Christ' may not have been qualities that came to him naturally, but he did school himself to cultivate them among his converts at Corinth and elsewhere. This restraint and moderation, however, have evidently been interpreted as weakness—as evidence that, in his heart of hearts, he knew he had no right to assert apostolic authority.

21b. Paul, **speaking as a fool**, can cap any boast that his opponents put forward. Cf. Phil. 3.4, where a similar claim is followed by a list of natural endowments and attainments not unlike that of verses 22f., with a dismissal of any such *cursus honorum*: 'whatever gain I had, I counted as loss for the sake of Christ' (Phil. 3.7).

22. Are they Hebrews?: Hebrews in the *NT* age is a more specialized term than 'Israelites'. In Ac. 6.1 it is used in distinction from 'Hellenists', which appears to denote Jews of Greek language and culture (cf. Ac. 9.29; 11.20 mg.), with associations outside Palestine. 'Hebrews', on the other hand, denotes Jews whose family ties were Palestinian, if they were not wholly resident in Palestine. Inscriptional references to a 'synagogue of (the) Hebrews' in Rome (*CIG* IV. 9909) and a similarly named one in Corinth (B. Powell, 'Greek Inscriptions from Corinth', *AJA* ser. II, 7 (1903), pp. 6of., no. 40) point to meeting-places for Palestinian (and probably Aramaic-speaking) Jews, over against others where Greek-speaking Jews from various lands of the Dispersion met (cf. Ac. 6.9). Philo uses 'Hebrews' to denote those who speak

Hebrew (*Dreams* ii.250; *Abraham* 28). It looks very much as if
Paul's opponents at Corinth were of Palestinian provenance.
So am I: cf. Phil. 3.5, where he calls himself 'a Hebrew born of
Hebrews'. In spite of his Tarsian birth, Jerusalem was the city of
his boyhood and early manhood, according to Ac. 22.3 (cf. W. C.
van Unnik, *Tarsus or Jerusalem: the City of Paul's Youth*, E.T. (1962)).
It is difficult to know how much credence to give to Jerome's
statement (*Commentary on Phm.* 23) that Paul's family came from
Gischala in Galilee. That his mother tongue was Aramaic is a
fair inference from Ac. 26.14, where the heavenly voice on the
Damascus road is said to have addressed him 'in the Hebrew
language' (cf. also the implication of Ac. 21.40; 22.2).
Israelites: an honourable term (Rom. 9.4), more general than
'Hebrews' (cf. 'of the people of Israel', Phil. 3.5); Paul may have
in mind a distinction between those who are Israelites by natural
descent from Jacob (Rom. 9.6) and one who is an 'Israelite indeed' (Jn 1.47).
descendants of Abraham: more comprehensive even than
'Israelites'; but 'not all are children of Abraham because they are
his descendants' (Rom. 9.7; cf. Gal. 3.29; Mt. 3.9 // Lk. 3.8;
Jn 8.33, 37, 39f.). 'According to the flesh' the boast in descent
from Abraham implied having been 'circumcised on the eighth
day'—one of Paul's grounds for 'confidence in the flesh', had he
been so minded (Phil. 3.5). So far as natural descent and religious
heritage were concerned, Paul could match his opponents' self-
confidence at every point.

23. But when he speaks of **servants of Christ**, he is dealing
with achievement, not endowment, and comparisons in this sphere
are particularly odious, so much so that he describes himself now
not merely as a 'fool' (*aphrōn*) but as **a madman** (*paraphronōn*), one
who is out of his senses. In calmer vein he has made a similar comparison in 1 C. 15.10, acknowledging that the credit for greater
achievement was due not to himself but to 'the grace of God'.
Here the comparison may well have been initiated by the other
side, but if he claims to be a **better** 'servant of Christ' than any
of them, it is not on such grounds as they might appeal to—
superior credentials, more converts and so forth. Had he chosen to
do this, an expansion of his concise summary in Rom. 15.18f.—
the preaching of the gospel and the planting of churches in the
provinces of Galatia, Macedonia, Achaia and Asia within the

space of ten years—would have been argument enough. But here his embarrassment at being forced into foolish comparisons of this kind makes him concentrate on sufferings rather than achievements, and he gives an amplified version of his appeal in Gal. 6.17 to his bearing on his body the *stigmata* of Jesus. How had he come by these marks? By **far greater labours, far more imprisonments** than his critics, **with countless beatings, and often near death** (cf. 4. 10–12; 1 C. 15. 31).

with far greater labours (*en kopois perissoterōs*): cf. 1 C. 15.10, *RV*: 'I laboured more abundantly' (*perissoteron . . . ekopiasa*). The **imprisonments** present an interesting problem, and incidentally remind us how many gaps are left by the narrative of Acts, for there the only imprisonment of Paul's recorded up to this time (if we date the composition of 2 C. 10–13 before the start of his last voyage to Palestine) is the occasion when he and Silas were locked up overnight at Philippi (Ac. 16.23–40; cf. 1 Th. 2.2). We cannot be sure where he underwent any of the other numerous **imprisonments** referred to here, but it is more than probable that at least one was endured in Ephesus, conceivably in connection with the 'affliction' mentioned in 1.8ff. Cf. H. Lisco, *Vincula Sanctorum* (1900); W. Michaelis, *Die Gefangenschaft des Paulus in Ephesus* (1925); G. S. Duncan, *St. Paul's Ephesian Ministry* (1929).

24–25a. The 'countless beatings' of verse 23 included five such experiences at the hands of Jewish authorities and three at (presumably) Roman hands. The Jewish beatings were probably inflicted by the sentence of the local court (*bêt-dîn*) attached to the synagogue in this or that Jewish community of the dispersion. The written law prescribed a maximum of forty strokes (Dt. 25.3); on the principle of 'setting a hedge about the law' to prevent its inadvertent infringement, tradition made the maximum thirty-nine. According to the later codification in the Mishnah tractate *Makkôt* (iii.10–15) the strokes were administered with a strap consisting of three hide thongs, two thirds on the back and one third in front; it is laid down that 'when they estimate the number of stripes that one can bear, it must be a number divisible by three'. None of these beatings is recorded in Acts.

Three times I have been beaten with rods: one of these occasions was at Philippi, when he and Silas were so beaten by the lictors (Gk *rhabdouchoi*, lit. 'rod-bearers') attendant on the two chief magistrates of the colony (Ac. 16.22f.). Whether the two other similar beatings were endured at the hands of Roman officials or not, we have no further reference to them.

once I was stoned: at Lystra (Ac. 14.19).

25b. Paul's experience of storm and shipwreck on his way to Rome (Ac. 27) was not the first of its kind; we should not have known of these earlier experiences but for his incidental mention of them here. It is difficult to fit them into any voyage described in Acts; once again, we realize how many substantial gaps remain in our knowledge of Paul's career.

a night and a day I have been adrift: lit. 'I have spent (*pepoiēka*, I have done) a *nychthēmeron* (a period of a night and a day).' **at sea:** Gk *en tō bythō*, 'in the deep' (*NEB* 'on the open sea'), clinging perhaps to a fragment of wreck (cf. Ac. 27.44a).

26–27. These two verses give a more general summary of the dangers and privations which beset him in the course of his apostolic activity; cf. 4.8–11 and especially 6.4f.; also 1 C. 4.9–13. **robbers:** bandits or brigands (Gk *lēstai*) such as infested the roads along which he made his **frequent journeys.** See W. M. Ramsay, 'Roads and Travel in the NT', *HDB* v (1904), pp. 375ff. The allusions to **danger from my own people, danger from the Gentiles, danger in the city** can be repeatedly illustrated from the narrative of Acts.

danger in the wilderness: Gk *erēmia*, unpopulated or sparsely populated territory, here mentioned by contrast with 'the city'.

false brethren: a term (Gk *pseudadelphoi*) which Paul uses in one other place (Gal. 2.4, its only other *NT* occurrence), with reference to counterfeit Christians who infiltrated into his company 'to spy out our freedom which we have in Christ Jesus' and if possible to impose a yoke of legal bondage on him and his converts.

through many a sleepless night: whether the sleeplessness was caused by bodily pain and material discomfort (cf. Ac. 16.25) or by concern for his friends and converts (cf. 6.5, 'watchings', which renders the same word *agrypniai* as is used here).

often without food: lit. 'in fastings (*nēsteiai*) often', of voluntary abstention from food (cf. 6.5 for the same word); the preceding **hunger and thirst** are involuntary.

28. These hardships are 'all in the day's work' for an apostle like Paul; what he finds more wearing is the **daily pressure** (Gk *epistasis*) **. . . of my anxiety for all the churches:** the

Corinthian correspondence bears more than adequate witness to
his **anxiety** for one church—burden enough for any man to bear,
but at the same time the manifold problems of his other churches,
arising from subversive doctrine, unseemly behaviour, internal
discord and the like, weighed upon him also.

29. Who is weak . . . ?: a reference to the 'weak brethren' (cf.
1 C. 8.7ff.; Rom. 14.1ff.) with whose tender and scrupulous conscience Paul had such patient sympathy, robust as his own sense
of liberty was. Cf. 1 C. 9.22: 'to the weak I became weak'.
Who is made to fall . . . ?: it was the 'weak brethren' who were
most prone to be tripped up (*skandalizesthai*) by the inconsiderate
example of the stronger; Paul, who declares his readiness to abjure
meat for ever if it is a cause of his brother's falling (1 C. 8.13), is
indignant (*pyroumai*, 'I burn', 'I am on fire') when others thought-
lessly lead a fellow-Christian to do what his conscience condemns.

A HUMILIATING MEMORY 11.30–33

30. Even to enumerate perils and privations endured in the
course of apostolic service might engender a proud and boastful
attitude—whatever superiority his opponents might claim, in
these things at least Paul could outdo them! Better to think of
things which hurt his pride; if he **must boast** at all, let him
boast of the things that displayed his **weakness**. One immediately comes to his mind—a humiliating and undignified experience, in which he cut such a ridiculous figure that the mere
thought of it killed any tendency to pride.

31. But first, as though he were about to make a higher claim
than any he had made thus far, he calls God to witness to the
truth of his words; cf. verses 10, 11; 2 C. 1.18; Gal. 1.20; Rom. 9.1.
he who is blessed for ever: cf. Rom. 1.25; 9.5.

32. the governor under King Aretas: Aretas (*Ḥāriṭaṭ*) IV,
originally called Aeneas, reigned at Petra over the Nabataean
Arabs from 9 B.C. to A.D. 40. He was father-in-law to Herod
Antipas; when the latter divorced his daughter in order to marry
Herodias, Aretas bided his time and, when a suitable occasion
arose, invaded Peraea and inflicted a serious defeat on Herod's
forces. His kingdom extended to the neighbourhood of Damascus;
it has even been held, because of the absence of Roman coins
from its numismatic record between A.D. 34 and 62, that the city
was at this time subject to him (as it had been to his predecessors

for some decades until the Roman conquest of 64 B.C.), but of this there is no positive evidence.

The **governor** is the 'ethnarch' (Gk *ethnarchēs*) who probably was the leader of the semi-autonomous Nabataean community in Damascus and acted as their spokesman and representative in dealings with the civic and provincial authorities. The Jews of Damascus would also be organized as an *ethnos* within the city, as they were in Alexandria, under the leadership of an ethnarch (Strabo, *ap.* Jos. *Ant.* xiv. 117). Whether the Nabataean ethnarch watched the city gates from inside or outside **in order to seize** Paul cannot be established from the wording here. The question arises why Aretas or his deputy should have shown this hostility to Paul: we probably have the answer in Gal. 1.17, according to which, immediately after his conversion and call to evangelize the Gentiles, Paul 'went away into Arabia'—presumably to preach the gospel to the Nabataeans—and then 'returned to Damascus'. It was after his return to Damascus that the ethnarch tried to arrest him, incensed no doubt by his activity in the Nabataean kingdom. Luke records the same incident, with one material and characteristic deviation—he says it was the Jews of Damascus who plotted against Paul and 'were watching the gates day and night, to kill him' (Ac. 9.23f.). It is not impossible that the leaders of these two ethnic groups in Damascus made common cause against him; if so, Paul (according to his custom) avoids accusing his own people (cf. Ac. 28.19b).

33. I was let down in a basket: by 'his disciples', says Luke (Ac. 9.25). The **basket** (Gk *sarganē*) 'was a large woven or network bag or basket suitable for hay, straw … or for bales of wool' (K. Lake and H. J. Cadbury, *The Beginnings of Christianity*, ed. F. J. Foakes Jackson and K. Lake, I. iv (1933), p. 106). The word in Ac. 9.25 is *spyris* (cf. Mk 8.8).

through a window in the wall: presumably in a house which was built on to the wall, away from any of the city gates. If ever Paul felt tempted to think too highly of himself, the memory of this inglorious escape was calculated to keep him humble; he records it here as compensation for his having boasted 'as a fool'.

AN ECSTATIC EXPERIENCE AND ITS SEQUEL 12.1–10

12.1. Paul turns to boast of another aspect of his weakness, but he approaches it indirectly. The reference to **visions and**

revelations of the Lord may suggest either that his opponents boasted of such experiences or that they decried his apostolic title because it was based on a 'vision'. Both implications may indeed be present, as though they said: 'Our visions are valid; his are illusory.' That Paul had such experiences is confirmed by the narrative of Acts which, in addition to his confrontation with the risen Lord on the Damascus road, records comparable visions at Jerusalem when he first returned there after his conversion (22.17–21), at Corinth (18.9f.), at Jerusalem during his last visit to that city (23.11) and on the voyage to Italy (27.23f.); other visions, but not of the Lord or his 'angel', are mentioned in Ac. 9.12; 16.9f. The experience described here cannot be equated with any recorded in Acts. Paul does not say whether on this occasion he saw the Lord or not; in fact he is more impressed by what he heard than by anything he saw. The genitive **of the Lord** should probably be interpreted as subjective, not objective: **the Lord** is the author of these **visions and revelations**.

2. So far is he averse from personal boasting that he begins to speak of himself impersonally, **I know a man in Christ**, although it becomes apparent in the course of his narrative that it was he who had the experience described.

fourteen years ago: reckoning back from the probable date of 2 C. 10–13 we arrive at the obscure period of Paul's career between his departure for Syria–Cilicia (Gal. 1.21) and his second post-conversion visit to Jerusalem (Gal. 2.1)—or, in terms of Luke's account, between his being shipped off to Tarsus from Caesarea (Ac. 9.30) and his being fetched by Barnabas from Tarsus to Antioch (Ac. 11.25f.). The identification of these **fourteen years** with the 'fourteen years' of Gal. 2.1 is untenable (cf. J. Knox, *Chapters in a Life of Paul* (1954), p. 78, n. 3).

caught up: the verb *harpazō* (primarily of a wild beast's seizing and rending its prey, as in Jn 10.12) makes it clear that the initiative was not Paul's; it is similarly used in Wis. 4.11; Ac. 8.39; 1 Th. 4.17; Rev. 12.5.

the third heaven: the 'heavens' were variously enumerated in Judaism, but the idea of seven heavens is commonest (cf. *Test. Levi* ii.7ff.; *Asc. Isa.* vi.13; vii.13ff.; TB *Ḥăgîgāh* 12b). Three heavens were deduced from 1 K. 8.27 (lit. 'the heavens and the heavens of the heavens'). Lucian (*Philopatris* 12), caricaturing Christians, says 'the Galilaean . . . who went by air into the third heaven and learned the fairest things has renewed us through water'. Whether Paul regarded **the third heaven** as the highest heaven is uncertain; he implies at least that in it 'Paradise' is located (cf. *Apoc. Mos.* 40.2; 2 Enoch 8.1).

whether in the body or out of the body: ecstasy, as the word originally signified, usually involved temporary detachment of the conscious mind from the body; Enoch, however, paid a bodily visit to the celestial realms and returned to earth (1 Enoch 12.1ff.; cf. 71.1ff.). The conditions of Paul's ecstasy on this occasion were such that he had no idea in which of these two states he experienced it: only **God knows**.

3. this man: lit. 'such a man', i.e. 'the man in question' (for this use of *ho toioutos* cf. 1 C. 5.5; 2 C. 2.6).

into Paradise: this word of Persian origin (*patri-daēza*, a walled enclosure) was borrowed by both Hebrew (*pardēs*; cf. Ec. 2.5, 'parks') and Greek (*paradeisos*); in LXX it is used of the earthly Eden (Gen. 2.8ff.). In Lk. 23.43 it is used of the present abode of the righteous departed, with no reference to its location; in Rev. 2.7 'the paradise of God' is the eschatological Eden (cf. *Test. Levi* xviii.10). The heavenly Paradise, the Eden above, appears in 4 Ezr. 4.7f.; 3 Bar. 4.8; TB *Ḥăgîgāh* 15b; *Gen. Rabba* 65 on Gen. 27.27, etc. To enter Paradise was a rare experience; in the story of the four rabbis who were granted this privilege early in the second century only Aqiba returned unscathed (TB *Ḥăgîgāh* 14b–15b). Paul did not return unscathed, as the sequel to his account makes plain.

4. Unlike the marvellous details of heavenly journeys in apocalyptic and gnostic literature, Paul's account gives no information except that **he heard things that cannot be told, which man may not utter**—things which it was impossible as well as impermissible to describe.

5-6. Paul preserves the curious distinction between himself as narrator and 'the man in question' (*ho toioutos*, as in verse 3) as recipient of the revelations. Looking objectively at the 'man in Christ' he can glory on his behalf, but considering himself subjectively he will glory only in 'the things that show his weakness' (cf. 11.30). Even if he did boast in his 'revelations of the Lord' he would not be boasting as **a fool**, for he would be **speaking the truth**, but he does not wish his converts to take him at his own evaluation, but on the basis of their personal experience of him (cf. 10.7).

7. and . . . by the abundance of the revelations: this phrase, with which verse 7 opens in Greek, must be attached to the end of verse 6 if, with Aleph A B G and some other authorities, we read *dio* ('therefore') after it and before **to keep me from being too elated**. But the phrase goes so much more naturally with **elated** that it is better, with P^{46} D and the majority of witnesses, to omit *dio* and construe as *RSV* does.

a thorn . . . in the flesh: this **thorn** or 'splinter' (Gk *skolops*) was evidently a distressing, not to say humiliating, physical ailment, which Paul feared might be a handicap to his effective ministry but which, in fact, by giving his pride a knock-out blow and keeping him dependent on divine enabling, proved to be an aid, not a handicap. Many and various attempts at diagnosis of this ailment have been made—including 'pain in the ear or head' (Tertullian), such troublesome characters as Hymenaeus and Alexander (Chrysostom), epilepsy (M. Krenkel, J. Klausner), convulsive attacks (M. Dibelius), ophthalmia (J. T. Brown, in *Horae Subsecivae* (1858)), malaria (W. M. Ramsay, E. B. Allo), sufferings caused by constant persecutions (J. Munck), attacks of depression after periods of exaltation (H. Clavier), the agony caused by the unbelief of his Jewish brethren (P. H. Menoud) or by the memory of his persecution of the church (A. Osiander, A. Schlatter). The very variety of these suggestions shows that certainty is unattainable, though some are more improbable than others. This **thorn . . . in the flesh** must at least have been something which first attacked him after the ecstatic experience described above; by **flesh** we should understand 'body', not 'the part of the soul which is not regenerate' (J. Calvin). There is probably a reference to this same affliction in Gal. 4.13f., where Paul speaks of a 'bodily ailment' (lit. a weakness or 'infirmity of the flesh', *AV*, *RV*) which was a 'trial' to his Galatian friends and might well have made them 'scorn or despise' him (spit in aversion), although they did no such thing.

a messenger of Satan: for Satan's agency in afflicting a Christian's body for his spiritual good, cf. 1 C. 5.5; Job provides an *OT* example. Through Satan God exercises his salutary paternal discipline on Paul, not, of course, by way of punishment (as in 1 C. 5.5) but with a view to his growth in grace and more effective service.

to harass me: the same verb (Gk *kolaphizō*) which is rendered 'buffet' (its literal sense) in 1 C. 4.11, a further indication that some recurring physical disability is intended.

8. Three times I besought the Lord: W. M. Alexander ('St. Paul's Infirmity', *ExT* 15 (1903–4), pp. 469ff., 545ff.) identifies Paul's ailment with 'Malta fever', and suggests that Paul was attacked by it (i) on the early occasion referred to here, (ii) on his first visit to South Galatia (Gal. 4.13f.), more particularly in Pisidian Antioch (Ac. 13.14), (iii) in proconsular Asia (2 C. 1.8ff.). The three occasions when he prayed for the removal of the ailment were the three occasions when he was attacked by it. It is a more natural inference from Paul's language, however, that his thrice-repeated prayer for its removal was offered soon after the first attack, and that after that he learned to live with it. His prayer was indeed answered, not by his deliverance from the affliction, but by his receiving the necessary grace to bear it.

9–10. he said: the tense is perfect (*eirēken*, lit. 'he has said'), implying perhaps that the words **My grace is sufficient for you** remain with him as an abiding source of assurance and comfort. **my power is made perfect in weakness:** the principle is the same as that of 4.7ff.; if Paul's preaching was so effective despite his physical weakness, then the 'transcendent power' was manifestly God's, not his own. The realization of this makes him **all the more gladly** glory in his **weaknesses:** if they are the condition on which **the power of Christ** rests upon him, he welcomes them, together with the **insults, hardships, persecutions and calamities** which are part of his apostolic lot (cf. 11.23ff.) —he welcomes them **for the sake of Christ**, for it is when he is **weak** in himself that he is **strong** with the strength of Christ.

SIGNS OF AN APOSTLE **12.11–13**

11. He has finished his 'foolish' boasting: it would not have been necessary for him to start it, had not his converts **forced** him to it by listening obsequiously to the boasting of others and failing to maintain the credit of their own apostle (cf. 5.12). Even if he was but a cipher, as his opponents alleged, yet the record of his service compared favourably with that of the **superlative apostles** to whom his critics appealed (cf. 11.5, where he has used almost identical language). Similarly in 1 C. 15.8ff. he maintains that even if he be, as his opponents alleged, a mere *ektrōma* compared with the original apostles, yet his commission as a witness to the risen Christ is as valid as theirs, and his achievement, by God's grace, superior to theirs.

12. Once more he appeals to the Corinthians' own experience of his apostolic quality (cf. 1 C. 9.1f.; 2 C. 3.1–4). They had seen **the signs of a true apostle** manifested before their eyes during the months in which Paul had evangelized their city, patiently enduring the opposition and attacks of his enemies there (Ac. 18.6f., 12ff.); they had seen **signs and wonders and mighty works** such as had marked the ministry of Jesus (Ac. 2.22) and of the Jerusalem apostles (Ac. 2.43; cf. the argument of Gal. 3.5); above all, through his ministry their lives had undergone a radical change for the better (cf. 1 C. 1.21). (Cf. T. W. Manson, *The Church's Ministry* (1948), pp. 50, 74, 100f.)

13. All the blessings that had come to the other churches founded by Paul they too had enjoyed; why should they feel resentment against him? Was it because he refused to **burden** them (*katanarkaō*, as in 11.9)? For **this wrong** he ironically begs their pardon (cf. 1 C. 9.12, 15ff.; 2 C. 11.7ff.).

A THIRD VISIT 12.14–21

14–15. for the third time: the second time (cf. 13.2, 'my second visit') was the 'painful visit' referred to in 2.1. The first time may have been his original coming to Corinth (Ac. 18.1ff.; 1 C. 2.1ff.); if that coming can scarcely be viewed as a 'visit' to the Corinthian church, then some intermediate visit, otherwise unchronicled, may be envisaged. This reference to an impending 'third visit' seems to rule out the identification of 2 C. 10–13 as part of the severe letter mentioned in 2 C. 2.3f.; 7.8, 12 (see pp. 166ff.), for that letter was sent to avoid the necessity of a painful visit. Here Paul is quite ready to pay them a visit which they will find painful if the situation warrants it (cf. 13.2). Again he lays bare his motives: he refuses to 'burden' them (*katanarkaō*); it is not their property, but themselves, that he is anxious to win. Why should he expect them to support him? They are his spiritual children (cf. 1 C. 4.15); **parents** make provision **for their children**, not **children** for **their parents**. He will most gladly **spend** (*dapanaō*) his resources and be expended (*ekdapanaō*) himself in order to secure their affection and allegiance. There is no

limit to his **love** for them; it is sad that their love for him is so
limited (cf. 6.11–13; 7.2–4; 11.11).

16–17. Granting that I myself did not burden you: here
a more ordinary verb (*katabareō*) is used than in verses 13 and 14
(see note on 11.9).

I was crafty: Gk *panourgos*; cf. 4.2, where Paul explicitly re-
nounces such conduct (*panourgia*, 'cunning').

got the better of you by guile: so some of them were saying,
perhaps because they felt that by sending Titus and his companions to deal with the final stages of their contribution to the
Jerusalem fund, Paul had 'put them on the spot'. He challenges
them therefore to say if in fact he took **advantage** of them
(*pleonekteō*, as in 7.2) in financial or other matters through any of
his messengers: his question is framed so as to require the answer
'No' (being introduced by the negative *mē*).

18. I urged Titus: the same language as is used in 8.6 (where
the verb is *parakaleō*, as here) and 8.17 (where *RSV* 'appeal' represents the derivative noun *paraklēsis*). The burden of proof rests on
those who distinguish Titus's mission here alluded to from that of
8.6ff. (on the implication of this for the setting of 2 C. 10–13 see
pp. 168f). Only one **brother** is mentioned here as accompanying
Titus, whereas two are mentioned in 8.18ff.; but one of these (probably the one of 8.18f.) is omitted here because he was not Paul's
representative but a delegate of the contributing churches.
(Titus's companions are both called 'messengers of the churches'
in 8.23, but the first-mentioned of the two was specifically appointed by the churches to act for them in the gathering and
administration of the contributions.) Paul challenges the Corinthians to say if Titus had conducted himself among them in any
way differently from himself: he knows there can be but one answer
to this. Neither in person nor through Titus did he **take advantage** of them.

19. Have you been thinking . . . ?: Or 'you have been thinking'; it is equally consistent with the context to construe this as a
question or as a statement.

that we have been defending ourselves: cf. 1 C. 4.3ff.; 2 C.
3.1ff. He is not concerned about his own reputation (as the apostle
of Christ he knows that it is to Christ alone that he is accountable),
but he is concerned, in a spirit of Christian responsibility (**before
God . . . in Christ**) to bring his converts to a better frame of

mind, to help them to assess men in their true proportion, and not to be taken in by the high-sounding claims of emissaries who have no such pastoral affection for them as he has. Neither does he wish them to accept himself at his own valuation: let them compare their personal knowledge of him with their knowledge of his critics (cf. verse 6). Submission to men who impose a subtle bondage on them will not lead to their **upbuilding**; what Paul is working for is their spiritual maturity, which can be fostered only in conditions of Christian freedom.

20–21. He does not wish at his next visit to find the same unhappy attitudes manifested as he did at his previous visit; he has no wish to repeat the experience of personal humiliation which was so painful for him and them alike on that last occasion (cf. 2.1–4).

I may have to mourn: Gk *pentheō*, as in 1 C. 5.2, perhaps with a similar hint of the excommunication of wrongdoers.

selfishness: Gk *eritheiai* (from *erithos*, 'hireling'), the self-regarding attitude and conduct of those whose one concern is their own advantage (cf. Gal. 5.20; Phil. 2.3). The word tended to take on something of the sense of *eris*, rendered 'quarrelling' in this verse (*RSV* translates it 'partisanship' in Phil. 1.17; cf. Rom. 2.8, where *ex eritheias* is rendered 'factious'). Several of the attitudes and practices listed here are included among the 'works of the flesh' in Gal. 5.19ff. or among the features of contemporary paganism in Rom. 1.29ff.; Paul would certainly feel 'humbled' if he found such things still rife among his converts at Corinth, together with the unrepented **impurity, immorality, and licentiousness** against which he had repeatedly warned them (cf. 1 C. 5.9ff.; 6.12ff.; 10.8). The persistence of such behaviour in the church would provide his legalist critics with a powerful argument against his reliance on the new life of the indwelling Spirit as the all-sufficient power to change his Gentile converts within and without from pagan ways to Christian ways.

CONCLUDING ADMONITION 13.1–10

13.1. the third time: cf. 12.14.

Any charge must be sustained . . . : the quotation of the ruling of Dt. 19.15 (cf. Num. 35.30; Dt. 17.6), requiring **the evidence of two or three witnesses**, may have a more general application here than in other *NT* contexts (cf. Mt. 18.16; 1 Tim. 5.19; Heb.

10.28) and refer to Paul's three visits; the third will be decisive
(so Calvin, *ad loc.*: 'my three comings will take the place of three
testimonies'). Cf. H. van Vliet, *No Single Testimony* (1958).

2. I warned those who sinned before and all the others:
a rare piece of positive information about his **second visit**—the
'painful visit' of 2.1. As against suggestions that 12.14 and 13.1
might mean only 'this is the third time I am *planning* to visit you',
this is clear evidence that a **second visit** actually took place; to
take *to deuteron* (lit. 'the second time', *RV*) with **I warned** and not
with **when present** involves an intolerable distortion of the construction, and it is almost as unnatural to translate *hōs parōn* in
this context by 'as if present'.

if I come again: i.e. 'when I come again'; no doubt is implied
about his coming.

I will not spare them: contrast the occasion mentioned in 1.23,
where in order to spare them he refrained from paying them a
visit as he had announced, and incurred criticism for changing
his plans.

3. you desire proof that Christ is speaking in me: because of his restraint (so unlike his opponents) they doubted
whether he was a full apostle, vested with all the authority of
Christ as the one who commissioned him (cf. 10.1, 8-11). 'You
shall have the proof you desire,' he says. '*I* may be weak in my
dealings with you, compared with my critics [cf. 11.21], but
Christ **is not weak in dealing with you**, and when I come I
shall be the vehicle of his power among you [cf. 12.9].'

4. he was crucified in weakness: but that was weakness by
worldly standards; in reality, Christ crucified is 'the power of
God', for 'the weakness of God is stronger than men' (1 C. 1.24f.).
lives by the power of God: cf. Rom. 6.4; Eph. 1.19ff. Those who
are united by faith to Christ share the 'weakness' of his passion
but also the power of his resurrection (cf. Phil. 3.10f.); Paul has
already spoken to them of himself in these terms (4.10f.) and does
so again: **in dealing with you** I shall manifest **the power of
God** which comes through sharing the risen life of Christ.

5. Did they demand 'proof' (Gk *dokimē*, verse 3) of Paul's
apostleship? Let them make proof (*dokimazō*) of themselves, to
test the genuineness of their **faith**. Rather than question if Christ
is speaking in Paul, let them question if Christ is living in themselves—as, of course, he is, **unless indeed** they **fail to meet the**

test: unless they are *adokimoi*, 'counterfeit' (which Paul does not believe they are).

6–7. Paul continues to play on the adjectives *dokimos* ('genuine') and *adokimos* ('counterfeit'). **I hope you will find out** that I am no 'counterfeit' apostle; but my prayer to God is **that you may not do wrong**, that you may come rather to a proper frame of mind and acknowledge the Christ who speaks in me, not that the genuineness of my apostleship may be confirmed **but that you may do what is right**—even though my apostleship should be proved counterfeit after all! Paul's self-effacing concern is not for his own vindication but for their winning the Lord's approval. Cf. 1 C. 9.27 for Paul's care to discipline himself lest he should become *adokimos*.

8. we cannot do anything against the truth, but only for the truth: probably a general maxim (cf. 1 Esd. 3.35, 38: 'Great is truth, and stronger than all'), quoted here with reference to the actual situation.

9. Paul will gladly appear **weak** in their eyes (cf. 10.10) and be really weak in himself provided that they **are strong** in Christ (cf. Eph. 6.10), not in their own estimation (cf. 1 C. 4.10, where the word is *ischyros*, as against its synonym *dynatos* here). If they **are strong** in the best sense, he will not need to assert the strength of his apostolic authority against them.

your improvement: Gk *katartisis*, restoration to wholeness; cf. *katartizesthe*, 'mend your ways', in verse 11 (the same verb is rendered 'be united' in 1 C. 1.10).

10. in order that when I come I may not have to be severe: cf. what is said about the 'tearful letter' in 2.3. Paul does not want a repetition of the painful experience which his second visit was for both himself and them.

the authority which the Lord has given me . . . : repeated from 10.8. It is necessary at times to use that authority **for tearing down** opposition to God's will, but the primary purpose for which he received it was **for building up** the people of God and the work of God.

FINAL EXHORTATION, GREETINGS AND BENEDICTION **13.11–14**

11. heed my appeal: Gk *parakaleisthe*, 'be exhorted' or, with *RV*, 'be comforted' (but if we treat it as middle rather than passive it might be rendered 'exhort one another', 'comfort one another' or, with *AV*, 'be of good comfort'). While the idea of 'comfort' takes us back to the beginning of the letter (cf. 1.3ff.), that of appeal or exhortation is more appropriate after the sustained argument of 10.1-13.10.

the God of love and peace: a designation not paralleled else-where in *NT*, although 'the God of peace' is common enough (cf. Rom. 15.33; 16.20; Phil. 4.9; 1 Th. 5.23; 2 Th. 3.16; also Heb. 13.20). If the Corinthians' party-spirit was due, as Paul believed, to deficiency in love, there would be special point in this designation.

12. Cf. 1 C. 16.20b.

13. Cf. 1 C. 16.20a. Since we cannot be sure where Paul was when he despatched 2 C. 10-13 we must remain uncertain of the identity of these **saints**, but most probably they belonged to one of the Macedonian churches.

14. The grace of our Lord Jesus Christ . . . be with you all: this, or something very similar ('. . . with you', '. . . with your spirit') is Paul's characteristic benediction at the end of a letter (cf. Rom. 16.20; 1 C. 16.23; Gal. 6.18; Phil. 4.23; 1 Th. 5.28; 2 Th. 3.18; Phm. 25); here **the grace of our Lord Jesus Christ** is amplified by **the love of God and the fellowship of the Holy Spirit**, so that we have language approaching later formulations of trinitarian theology (see note on 1 C. 12.4-6). The first two genitives are certainly subjective, and so probably is the third: **the fellowship** is that which **the Holy Spirit** creates and main-tains in being (cf. perhaps Phil. 2.1; also Eph. 4.3, 'the unity of the Spirit'). *RSV* mg., however ('participation in the Holy Spirit'), treats this genitive as objective. While it does not make much practical difference to construe it thus (joint participation in the Spirit inevitably implies spiritual fellowship one with another), it is more natural to treat all three genitives as subjective. Paul turns his Corinthian friends, impoverished by their party-spirit, to contemplate the unlimited wealth of blessing which God makes available to them in Christ by the power of the Spirit.

Appended Note

Of the sequel to this letter we know hardly anything. A comparison of Rom. 16.1, 23 with Ac. 20.2f. suggests that the place in 'Greece' where, according to Luke, Paul spent three winter-months pre-ceding his last voyage to Jerusalem (a voyage on which he was accompanied by representatives of several of his Gentile churches) was actually Corinth, the city in which Gaius, his host, was resident (1 C. 1.14) and of which Erastus was treasurer (especially if he can be identified with the Erastus of a Corinthian inscription uncovered in 1929, who laid a marble pavement at his own expense 'in consideration of his aedileship'). We cannot say whether a full reconciliation had been achieved between Paul and his Corinthian converts by this time, but his letter to the Romans, which (or at least that edition of it which included chapter 16) was evidently sent from Corinth (carried by Phoebe, 'a deaconess of the church at Cenchreae'), presupposes a calm atmosphere, untroubled by 'fighting without and fear's within'. Perhaps the severe warnings of 2 C. 10–13, like the earlier 'tearful letter', had a salutary effect—for the time being. But it is not clear that the church of Corinth sent a delegate to go with Paul to Jerusalem, carrying its contribution to the mother-church—no Corinthian appears in the list of Ac. 20.4 (which, however, need not be exhaustive). If Corinth did in fact send a contribution, it may have been entrusted to the unnamed 'messengers of the churches' of 2 C. 8.18–23.

When, forty years later, we next have information about the Corinthian church—in the 'godly admonition' addressed to it by the Roman church and traditionally known as the first letter of Clement (of Rome)—it has not made much progress towards maturity and stability; dissension and anarchy have manifested themselves within its ranks once more. The Corinthian church of the first century is a perpetual reminder to us that Christianity in the apostolic age was not marked by ideal unity and purity from which later generations declined.

INDEX OF PERSONAL NAMES

INDEX OF PLACES AND PEOPLES